Psychology SL&HL
FOR THE IB DIPLOMA

Jacob Solomon

PEAK

Published by:
Peak Study Resources Ltd
1 & 3 Kings Meadow
Oxford OX2 0DP
UK

www.peakib.com

Psychology SL&HL: Study & Revision Guide for the IB Diploma

ISBN 978-1-913433-09-3

© Jacob Solomon 2021

Jacob Solomon has asserted his right under the Copyright, Design and Patents Act 1988 to be identified as the author of this work.

All rights reserved. No part of this publication may be reproduced, stored in a retrieval system, or transmitted in any form or by any means, without the prior permission of the publishers.

PHOTOCOPYING ANY PAGES FROM THIS PUBLICATION,
EXCEPT UNDER LICENCE, IS PROHIBITED

Peak Study & Revision Guides for the IB Diploma have been developed independently of the International Baccalaureate Organization (IBO). 'International Baccalaureate' and 'IB' are registered trademarks of the IBO.

Books may be ordered directly from the publisher (see www.peakib.com) and through online or local booksellers. For enquiries regarding titles, availability or retailers, please email books@peakib.com or use the form at www.peakib.com/contact.

Printed and bound in the UK by:
CPI Group (UK) Ltd, Croydon CR0 4YY

www.cpibooks.co.uk

Cover image: adapted from illustration by Pilck, via Adobe Stock

Preface

Dear ....

This book is written for you, the IB student in psychology, so go ahead and write your name above and make this *your book*.

The purpose of studying psychology is to interact with other people and situations at a deeper, more comprehending, and better-informed level. It may even lead you to a career and to your life's calling. In the meantime, you have to pass IB psychology. These notes are put together to help you to do just that.

This book is designed specifically to help you to review the material of the course. The word revision literally means to see again. By presenting the material in brief, review form, you should get the overall feel and perspective of how the topics you have studied come together. That includes their perspectives, wide variety of methods used, and how the ideas and findings relate to one another. In short, you should see the wood, despite the trees.

The reality of the IB psychology exam is that you are expected to recall and apply a large database of theory, methodology, and research studies. Though there is considerable material on each area of the IB syllabus, this guide refers to the theory and research commonly selected and used in the IB psychology program. ***I have endeavoured to select review material from the theory and research that you are most likely to have come across in classes and in reading assignments.***

Please bear in mind that the whole course is underpinned by two essentials: method and ethics. Exam questions in all papers frequently combine method and ethics with the topic content.

Please e-mail me via Peak Study Resources using feedback@peakib.com with any suggestions for inclusion in later editions of this work. There may also be occasional updates or supplements which you can find by visiting the psychology resources page on the Peak website at www.peakib.com (or scan the QR code on the back cover).

If this study guide helps you pass your exam, I'll be happy. If it increases your clarity in psychology, I'll be delighted. And if it helps you to know yourself a little better, I'll be thrilled.

Wishing you every success! (But remember that success comes before work in the dictionary only.)

Jacob Solomon

Contents

Preface iii
About this book vii
Navigating the guide vii

Chapter 1: The biological approach to understanding human behaviour 1

1.1 Introduction to the Biological Approach 2
1.2 The Brain and Behaviour 2
1.3 Hormones and Their Effect on Human Behaviour 13
1.4 Pheromones and Their Effect on Human Behaviour 15
1.5 Genetics and Behaviour 17
1.6 Evolutionary Explanations of Behaviour 22
1.7 The value of animal models in research to provide insight into human behaviour (Higher Level only) 24
1.8 Ethical Considerations in Animal Research (Higher Level only) 27
1.9 Research Methods, Designs, and Techniques Used in the Biological Approach to Understanding Behaviour 28
1.10 Strengths and Limitations: Biological Approach 28
1.11 Ethical Considerations: Research Methods Used in the Biological Approach 29
Exam-style Practice Questions: The Biological Approach 29

Chapter 2: The Cognitive Approach to Understanding Human Behaviour 30

2.1 Introduction to the Cognitive Approach 31
2.2 Cognitive Processing: Models of Memory 31
2.3 Cognitive Processing: Schema Theory 37
2.4 Cognitive Processing: Thinking and Decision-Making 41
2.5 Reliability of Cognitive Processes: Reconstructive Memory 43
2.6 Reliability of Cognitive Processes: Biases in Thinking and Decision-Making 44
2.7 Emotion and Cognition: The Influence of Emotion on Cognitive Processes 46
2.8 Cognitive Processing in the Digital World (Higher Level only) 48
2.9 Research Methods Used in the Cognitive Approach to Understanding Behaviour 53
2.10 Strengths and Limitations: Cognitive Approach 53
2.11 Ethical Considerations: Research Methods Used in the Cognitive Approach 54
Exam-style Practice Questions: The Cognitive Approach 55

Chapter 3: The Sociocultural Approach to Understanding Human Behaviour 56

3.1 Introduction to the Sociocultural Approach 57
3.2 The Individual and the Group: Social Identity Theory 57
3.3 The Individual and the Group: Social Cognitive Theory 60
3.4 Cultural Origins of Behaviour and Cognition 67
3.5 Cultural Attitudes on Individual Attitudes, Identity, and Behaviours: Enculturation and Acculturation 71
3.6 The Influence of Globalisation on Behaviours (Higher Level only) 76
3.7 Research Methods Used in the Sociocultural Approach to Understanding Behaviour 80

3.8 Strengths and Limitations: Sociocultural Approach to
Understanding Behaviour ... 80
3.9 Ethical Considerations: Sociocultural research to Understanding Behaviour 81
Exam-style Practice Questions: The Sociocultural Approach   82

Chapter 4: Approaches To Researching Behaviour (HL) 83
4.1 Introduction to Research Methods in Psychology   85
4.2 Elements of Researching Behaviour   88
4.3 Analysing Data   92
4.4 Evaluating Research   94
4.5 Drawing Conclusions   95
4.6 Your Paper 3 Examination (Higher Level only)   96
Stimulus Response Practice Question: Paper 3   96

Chapter 5: Paper 2 Option – Developmental Psychology 98
5.1 Influences on Cognitive and Social Development   99
5.2 Developing an Identity   106
5.3 Developing as a Learner   114
5.4 Ethical Considerations   120
5.5 Key Research   120
Essay-response Exam Questions: Developmental Psychology   122

Chapter 6: Paper 2 Option – Abnormal Psychology 123
6.1 Factors influencing diagnosis   124
6.2 Etiology of abnormal conditions   132
6.3 Treatment of disorders   139
6.4 Ethical Considerations   146
6.5 Key research studies   147
Essay Response Practice Questions: Abnormal Psychology   148

Chapter 7: Paper 2 Option – Human Relationships 149
7.1 Personal Relationships   150
7.2 Group Dynamics   159
7.3 Social Responsibility   166
7.4 Ethical Considerations   172
7.5 Key research studies   173
Essay Response Practice Questions: Psychology of human relationships   175

Chapter 8: Paper 2 Option – Health Psychology 176
8.1 Determinants of Health   177
8.2 Health Problems   184
8.3 Promoting Health   191
8.4 Ethical Considerations   196
8.5 Key research studies   196
Essay Response Practice Questions: Health Psychology   198

About this book

This is a study and revision guide that is designed to help you. During the course you have probably studied some areas in more depth than others. You may be in the situation of "We covered so much that I don't know where to start to prepare the exam." So this book should help you get what you need to know to the level that you can answer the range of questions set in the exams: both the short-answer questions (typically 300 words) and essay response questions (typically 800 words).

Navigating the guide

This guide is structured to enable you to study efficiently:

- key terms are highlighted in bold,
- significant studies appear as a discrete section in the text,
- cross references provide links between linked topics and studies spanning more than one area of research, and
- practice questions follow the relevant sections of text.

We use icons to help you quickly and easily identify different types of information.

Key to icons used in this study guide

Chapter 1: The biological approach to understanding human behaviour

Overview

Our studies in the biological approach focus on the biological correlates to behaviour that may be detected within the nervous (central and peripheral) systems, and the endocrine (hormone) systems.

This approach takes into account that different areas of the brain carry out different functions (brain function localisation), which work in harmony with the communications between the nerve cells throughout the body. This in turn influences our psychological as well as physical functioning. We also produce hormones, biochemical substances carried by the blood system that can affect our own behaviour. Whether or not we can also produce pheromones, that affect the behavior of other people, is still debated among researchers.

In addition, we consider the role of how genes can influence behaviour patterns. We also look at how behaviour patterns can influence genes: over generations, genotypes (the genetic composition) appear to evolve in response to environmental changes and challenges that the less fit do not survive.

If you are a Higher Level student, you will also consider the ethically controversial issue of research using animals to understanding human behaviour. Studies that could not be conducted on humans have contributed considerably to our understanding and treatment of conditions such as memory-afflicting Alzheimer's disease, but are subject to practices minimising animal use and animal suffering.

> Understand that the biological approach views thinking and behaviour as coming from the workings of the nervous system (from the brain to neurotransmitters), hormone (endocrine) system, and genes. The biological approach is based on investigating the biological correlates to behaviour. Bear in mind that the relationship between biology and behaviour is a complex one of mutual causality; research studies indicate that biological elements can influence behaviour, and also that behaviour can influence biological elements.

KEY QUESTION

What contribution do the nervous system, hormone system, and genes make to thinking and behaviour?

Learning objectives of this unit include an understanding of:
- The role of the brain in influencing behaviour (SL and HL)
- The role of hormones in influencing behaviour (SL and HL)
- The role of genetics in influencing behaviour (SL and HL)
- The role of animal research in influencing behaviour (HL only)

1.1 Introduction to the Biological Approach

The biological approach views cognitions, emotions and behaviours as products of our nervous system, and endocrine system, and genes.

Biological principles of interest to psychologists include:

- There are biological correlates to behaviour. These may be detected within nervous (central and peripheral, neurotransmitter) systems, and the endocrine (hormone) system.
- Different areas of the brain carry out different functions (brain function localisation).
- Synapses (gaps) exist between nerve cells. Different neurotransmitters carry different neural transmissions (messages) from one synapse to another, according to our psychological functioning.
- Hormones carried in the cardio-vascular (blood system) influence our psychological functioning, and possibly (as pheromones) the behaviour of others.
- Genes influence behavioural patterns.
- Over generations, genotypes (the genetic compositions) evolve in response to the evolutionary process of adapting to the environment.
- (HL only) Research using animals can inform human behaviour.

The biological approach thus emphasises that cognitions, emotions and behaviours are products of our biological correlates.

1.2 The Brain and Behaviour

Our understanding of the brain is progressing rapidly. **Brain function localisation**, the idea that different parts of the brain carry out different physical and psychological functions, has been known for close to 200 years. The case of railway worker Phineas Gage (1848) showed that brain functions are localised. An explosion sent a pole right through his brain. He lost some, but not all his mental capacities. That indicated that different parts of the brain have different functions, as shown in Figure 1.1. Indeed, sources of information on the brain and behaviour include (i) patients who have survived brain injury with impairments in some functions yet no effect on others, (ii) patients who have undergone brain surgery, and (iii) participants in research undergoing brain scans whilst performing particular tasks.

In addition, the functions of different parts of the brain are grouped in two physical hemispheres: the left hemisphere and the right hemisphere. These are summarised in Figure 1.2 which shows that **left-brain** functions tend to dominate in language and logical reasoning while the **right-brain** has the major role in aesthetics, intuition, and creativity.

Moreover, the brain has three concentric layers, starting from the central core of the brain and moving outwards. At a simple level, the central core controls involuntary physical and psychological processes. The next layer incorporates the limbic system which handles emotions and memory. The top, the outer cerebrum, regulates the higher mental processes, which in turn are grouped in the left and right hemispheres.

1. THE BIOLOGICAL APPROACH TO UNDERSTANDING HUMAN BEHAVIOUR

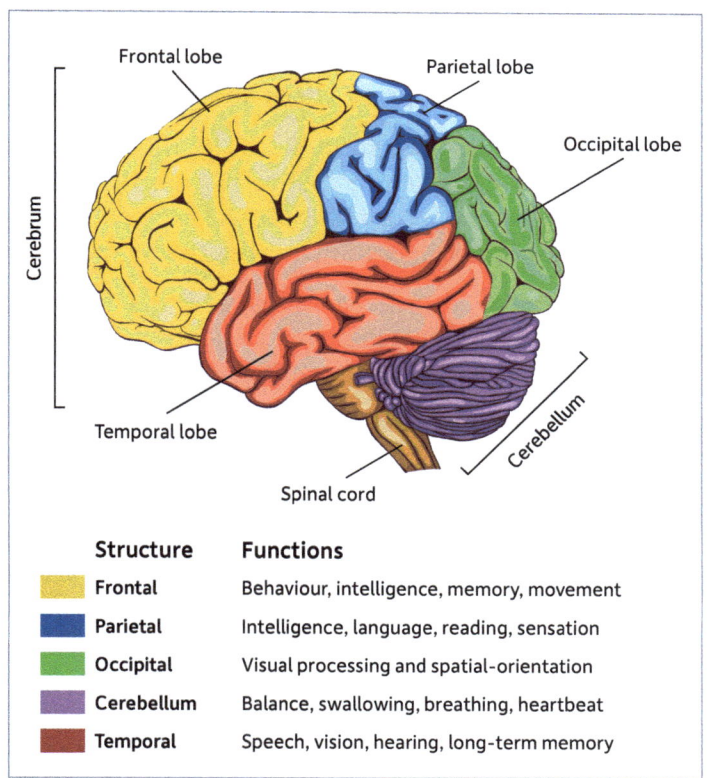

Figure 1.1: **Side view of the human brain, showing brain function localisation**

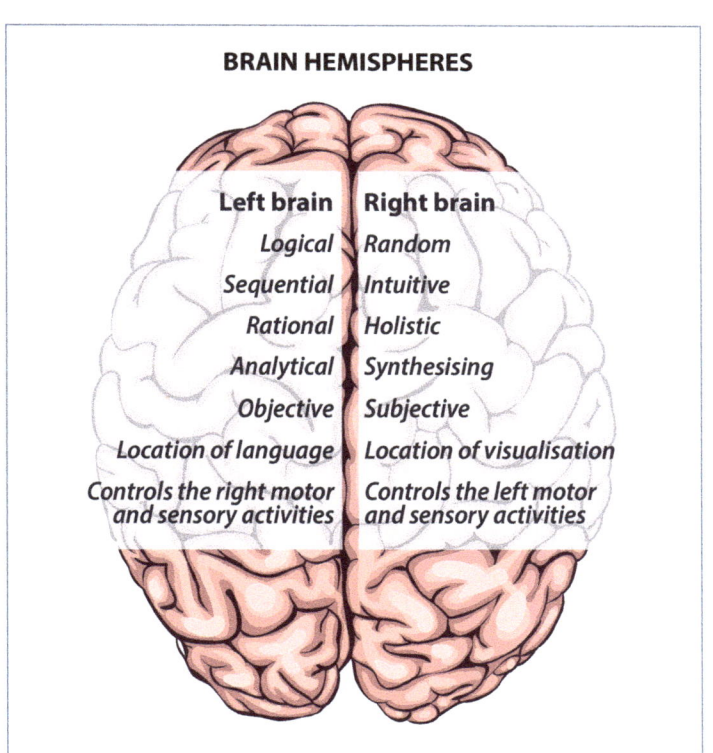

Figure 1.2: **Top view of the human brain, divided into left brain and right brain**

Bear in mind that the brain is actually far more complex. Specific functions of the brain tend to be spread into different parts of the brain, as evidenced by the following case study.

RESEARCH STUDY

Milner et al. (1966–2008): the Case Study of HM (Henry Molaison, 1926–2008)

The aim of the study was to research the role of the hippocampus on memory: brain function localisation. It exemplifies the use of *research methods* in the biological approach: the in-depth *case study*. It also exemplifies the use of a range of *techniques* in the biological approach: cognitive testing, interviewing, observation, and brain scanning.

This is illustrated in the case-study of HM (Henry Molaison, 1926–2008). It was a longitudinal study, researching the same participants over an extended period. In this case, HM was the one and only participant.

HM fell off a bicycle at the age of seven and suffered an injury that was believed to be causing his subsequent, continued serious epileptic seizures. In 1953, doctors removed the tissue from the medial temporal lobe of the brain (there was no effective drug treatment at the time), including much of the hippocampus.

This operation seriously affected his memory capacities. Observing and interviewing HM indicated that he was unable to form most types of new memories, including event recall and the faces of people that he had recently met, though he could still form spatial memories: cognitive testing showed that he could draw a plan of his new home. He could also form short-term memories; he had the necessary working memory to hold a conversation though he would forget it very soon afterwards, unable to convert short-term memories into permanent, long-term memories that he would be able to recall months or even days later. HM could still recall information acquired before the operation, making his situation a case of anterograde amnesia. All this indicates complex brain function localisation: that more than one locality of the brain is involved in the single function of memory.

HM's brain was MRI scanned in 1992 and 2003, showing that the damaged area included the parts of the brain that handle memory and emotions, including the hippocampus and amygdala regions. This helped to explain why HM seemed to be unable to transfer information from short-term to the long-term: the damage to the hippocampus and amygdala would have interfered with the work of acetylcholine, a key neurotransmitter (see section 1.3) in memory formation. However, the fact that HM's memory functioned at all indicated that memory functions are more widely distributed throughout the brain than previously thought, and not just in the hippocampus and the amygdala. For example, his ability to take part in a conversation indicated that the short-term memory may not be located in the hippocampus, though his inability to convert short-term memory to long-term memory would indicate that the necessary mechanism is located in the hippocampus. The study indicated that the hippocampus' role is in memory transfer rather than memory storage.

1. THE BIOLOGICAL APPROACH TO UNDERSTANDING HUMAN BEHAVIOUR

Strengths and limitations of Milner et al. (1996–2008)

Strengths	Limitations
1. The **longitudinal** nature of the case study meant that different aspects of the study could be observed over time, making it possible, for example, to confirm the areas in which HM's memory system functioned and did not function. 2. More than one method was used: cognitive testing, interviewing, observation, and brain scanning. These different methods could be used to check the validity of the findings; an example of **method triangulation** (Chapter 8, section 8.5). 3. Ecologically valid: HM was studied in his natural environment.	1. HM's cognitive impairments may have been influenced by the medication he taken to treat his epileptic condition as well as the actual damage. 2. Difficulties in transferring the findings from a single case study, although the findings have been supported by several other similar case studies, e.g. Clive Wearing (Chapter 2, section 2.2.1).

Examples of further studies on brain study localisation are in section 1.2.1 (Harris and Fiske, 2006), and in section 1.2.2 (Kim and Hirsch, 1997)

1.2.1 Modern techniques used to study the brain in relation to behaviour

Studies of the brain and behaviour have become much clearer with *modern methods of brain scanning*, which became used more widely from the 1960s. It enables researchers to see images of the soft tissue making up the brain whilst the patient is alive.

The pioneer developments in this field were **electroencephalography** (EEG) that made it possible to study the electrical activity happening across the surface of the brain, and **computerised tomography** (CT) that enabled the identifying of brain damage and abnormal brain structures. Their use began in the 1950s. CT scanning focused X-rays to produce static images of the brain. These was followed by the development of the higher resolution, second-generation **magnetic resonance imaging** (MRI), which in turn gave way to the very expensive **positron emission tomography** (PET) and **functional magnetic resonance imaging** (fMRI). fMRI systems produce series of multi-dimensional images that can trace activity within the brain, including which parts of the brain are operating when a person is performing a specific task. Unlike the MRI, which shows the structure of the brain, the fMRI can show the functioning of the brain. The extremely complex brain mapping produced by such devices tends to indicate that no one part of the brain is exclusively responsible for a specific function. In research, brain scanning is limited by suitability for the particular task, cost, and availability. Their workings and debated strengths and limitations for research in psychology are considered in the following two research studies.

Types of brain scanning are techniques of investigation, but not methods of investigation

RESEARCH STUDY

Davidson et al. (2004)

This study focuses on electronic methods of studying the brain. Davidson et al. researched the influence of the practice of meditation's influence on brain activity and brain structure. The team used an EEG to compare the gamma waves (highest-frequency brainwaves, associated with the most intense concentration) of those with established training and experience in meditation with those without.

This was achieved by comparing the brain gamma wave activity between eight monks (the test group) to whom meditation was part of life, and ten students (the control group) who were given one week of meditation training before the study. For the study, all participants were required to create a deep feeling of compassion without focusing it on any particular person.

The EEG findings showed the monks to have a much better organised and a much higher degree of gamma wave activity. The brains of the students showed only a slight increase in gamma wave activity following the week's training in meditation.

The study suggests that a mind trained in meditation becomes biologically more suited to meditate. It will have a much fuller experience of its potential benefits when applied to relieving stress and physical pain. On a wider basis, this suggests that a mind experienced in any particular skill becomes biologically adapted to carrying out that skill. However:

- The results were entirely correlational: the higher level of gamma waves in the monks' brains may be a product of non-meditation experiences.
- The information scanners' coloured light responses may exaggerate the different activities in the brain.
- The brain areas might light up on the machine for reasons other than those supposed by the investigator.

RESEARCH STUDY

Harris and Fiske (2006)

This study addresses two objectives: electronic methods of studying the brain, and the localisation of the functioning of the brain

This study may also be included when studying the Human Relationships option (Chapter 7), in the topic of Prejudice and Discrimination, as biological evidence of evolved mechanisms in brain that support prejudice and discrimination against an out-group.

As it uses biological evidence, it is unsuitable for the stereotyping component in cognitive psychology (Chapter 2).

Harris and Fiske aimed to find biological support for stereotyping and prejudice capacities in different parts of the brain.

Twenty-two Princeton University undergraduate students participated. In anticipation of the research main task, they were given some practice in computer-selecting to choose from one of four reactions to a series of photographs: pride, envy, pity, or disgust. This was to ensure that student responses would accurately reflect their reactions to the series of pictures in the main study.

Each participant was then connected to an fMRI scanner and shown a total of 60 photographs of people in all positions in life: older people, famous sports people, disabled people, wealthy people, drug addicts, and homeless people. The fMRI scanner works by showing changes in the flow of blood to areas of the brain, demonstrating the level of the use of oxygen connected with its neural activity. The scanner registered the brain image responses to the photographs. The students also indicated their response by choosing one of the four emotions for each photograph, as in the practice session.

The findings of the study showed increased activity in the medial pre-frontal cortex when viewing people. This is the part of the brain that is known to be active when we are thinking about other people. However, the fMRI scans showed no increased activity in the

1. THE BIOLOGICAL APPROACH TO UNDERSTANDING HUMAN BEHAVIOUR

medial pre-frontal cortex when students viewed pictures of addicts or homeless people. The scans did, however, show additional activity in the amygdala and the insula, which are similarly aroused when reacting with disgust at rotting garbage.

The researchers concluded that biological correlates indicate the working of stereotyping and prejudice, as the lack of any reaction in the pre-frontal cortex appeared to indicate that they did not emotionally react to the addicts and homeless as fellow human beings.

Strengths and limitations: Harris and Fiske (2006)

Strengths	Limitations
1. The study showed correlates between stimulus (the different photographs), the participants' responses and the fMRI data showing activity in different distinct regions of the participant's brains. 2. The use of the fMRI enabled the recording of activity throughout the brain.	1. Small size of sample, owing to the time and expense of fMRI scanning 2. Possible bias in the sample as the participants were all American students in an Ivy League University, whose negative stereotypes may have been affected by previous experiences not shared by the general population. 3. In addition, the fMRI finds are correlational, unable to demonstrate cause and effect. Furthermore, the findings indicating brain localisation do not exclude the possibility of neural networks that additionally enable other parts of the brain to be involved in processing the stimuli. This is a general limitation with brain scanning: it can register brain activity, but not yet demonstrate cause and effect.

1.2.2 Localisation of function of the brain: examples of modern research studies

- Harris and Fiske (2006) – see above in this section
- Maguire et al. (2000) – see below in this section
- Draganski et al (2004) – see below in this section
- Fisher et al (2005) – see below in this section
- Baumgartner et al (2008) – see section 1.3

RESEARCH STUDY

Kim and Hirsch (1997)

Kim and Hirsch used fMRI (functional magnetic resonance imaging) to see how the brain processes language in bilingual people, and that brain functioning tend to be localised. One group had learned a second language as children. The other had learned a second language later in life. Both groups had to think about what they had done the day before, first in one language, and then in the other.

Kim and Hirsch investigated the Broca's area, in the left frontal lobe of the brain, which manages speech production, and the Wernicke's area, in the rear of the brain, which processes the meaning of language. Both groups of people used the same part of the

Wernicke's area no matter what language they were speaking. But their use of the Broca's area differed. Those who learned a second language as children used the same region in the Broca's area for speaking both languages. But those who learned a second language later in life made use of a distinct additional region in Broca's area for their second language, close to the one activated for their native tongue.

This suggests that language is being hard-wired during early childhood development. Once that wiring is complete, the management of a new language must be handled by a different part of the brain.

Thus, it appears from this research that (a) the part of the brain used for language learning is indeed localised (b) knowing more than one language from childhood does not affect efficacy in either, and (c) learning to speak a language later in life requires much more brain activity.

Strengths and limitations: Kim and Hirsch (1997)

Strengths	Limitations
1. Scanning appears to confirm that both the Broca's and the Wernicke's areas do serve distinct and specialised functions in language comprehension and in speech production. 2. It helps to explain why post-childhood learners of a foreign language tend to make errors based on mother-tongue influence.	1. Differences in language-learning ability may be connected with the way the learner interacts with the language. Mothers teaching an infant to speak are very tactile, auditory, and visual. High school foreign language teachers tend to be less so. 2. Early learners do not bring to language learning the fears of learning vocabulary and grammar.

The additional evaluation in Harris and Fiske (2006) of fMRI scanning may also be applied to this study, see section 1.2.1.

1.2.3 Neuroplasticity and its Effect on Human Behaviour

The findings of Davidson et al. (Section 1.2.1) may also be explained by **neuroplasticity**, the growth and development of specialised **neural networks** through repetition of physical and mental tasks over time. Neural networks are interconnected groups of neurones that carry out specific functions when activated. The development of neural networks though both repetition and **neural pruning** are influenced by both genetic and environmental factors. Neural pruning is where neurons and connections that are not regularly used tend to die, so that they do not block the transmissions through the neural networks.

Neural networks and neural plasticity can enable us to support and improve skills. Biologically, the **dendrites** (branches) of the neurons grow in numbers and connect with other neurons. The brain adapts to the challenges placed on it by **dendritic branching**: a process that continue throughout life. For example, you might find mathematics very difficult. With regular and repeated practice, the part of the brain that deals with mathematics on a challenging basis 'thickens', and handles mathematics more effectively. Thus, the more you exercise your brain, the more powerful it becomes.

Conversely, lack of stimulation can prevent development of neural networks. Perry (1997) compared the CT brain scans of three-year-olds with normal degrees of human interaction with those who had suffered extreme neglect. Findings: (a) on the whole,

1. THE BIOLOGICAL APPROACH TO UNDERSTANDING HUMAN BEHAVIOUR

the brains of severely neglected children tended to be smaller than those who had been normally nurtured, and (b) there were large ventricular spaces in the brains of the neglected children, which would interfere with moods, sleep, and regulation of anxiety. Some of the neurons of children lacking social interaction would not make enough connections to remain functional and will wither. Thus, the lack of early-learning activities and demanding education could mean an overall poorer life's experience with a less sophisticated and developed brain.

The presence of more neurons in the brain does not necessarily promote clearer thinking. Sowell et al. (1999) demonstrated the widespread tendency for feelings of confusion in adolescents corresponds with the MRI-detected high density of synaptic connections (sections 1.2.4 and 1.4), particularly in the parietal and frontal lobes compared to adults. Those which are less used tend to die towards the end of adolescence, indicating that "brains are believed to develop mainly by a **pruning** of their neural thickets to form orderly processing path" (McCrone, 2000), as considered at the beginning of this section.

 RESEARCH STUDY

Maguire et al. (2000)

Maguire et al. (2000) investigated whether brain plasticity could be detected in the brains of people who intensely studied spatial navigation. It focused on a test group of 16 right-handed active male London taxi drivers who passed The Knowledge (the examination required for taxi drivers to enter the profession) no less that 18 months previously. The MRI brain scans of the taxi drivers were compared with 50 male non-taxi drivers of similar age. The researchers found a significantly greater amount of grey matter signifying the development of neural networks in the posterior hippocampuses of the brains of the taxi drivers, whose volume seemed to correlate positively with the number of months working as a London taxi driver. The study concluded that regular and intensive practice in the spatial navigation of London's very complex street network stimulated neuroplasticity within the memory-handling hippocampus.

> This study can also be used for localisation of brain function.

The study had the strengths of the support of MRI scans that indicated a substantially increased volume of grey matter in the hippocampus that incorporated the complex mental map for driving in London. It is all the more significant in being supported by the positive correlation between months of post-Knowledge taxi driving, and volume of grey matter. However, the possibility of those who chose to become taxi drivers having pre-existing well-developed spatial abilities cannot completely be ruled out. In addition, at 16, the number of participants in the test group was relatively small.

 RESEARCH STUDY

Draganski et al. (2004)

Draganski et al. (2004) was an experimental study that investigated whether a new motor skill – learning how to juggle, would show correlating structural changes in the brain. It was **independent measures** in design, meaning that participants were allocated to the test group or the control group. There were 24 volunteer participants, aged 20–24, 3 male and 21 female.

> This study can also be used for localisation of brain function, neural network development through dendritic branching, and neural pruning.

None of the participants had any experience in juggling. Those in the test group only were given three months coaching in a three-ball juggling routine. At the end of that time they could do it. After that, they were instructed not to do any juggling for the next three months. Those in the control group were not given any coaching at any stage.

All participants, test and control, were MRI-scanned before the coaching period, after the three months of training, and after the three month no-juggling period.

The scans showed no significant differences between the test and the control group in the initial scans. The second scans showed a significant increase in grey matter, developments of neural networks, in the mid-temporal area in both hemispheres in the test group. This region is associated with visual memory: observing movements and then remembering how to do them. The third scans after the three-month no-juggling period saw a decline in grey matter in that part of the brain, indicating neural pruning. There were no grey matter changes in the control group.

The study concluded that learning that new skill using visual memory had the correlate of increased grey matter, supporting development of neural networks and featuring dendritic branching. Not using that skill for three months had the correlate of decreased grey matter, supporting neural pruning.

The study had the strengths of being experimental in design, demonstrating cause and effect. The brain scanning showed biological correlates in the areas of the brain associated with creating visual memory. However, the participating volunteers was gender biased group (21 females, 3 males). The sample was also small, reflecting a general issue with the expense and time-consuming nature of brain scanning.

1.2.4 Neurotransmitters and their Effect on Human Behaviour

Psychology's interest in neurotransmitters is that these chemical substances coordinate to promote a wide and complex range of human emotions and behaviours. A person's biological and psychological situation can affect the rate of firing (the release) of neurotransmitters. Any one **neuron** (nerve cell) may be working with some 10,000 **synapses** (tiny but significant clefts or gaps between one neuron and other neurons, typically about one millionth of a centimetre) with many thousands of other neurons. It is the synapse that makes it possible for a neuron to pass an electrical or chemical signal to another cell. Drugs such as nicotine can stimulate neurotransmitter activity, and also inhibit neurotransmitter activity by covering the ends of the synaptic sites.

Neurotransmitters are chemical substances found in the terminal buttons of a neuron, and are biochemical in structure. They enable stimuli (such as pricking your finger on a red rose) to be processed and reacted to by the central nervous system (brain and spinal cord). Every stimulus or unit of information has a different feeling, because of the way they communicate with the brain and the way the brain responds to that communication. Neurons are not joined together in one long chain, but each one is separated from the adjacent ones by the synaptic clefts.

It is the ***existence of synapses that make neurotransmission possible***. Neurotransmission, the communication between neurons, is an electro/biochemical process. The neural impulse is electric. As it travels along the **axon** (the body of the neuron) it releases neurotransmitters that are stored in the terminal buttons of the neuron. These jump across the synaptic clefts, and are absorbed by the receptor sites of the receptors (dendrites) of one or more adjacent neurons, rather as a key fits into a lock. The neurotransmitters may then be **re-uptaken** by the terminal buttons for further use, or broken down by enzymes. The whole process of neurotransmission repeats itself from neuron to neuron, and to/from/within the central nervous system (brain and spinal cord). Psychiatrists can prescribe drugs designed to stimulate neurotransmission where the natural mechanisms

1. THE BIOLOGICAL APPROACH TO UNDERSTANDING HUMAN BEHAVIOUR

are insufficient, or inhibit neurotransmission where the natural mechanisms are excessive.

Neurotransmitters that increase the likelihood of a neuron firing crossing the synapse are **excitatory** (e.g. memory-forming acetylcholine, considered below), and those that decrease the likelihood of a neuron firing crossing the synapse are **inhibitory** (e.g. GABA, gamma-aminobutyric acid, which inhibits memory forming activity in the hippocampus and in the frontal lobe, making it easier to block out intrusive thoughts when concentrating). Neurotransmitters that only indirectly affect the neuron are **metabotropic**, which are classified separately to excitatory and inhibitory. Dopamine and serotonin are examples of metabotropic neurotransmitters.

The effects of neurotransmitters (whether excitatory or inhibitory) activity may be speeded up by **agonists**, and slowed down by **antagonists**. If the neurotransmitter is excitatory, an agonist will increase the excitatory effect, and an antagonist will decrease the excitatory effect. If a neurotransmitter is inhibitory, an agonist will increase the inhibitory effect of the neurotransmitter, whereas an antagonist will decrease the inhibitory effect.

Chemicals that cause an agonist or an antagonist reaction by attaching themselves to receptors in the brain occur naturally as e.g. hormones, and in manufacture, e.g. in drugs. The influence of agonists and antagonists on neurotransmitter functioning is exemplified by the research of Martinez and Kesner (1991) in Section 1.7, an experimental study using rats on how agonists and antagonists influence the work of **acetylcholine**, an excitatory memory-forming neurotransmitter. This section includes a later study with similar objectives with human participants, Antonova et al., 2011, focusing on antagonists.

There are many neurotransmitters and only a relatively small number have been identified. For example, **dopamine** is a metabotropic neurotransmitter that helps to control the brain's reward and pleasure centres. Increased dopamine levels in the brain mean increased stimulation. For happy experiences, dopamine release sets the pleasure circuit in action. Dopamine is manufactured in the brain, in the nerve cell bodies located within the ventral tegmental area (VTA), and is released in the nucleus accumbens and the prefrontal cortex.

Dopamine is 'fired' when, for example, you see restaurant advertisement and you immediately get the pleasure that you associate with that food – without eating any of it.

Serotonin is also a metabotropic neurotransmitter, employed by the nervous system in mediation of pain, sleep control, and regulation of mood. High levels of serotonin are associated with feelings of well-being and happiness, and of being at peace with the world.

RESEARCH STUDY

Fisher et al. (2005)

Fisher et al. (2005) investigated the influence of dopamine on love. The study investigated whether people in love would show increased dopamine action in the parts of the brain associated with motivation. The study hypothesised that falling in love is a motivation system that leads to emotion.

The participants were 7 male and 10 female young adults (aged 18–26) who were in the courtship stage (average 7 months; range 1–17 months). The researchers obtained two sets of data on nature, intensity, and duration of each participant's being in love. Firstly, the interviewed each participant using a semi-structured format. Secondly, each participant

This study can also be used for electronic methods of studying the brain, and the localisation of the functioning of the brain.

expressed the degree of intensity of the love relationship by completed a "Passionate Love Scale" (PLS).

The study itself used a fMRI scanner on each participant. In the scanner throughout the test, the participant viewed the photograph of the person they were in love with for just 30 seconds. They were then asked, as a distraction, to count backwards in sevens from a high number for 40 seconds. Next, they viewed a picture of someone they knew for 30 seconds. Finally, another countdown test, lasting 20 seconds.

The fMRI scans showed different parts of the brain involved when viewing the picture of the beloved, and the picture of the acquaintance. Looking at the beloved, but not at the acquaintance activated the right VTA (ventral tegmental area), which is a dopamine-rich area of the brain that produces intense pleasure, motivation, and focused arousal.

The strengths of the study are that dopamine action in the VTA did increase with viewing the photograph of the beloved, which may indicate that dopamine as a neurotransmitter is designed to power our motivation system in anticipation of pleasures and rewards. The study is limited by the difficulty in determining cause and effect: initially, is it the dopamine affecting love or the love affecting dopamine? Also, our knowledge of the workings of neurotransmitters are limited: it is not clear which other neurotransmitters might be working together with the dopamine and the degree that they be affected by agonists that increase their effect or antagonists that decrease their effect.

RESEARCH STUDY

Antonova et al. (2011)

This study aimed to examine the role of **acetylcholine**, and **excitatory neurotransmitter** on spatial memory. *The IB accepts cognitive process including memory as a type of behaviour.* It is a pioneer piece of research on humans: previous studies (such as Martinez and Kesner, 1991) used rats, with the problem of how far the findings can be generalised to humans.

This study can also be used to explain the role of an excitatory neurotransmitter (acetylcholine), and an antagonist (scopolamine) in a short answer question. The antagonist function will not be directly examined in an essay response question.

The study of Martinez and Kesner (1991) in Section 1.7 contains an additional study on the role of acetylcholine in memory using rats that focuses on both agonists (use of physostigmine) and antagonists (use of scopolamine). Although it is placed in the HL section, it is vital for both HL and SL students.

There were 20 male adult participants. The study was experimental, using a repeated measures design. Participants were randomly divided into two groups.

In the first stage, half were injected with scopolamine, an antagonist. The other half were injected with a placebo. Each participant was then put into an fMRI scanner to record brain activity, with the task of memorising spatial information from a screen on how to navigate a complex arena to get to a pole. Once they had observed, the screen was switched off for 30 seconds, with the participant instructed to mentally rehearse the route to the pole. The screen then switched on, and the participant was then required to find the way from a different start using a joystick, making use of previously gained knowledge of the arena to get to the pole. It was hypothesised that those injected with scopolamine would perform the task substantially less successfully, as scopolamine had an antagonist effect of the acetylcholine memory-forming neurotransmitters.

In the second stage, about a month later, the participants carried out the same procedure again. Those who had been injected with scopolamine in the first phase were injected with a placebo, and vice-versa. It was thus repeated measures in design, as the same participants took part in both the test condition and the control condition.

The results were in two parts. The fMRI scans showed significantly less hippocampal activity when the participants were injected with scopolamine than when injected with a placebo. The actual performance in the navigating-the-arena-to-the-pole task was overall poorer, but the difference was not sufficient to be statistically significant.

1. THE BIOLOGICAL APPROACH TO UNDERSTANDING HUMAN BEHAVIOUR

The team concluded on the evidence of the fMRI scans that the efficiency and abundance of neurotransmitter acetylcholine can improve the memory process. Its application is that similar drugs can help people to improve their memories

Strengths and limitations: Antonova et al. (2011)

Strengths	Limitations
1. The research used two techniques simultaneously: brain scanning and computer testing, enabling one to be a check on the other (method triangulation, see Chapter 8, Section 8.5) 2. The study was repeated measures in design, so the problem of possible differences between the participants was eliminated as all participated in the test and control condition.	1. Small size of the sample due to the logistics and expense of using the fMRI raises the question of the degree the findings can be generalised. 2. The unfamiliar procedures of injections and being confined to the fMRI could have caused memory-interfering stress.

1.3 Hormones and Their Effect on Human Behaviour

Hormones are chemicals released by the various glands (e.g. adrenal gland, pineal gland) into the blood stream, where they are carried to their place of need. They regulate medium and long-term changes in the body. Some hormones can also act as neurotransmitters (Section 1.2.4 above), such as dopamine and oxytocin.

1.3.1 Oxytocin

Romantic love according to the anthropological research of Fisher (2004) is not an emotion, but a hormone-based motivation system. This can create a craving, to enable lovers to mate, feel very close to each other, and produce offspring. Oxytocin is released with touches and hugs, especially in sex.

Oxytocin is secreted by the hypothalamus and released in two ways: (a) through the pituitary gland into the bloodstream functioning as a hormone, and (b) into the central nervous system (brain and spinal cord) where it connects with oxytocin receptors – functioning as a neurotransmitter.

RESEARCH STUDY

Baumgartner et al. (2008)

Baumgartner et al. experimentally investigated the function of oxytocin as an active hormone in economic decision-making – aimed to investigate the role of oxytocin (IV – independent variable) in causing a cheated partner to forgive and continue the trust that had existed in the relationship (DV – dependent variable).

The test group was given an oxytocin supplement, and the control group a placebo. Both groups then played a trust game. The 'investor' players received a sum of money which they were told to either keep or share with a second 'trustee' player. If the sum was shared, it would be tripled. The 'trustee' player could share the money (trust) or could keep the money (betrayal). The participants played against different 'second players' in the trust game, and then against a computer in a similar risk game. The trust was betrayed in half the games. The players received feedback at once from those conducting the experiment. Those who had taken oxytocin continued to invest (forgave, continued to trust despite betrayal) at the same rate when playing with people (but not the computer), even though they knew that they had been cheated. Those on the placebo invested less.

fMRI brain scans showed that the test group showed a decreased response in the highly-concentrated oxytocin receptor amygdala section of the brain, and in the caudate nucleus in the brain (involved in reward-related responses, and learning to trust).

Strengths and limitations: Baumgartner et al. (2008)

Strengths	Limitations
1. Experimental nature of study; the control was given a placebo. The set up made it possible to indicate cause and effect 2. Shows biological input to people forgiving and restoring trust within relationships. 3. Can show why being in love may blind to very serious faults in one's partner.	1. The areas of the brain scanned did show decreased action, but the connection with oxytocin was entirely correlational. There was no scientific explanation of the physiological work of oxytocin supplement. 2. The effects of nasal spray oxytocin, and naturally produced oxytocin may differ.

1.3.2 Melatonin

Melatonin is produced by the pineal gland. It is secreted as a reaction to the dark and inhibited by light. It affects human behaviour in helping us to sleep. Its precise function is to communicate with the pituitary gland, which in turn sends out other hormones that make it difficult to stay awake. Thus, people tend to sleep more during the long winter nights than in the shorter summer nights, and less if there is a light on in the bedroom.

SAD (seasonal affective disorder) is a type of depression occurring at the beginning and end of winter, which seems to be related to melatonin levels. Associated behaviours include fatigue, irritability, problems concentrating, loss of sex-drive, and insomnia.

RESEARCH STUDY

Avery et al. (2001)

Avery et al. used a laboratory experimental method to investigate the function of melatonin in the behaviours of 95 SAD patients, who were divided into three groups. The first received 'dawn simulation' – an artificial-lighting-produced false dawn starting at 4:30 am (involving timing the bedroom lights to come on gradually during the hour or so before awakening). The second was given bright light therapy, and the third a placebo dim red light at dawn. That last group, the control, was put under the impression that the dim red light would help their SAD symptoms. In reality, the dim red light would not have stopped the melatonin secretion and removed the SAD symptoms. All patients were interviewed, and the interviews were structured and standardised. Results: those given dawn simulation and bright light therapy were able to fit their sleep patterns with their normal routines by stopping the sleep-promoting melatonin. Dawn simulation was actually more effective: it happened without the side-effects of the headaches and nausea of the bright light therapy group. Those who were given the placebo were not deceived, and in most cases the SAD continued.

1. THE BIOLOGICAL APPROACH TO UNDERSTANDING HUMAN BEHAVIOUR

Strengths and limitations: Avery et al. (2001)

Strengths	Limitations
1. It was a laboratory experiment that indicated that the natural functioning of the hormone melatonin is influenced by the presence of light. Bright light therapy and dawn stimulation could regulate the sleep patterns, apparently by stimulating a rise in melatonin levels. 2. It can be applied to sleep problems such as those caused by jet lag: melatonin is now available in pill form.	1. The types of therapy that the participants knew they were receiving could have affected their self-reporting during interview. 2. The study was confined to SAD patients. It did not extend to the situation of people who lived in such environments whose sleep patterns remained undisturbed and thus did not seem to react to melatonin in the same way.

1.4 Pheromones and Their Effect on Human Behaviour

Pheromones are chemical messengers that animals produce and release into the environment that are designed to influence the behaviour of other nearby members of the species. They can signal, for example, danger, presence of food, or invitation for sexual activity. Their presence is well established in species of insects, and apparent in pigs. The androstenone that pigs secret through their sweat glands seems to function as a pheromone in signalling aggression or sexual attraction. However, the vomeronasal organ, the part of the olfactory (smell) system that seems to be detecting the androstenone from pigs appears to be non-functional in humans. There is no current study that conclusively demonstrates that humans exude substances that biologically act as pheromones.

Currently, the debate on human pheromones includes:

- The highly complex nature of human odour receptors questions whether human behaviour is influenced by the smell as a whole or by specific chemicals functioning as pheromones. Mere smell is not a pheromone.
- The fact that bacteria combine with substances secreted by the body raises the question as whether the behaviour is influenced by the bacteria combining with specific chemicals rather than specific chemicals functioning as pheromones.
- Complications in generalising any findings on pheromones influencing behaviour when taking into account cultural variations as to what constitutes a pleasant, attractive smell.
- Failure to discover a single, naturally-produced human-secreted substance whose functioning as a pheromone has been conclusively demonstrated.

 RESEARCH STUDY

Gelstein et al. (2011)

Gelstein et al. experimentally investigated whether sadness-emitted human tears would emit pheromone-type chemosignals that would reduce the sex drive of potential mates. The researchers in the experimental study used two solutions that were indistinguishable to the all-male participants. One, for the test condition, contained sadness-produced human tears that were generated by two young women watching a sadness-inducing movie. The other, for the control condition, was salt water.

The male participants were exposed at close quarters to drops from the solutions, which were held by a pad close to the nose. The test participants' solution was the tears. The control participants' solution was the salt solution. Both groups then viewed a series of ambiguous pictures of attractive and less attractive people of the opposite sex, and they then rated their attractiveness. Part of the research also offered involved the participants being connected to an fMRI scanner that registered the parts of the brain that were responding to those stimuli. The study was repeated soon afterwards, with the test group becoming the control group with the saline solution and the control group becoming the test group with the tears. Thus all participants participated in both the test and control modes, a repeated measures design.

The results found lower sexual arousal in the test mode participants whose sexual interest seems to have been weakened by closeness to the tears. The researchers concluded that there was indeed a possibility that the sadness-produced tears could contain pheromones that would biologically lower the sex-drive of nearby would-be suitors.

Strengths and limitations: Gelstein et al. (2011)

Strengths	Limitations
1. The study was a controlled, repeated-measures experiment whereby all participants underwent both the test and the control conditions. 2. It was supported by fMRI correlates.	1. Reproductions of this study have not shown the same results. 2. No biochemical substance in the study was demonstrated to be acting in the capacity of a pheromone.

RESEARCH STUDY

Hare et al. (2017)

Hare et al. experimentally investigated whether androstadienone (AND) and estratetraenol (EST), two putative (thought to possibly be) human sex pheromones would indeed positively influence judgement of gender, sexual attraction, and probability of unfaithfulness.

The first phase involved 46 heterosexual participants of both genders. All had a cotton ball taped under the nose throughout the task. On the first day, the cotton balls of the test participants were moistened with clove oil containing AND and EST, and those of the control group with clove oil only. They were exposed to five morphs: gender-neutral faces, and all participants had to state whether each morph was male or female. The researchers hypothesised that sensing AND or EST would prompt the viewer to see the opposite sex in the morph. On the second day, the experimenters repeated the procedure, but unknown to both the participants and to those actually administering the experiment, those who were exposed to the test condition on the first day received the control clove oil only, and vice-versa. Thus, on the second day, the test group had become the control group, and the control group had become the test group, a **repeated measures design**. The study was **double blind**, as neither the experimenters nor the participants knew who was in the test condition and who was in the control condition.

The second phase involved 94 heterosexual participants of both genders. The experiment was of similar design over two days, using the cotton balls with clove oil, with or without the AND and EST, double-blind, and repeated measures in design. However, in this phase, instead of morphs, participants were shown photographs of faces of the opposite sex, and asked to rate their attractiveness and likelihood of sexual unfaithfulness.

1. THE BIOLOGICAL APPROACH TO UNDERSTANDING HUMAN BEHAVIOUR

The results indicated that neither AND nor EST functioned as pheromones. There was no difference between the test and the control groups in the gender identification of morphs, perceived attractivity and perceived unfaithfulness of the owners of the faces of the opposite sex. The researchers concluded from this study that there was no support for most likely candidates AND and EST functioning as pheromones.

Strengths and limitations: Hare et al. (2017)

Strengths	Limitations
1. The study was a controlled, repeated-measures experiment whereby all participants took part in both the test and the control conditions. 2. There were a relatively large number of participants. 3. Its validity was enhanced by the double-blind nature of the procedures.	1. Low ecological validity due to the laboratory set-up. 2. The action of the putative pheromones AND and EST may have not been activated by the particular tasks chosen by the researchers.

Wedekind (1995) in Chapter 7 (Section 7.1.1) may be used a further study on the possible existence and functioning of pheromones.

1.5 Genetics and Behaviour

A gene is a unit of **deoxyribonucleic acid** (**DNA**) that is found on a thread-like chromosome. Genes are the units that contain the genetic information that is passed from one generation to the next. These not only affect physical characteristics, but appear to influence behavioural patterns as well. Collectively, all the genes that a person has form the individual's **genome**.

1.5.1 Key Principles of Psychology's Involvement in Genetics

Genes influence behaviour

Genes influence the inheritance of biological characteristics that may in turn influence behaviour. Typically, a specific behaviour pattern is a product of both the combination of specific genes, and the environment. The evidence for links between genes and specific behaviours requires taking environmental factors into account, as in the next principle.

The presence of genes that could influence a behaviour does not necessarily mean that behaviour will be expressed

Psychological factors within the environment such as stress and other elements that activate hormones, cultural influences, and also diet and exercise can switch on or switch off gene-functioning. The study of such elements that regulate the switching on and switching off genes is called **epigenetics**. Having genes for a behaviour does not necessarily mean that behaviour will occur. Indeed, sometimes genes are permanently switched off, usually due to the biochemical process of **methylation** of the DNA molecule as part of the development process, and may never be expressed in the future. Methylation happens within the life cycle of some genes where methyl groups combine with the DNA molecule, and can change the activity of a DNA segment without changing the sequence. In addition, **mutations** can occur where actual alterations of the DNA take place.

Genetics link with evolutionary theory

Those whose genes support the behavioural traits that are most compatible with the environment are the ones who are most likely to survive, successfully attract a partner, and reproduce. However, successfully adapting to the environment also influences chances of survival and mating opportunities. This point is expanded later in this section in Komori et al. (2009).

1.5.2 Methods of Investigation into Genetically-based Theories of Behaviour

Methods that psychology uses to investigate genetically-based theories of behaviour have considerably advanced in the 21st century with genetic mapping, although some earlier studies continue to be of value.

Genetic similarities: Twin studies, and kinship (family) studies

Genetic similarities are referred to as relatedness: the higher the genetic similarity, the greater degree of relatedness. The degree of relatedness between the participants of the study has to be taken into account when evaluating the validity of a twin study, or a kinship study. A kinship study investigates the incidences of particular behaviour(s) among members of the family over generations.

The twin studies approach takes the view that the relative importance of genes (nature) versus different environments (nurture) can be best studied using the rare instances of where twins have been brought up separately from each other.

Studies in genetic similarities include comparing the behaviours of monozygotic (MZ) twins, dizygotic (DZ) twins, siblings, and natural and adopted children. MZ twin studies are of particular interest to researchers as in terms of relatedness they share 100% of their genes, which suggests a likelihood of higher **concordance rates** (probability that the same trait may be present) in intelligence and behaviour than with DZ twins and those more distantly related, and that any differences in MZ twins are likely to be due to different individual experiences of the environment. In contrast, DZ twins and siblings are likely to be sharing 50% of the genetic information.

Both twin and family studies make it possible to compare the behaviours of those brought up together and who have been brought up apart, in order to assess the role of specific psychological elements. This enables researchers to deduce the relative importance of genes and the environment in influencing a particular behaviour pattern.

RESEARCH STUDY

Bouchard et al. (1990) aka The Minnesota study of twins reared apart

This longitudinal study began in 1979. Participants were 137 pairs of twins (81 identical, 56 non-identical, some reared apart and some reared together), recruited worldwide.

It aimed to investigate the degree that genes determine intelligence. In linking intelligence to behaviour, a more intelligent person is likely to interact on a deeper level with the environment and society. It was designed as a twin study. Its rationale was that the relative importance of genes (nature) versus different environments (nurture) can be studied using the rare instances of where twins have been brought up separately from one other as they would be sharing the same genes.

The participants were assessed for intelligence though some 50 hours of testing and interviewing. The twin study indicated that 70% of intelligence and behaviour patterns appeared to be influenced by genetic factors and 30% to other factors. The MZ twins' similarities even when separated showed significantly higher concordance rates than DZ twins even when raised together.

The study had the strength of being was cross-cultural, as its participants were recruited worldwide. It incorporated both interviewing and a variety of tests which had a triangulatory function supporting the validity of the data. Its limitations include problems in generalising the findings of the study as participants were recruited through media publicity. There was no adequate method of ascertaining the frequency of contact between the twins before the study. There is also the likelihood that twins brought up together do not necessarily experience their environments in the same way. In addition, the data found was correlational and thus unable to establish cause and effect.

RESEARCH STUDY

Hutchings and Mednick (1975)

Hutchings and Mednick is a pioneer adoptive study on the influence of genetics on criminal behaviour. It studied 14,000 adopted children, investigating whether criminal behaviour was more likely to have been learnt from the adoption environment, or if it was guided by specific genes towards criminal behaviour. It found that a relatively high proportion of boys with criminal convictions had biological parents with criminal convictions. This suggests a possible genetic link between genetics and aggressive behaviour.

Specifically, this study found that if both the biological and adoptive fathers had criminal records, more than a third of the sons would also have criminal records. If just the biological father had a criminal record, it would drop to about a fifth. Where the adoptive father had such a record it dropped further to 11%, a ninth. Where neither father had one (the control), 10% of the sons had a criminal record.

Conclusion: genetics (nature) played a somewhat greater (but certainly not exclusive) role than upbringing (nurture) in influencing criminal behaviour. The study had the advantage of access to a large number of records of adopted children. It was ecologically valid as the participants' behaviours considered were those taking place in their own environment. However, the study may be criticised:

- Children who are adopted are often placed in a similar environment to their natural parents.
- Genes seem unlikely to account for criminal behaviour peaking in the 20s age-group, and then sharply declining.
- Legal definitions of different types of crime are unlikely to conform to genetic structures.

> This study can also be used for genes and behaviour.

RESEARCH STUDY

Weissman et al. (2005)

This was a 20-year longitudinal kinship (family) study to research the role of genes in influencing depression over three generations. It examined the family incidence of depression in grandchildren by gathering information about their parents and grandparent's experience or non-experience of depression. It was a prospective study, as it involved studying the children and grandchildren of depression to see whether they would develop a similar condition.

The core sample consisted of adults in two categories, diagnosed with major depression, and non-diagnosed with major depression. They and their children were interviewed four times during the period of the study, by which time the children had become parents, and the parents had become grandparents. In total, there were 161 grandchildren and their parents and grandparents participating in the study. The children were evaluated twice, by a child psychiatrist and a psychologist.

Mental health professionals, who had neither access to information on the individual participant's mental health nor access to data from previous interviews, conducted the interviews. It was thus a blind study, to ensure its credibility.

The results indicated that mental health issues in the third generation were (i) most likely where both parents and grandparents had been diagnosed with depression, with more than half showing symptoms of mental health concern (mostly anxiety) by age 12 (ii) in those circumstances, more likely to display extreme symptoms where parental depression was more severe (iii) not significant in incidence where there was parental depression, but no grandparental depression.

This research indicates the importance of a family study extending more than two generations, as the parent's genes passed on to the children appear to be moderated by those of the grandparents.

The study had the strengths of being longitudinal in design and extending over three generations. Those conducting the interview were in the blind condition. Its limitations include not having identified any specific genotype, and the variations of the amount of time the children spent with their grandparents.

1.5.3 Linkage analysis

Linkage analysis is where the nature of specific behaviour patterns is correlated with variations within the genes. This can involve **genome-wide association studies (GWAS)**, the use of a large genetic database to research whether a particular variant is associated with a specific trait.

RESEARCH STUDY

Caspi et al. (2003)

This study can also be used for how a specific gene, 5-HTT, influences behaviour.

This is a pioneer study in linkage analysis. Its aim was to examine whether the degree of an individual's susceptibility to depression following stress is influenced by the person's genetic makeup.

This study focused on the role of serotonin in depression together with the role of genes in determining the availability of serotonin. Serotonin functions as both a neurotransmitter and a hormone. Low serotonin levels are associated with symptoms of depression, having negative effects on mood, appetite, sleep, and sexual desire. The study was grounded in the diathesis-stress model, holding that major depression and other abnormal conditions are products of both the genotype (genetic structure) and the environment. The hypothesis of the study was that a mutation of the low-level serotonin transporter gene 5-HTT influenced susceptibility to depression. The particular mutation was at least one 5-HTT allele being short instead of long.

The aim of the study was to investigate the influence of genetic make on susceptibility to depression.

The study involved 847 26-year-old participants, in New Zealand. All of them had regular health check-ups until age 21. They were divided into three groups according to genotype according to genotype: two long alleles (control), one long allele and one short allele (test), and two short alleles (test).

Each participant self-reported through responding to a questionnaire that was designed to assess two variables: (a) the amount of stress experienced in work, health, and relationships, and (b) the presence or absence of symptoms of depression.

The researchers found that participants in the test groups (with one or two short alleles) showed significantly more symptoms of depression than those in the control group with two long alleles, but this was only true where they had been exposed to major stressful life events, not otherwise. The team concluded that there is a link between genotype and depressive symptoms that could express themselves through experiencing stressful events.

Strengths and limitations: Caspi et al. (2003)

Strengths	Limitations
1. It was controlled, it used a large sample, and it applied a biologically-based quantitative method of linkage analysis. 2. The questionnaire covered a wide range of environmental elements that might promote genetic expression.	1. Many individuals with two long alleles have received diagnoses of major depression. 2. It is not clear what exactly caused the depression in each case: the genetic mutation or the stressful environmental conditions. 3. 5-HTT is a serotonin transporter gene, whose study in this context accepts the serotonin hypothesis. This holds that lower activity on the serotonin pathways plays a causal role in the development of depression. The serotonin hypothesis is not well supported by research and is thus not accepted by all biological psychologists.

1.5.4 Ethical Considerations: Genetics-based Research

The most widespread aim of research in human genetics is to identify particular genes involved in heredity diseases, but furthering understanding of human behaviour is also very important. Its potential for improving the overall quantity and quality of life has to be balanced with the following ethical issues:

- Danger of information leaks on 'adverse' genetic characteristics creating difficulties in finding a partner, getting a job, or the terms of a medical insurance policy. The researcher has to guarantee confidentiality, with a signed consent document showing the participant's clear understanding of the study and its implications.
- Possibility that a participant has unknowingly been adopted.
- Participant anonymity protects, but can prevent any follow-up study.
- The importance of the discovery of a previously unknown genetic disorder might well be over-exaggerated by the participant, or taken out of proportion/context.
- Cultural issues are extremely sensitive with many ethnic groups. Typically, the elders of the society must be consulted for permission to work with members of their group.

1.6 Evolutionary Explanations of Behaviour

Evolution holds that it is the fittest that survive and pass their genes on to the next generation. Psychology focuses on the key concept of those whose genes support the behavioural traits that are most compatible with the environmental are the ones who are most likely to survive, successfully attract a partner, and reproduce.

RESEARCH STUDY

Komori et al. (2009)

The purpose of this study was to investigate whether having facial symmetry (which in turn is likely to have a genetic input) makes an individual more attractive to the opposite sex. Facial symmetry has also been associated with the positive evolutionary qualities of good health and reproductive fitness, although those links have more recently been questioned in studies such as Pound et al. (2014).

The study aimed to investigate whether increased levels of facial symmetry and averageness (degree of similarity to the gender norm) linked to increased physical attractiveness to the opposite sex.

Conducted in Japan and in Japanese, each of 56 men and 58 women viewed a series of pictures of different people of the opposite sex and were required to rate the attractiveness of each person on the photograph on a semantic scale according to their first impression. The researchers had used geometric morphometrics measures to determine both the degrees of averageness and symmetry of each face.

The results indicated that for male faces symmetry and averageness positively affected attractiveness ratings. For female faces, averageness affected attractiveness, but symmetry did not.

The researchers concluded that facial symmetry and masculinity in a man's face induced perceptions of male masculinity and health which ultimately afforded mating opportunities. The study also indicated that women who were closer to the feminine averageness were most attractive to men.

1. THE BIOLOGICAL APPROACH TO UNDERSTANDING HUMAN BEHAVIOUR

Strengths and limitations: Komori et al. (2009)

Strengths	Limitations
1. The participants were a relatively large sample recruited from a panel of a market research company. 2. The averageness and symmetry of the facial images were standardised by geometric morphometrics procedures, to the degree that each of 72 facial feature points on the face deviated from the gender average and from the opposite side of the face.	1. The Japanese location of study leaves open the extent that its findings can be generalised to other cultures 2. The information in this study was based on superficial initial reactions only. Evolutionary factors can perhaps explain first impressions rather than the deeper qualities that bring mating couples together. 3. The study was on the basis that facial symmetry is a positive evolutionary quality, which has since been questioned (as above)

RESEARCH STUDY

Buss et al (1990)

The work of Buss et al. under the title of the International Mate Selection Project obtained data from some 10,000 participants from 33 countries using a multi-lingual questionnaire designed to identify the characteristics most desired for an exclusive relationship with the person of the opposite sex.

The purpose of this study was to investigate sexual selection evolutionary theory. That holds that survival from one generation to next is dependent on having the desirable characteristics to be selected as a mate, with the best choices available to those who have developed particular characteristics. The study aimed to investigate which characteristics promote sexual selection, and the degree that they vary from culture to culture.

The male respondents reported factors that were biologically determined and would tend to optimise reproduction, with culture placing limits on availability. Irrespective of upbringing and way of life, men prized youth and physical attraction, virginity tending to be a limiting factor in the more traditional societies only. Associating pleasing appearance with health, the findings supported the theory that men compete for the women that will most enhance their genetic material, and that are physically in the best position to bring up children. Characteristics reported as being most valued by females were also biological: they wanted the male partner that was physically and by extension economically able, supporting the theory that females desire the opposite-gender partner that can provide the desired optimum levels of security and support.

Strengths and limitations: Buss et al. (1990)

Strengths	Limitations
1. It is cross-cultural, linguistically sensitive, and it used a large sample. 2. It emphasises the important of economic success as a human evolutionary strategy, particularly in males.	1. Relied on self-reporting, with possibilities of translation inaccuracies 2. Possibility of respondents finding themselves influenced by perceived demand characteristics of the researchers.

1.7 The value of animal models in research to provide insight into human behaviour (Higher Level only)

The purpose of animal models in psychology is to obtain data on animal behaviour and then apply the findings to understanding human behaviour. An animal model is the use of non-human species in research, whose findings are then extended to humans. Despite the increasing availability and prevalence of brain scanning in research, psychologists continue using animals for research for the following reasons:

- Genetic and physiological similarities to humans: particularly useful for testing and refining psychiatric drugs before putting them on the market.
- Short life cycles: using mice makes it possible to study several generations over a short period. Faster aging in animals enables simulations of the human life cycle for the study of, for example, the effect of childhood deprivation on behaviour patterns as an adult.
- May be used in situations that would be impractical or unethical for human participation, such as isolation. They may also be killed using humane methods for autopsies that might provide more information than brain scans.
- They can be of considerable value in projects researching human life-enhancing and life prolonging treatments, for example treatment of Alzheimer's.

> **Ethical Considerations: Animal Research**
>
> The use of animals in research has posed severe ethical problems that are considered at the end of this chapter. The EU statistics of 2011 showed that overwhelming majority of the 11 million animals used in medical and psychological research are rodents, mainly mice. Primates such as chimpanzees, baboons and other monkeys are far more rarely used and had declined by a third since 2008.

The use of animal models in psychology has contributed to understanding of many aspects of human behaviour, of which three are considered below:

1. Rosenzweig et al. (1972) on whether a more stimulating environment enables the brain to support a more complex range of behaviours
2. Martinez and Kesner (1991) on memory recall influencing behaviour.
3. Leinenga and Gotz, (2015) on the use of ultrasound technology to treat Alzheimer's disease patients.

RESEARCH STUDY

Rosenzweig et al. (1972)

Rosenzweig et al. studied neural development as a result of stimulating environments, using laboratory rats. The aim of the experiment was whether the presence or absence of being in an exciting and stimulating environment influenced brain plasticity; in this case the development of more complex and highly functional neural developments in the cerebral cortex of the brain. That in turn would promote a more sophisticated repertoire of behaviour from the rats.

The procedure used rats with similar genotypes as they all came from the same litter. Each rat was allocated to one of three groups for a 30-day period, making it an independent measures study: (i) controlled environment with three rats to the cage, and no objects

1. THE BIOLOGICAL APPROACH TO UNDERSTANDING HUMAN BEHAVIOUR

to play with (ii) experimental impoverished environment where each rat was in an individual bare cage, and no objects to play with (iii) experimental enriched environment with a maze and a range of toys to play with. The rats were then killed using standard human procedures and studies were made of the brains of the rats in the control and test conditions.

The researchers found that the rats from the test-enriched conditions had significantly thicker and heavier cortexes than those in the test impoverished condition, and that their active nervous system was denser and transmitted memory-assisting neurotransmitter acetylcholine more efficiently.

This pioneer study concluded that consistent interaction with a stimulating environment promotes brain plasticity. Generalised to humans, this supports the importance of providing exciting, interactive, and challenging environments for children from a very early age. It may also indicate that growing up in stimulus-lacking poverty situation can hinder brain development, with a poorer mental capacity to apply to learning, and sophisticated and informed decision-making.

Strengths and limitations: Rosenzweig et al. (1972)

Strengths	Limitations
1. The research was in a fully controlled laboratory setting, enabling the establishment of cause and effect. 2. The findings in neuroplasticity are supported by later brain scanning studies with human participants, e.g. Maguire et al. (2000) (Section 1.4). 3. The privations and deaths suffered may well be justifiable in modern ethical terms in view of the value of the study to human behaviour and the lack of sophistication of brain scanning at that time.	1. A follow-up study by the researchers indicated that it was unclear whether the primary factor in brain development was playing with the toys or the company of other rats. It observed that rats placed in solitary conditions with toys tended to leave the toys alone. 2. The findings on rats may not be readily generalised to humans, as, for example, rats to do have the granular prefrontal cortex of human beings.

 RESEARCH STUDY

Martinez and Kesner (1991)

This study researched the workings of the nervous system, but focused on the role of **acetylcholine**, a neurotransmitter involved in memory. Its objective was to investigate the ways in which acetylcholine influences the formation of memory.

The procedure was experimental, and used rats bred for laboratory purposes. Each rat was allocated to one of three conditions: (i) control sample, rats not injected with any substance (ii) test sample whereby the rats were injected with **scopolamine**, a drug that blocks acetylcholine receptors, having antagonist effects on the nervous system including memory formation (iii) test sample whereby the rats were injected with **physostigmine**, a drug that has an agonist effect on the effectiveness of acetylcholine, preventing its breakdown and thus enabling the memory process to be more effective.

Each rat was placed in a maze with food at the end. The researchers recorded the time taken to complete the maze.

The researchers found that those injected with scopolamine (with antagonist effects on the work of acetylcholine in memory formation) took the longest to complete the maze. Those injected with physostigmine (with agonist effects on the work of acetylcholine in

This study might be used to explain the role of an agonist and an antagonist in a short answer question. However, Antonova et al. (2011) in Section 1.2.4 could be preferable as the participants there were humans.

memory formation) took the least time to complete the maze. The control group's average time was in between the two differently-treated test groups.

The team concluded that the efficiency and abundance of neurotransmitter acetylcholine can improve the memory process. Its application is that similar drugs can help people to improve their memories.

Strengths and limitations: Martinez and Kesner (1991)

Strengths	Limitations
1. The research was in a fully controlled laboratory setting, enabling the establishment of cause and effect. 2. The study is easily replicable. 3. Ethically, the privations and deaths suffered may well be justifiable in modern ethical terms in view of the value of the study to human behaviour and the lack of sophistication of brain scanning at that time.	1. It could be argued that it was the getting an injection as well as what they were injected with that affected the time the rats took to get through the maze. This point was addressed in Rogers and Kesner (2003), a later, similar study, which included a group of rats being injected with a saline solution as a placebo, a substance that does not have any effect and can be used a control as in this study. 2. The findings on rats may not be readily generalised to humans, as, for example, rats do not have the granular prefrontal cortex of human beings.

RESEARCH STUDY

Leinenga and Gotz (2015)

This study has involved the use of non-invasive ultrasound technology on animals with the objective of treating human Alzheimer's disease patients. Its aim is to restore human memory functions, by clearing the brain of neurotoxic amyloid plaques. That allows blood proteins to enter the brain and clear out the clusters of protein deposits that appear to have reduced effective cognitive functioning.

The procedure used genetically modified mice which had been bred to develop the brain deposits that interfered with cognitive functioning. The researchers applied ultrasound treatment that enabled small proteins from the bloodstream to temporarily enter the brain, stimulating the cells that could clear the deposits that caused Alzheimer's disease lack of cognitive functioning.

The mice performed three cognitive tasks before and after the treatment: a maze, an exercise in remembering newly encountered objects, and another exercise in remembering places to avoid. As such, it was a baseline study, of repeated measures design. The results showed a significant cognitive improvement in three quarters of the mice.

The study concluded that the success of ultrasound treatment on mice justified further research with the ultimate objective of addressing Alzheimer's in humans.

1. THE BIOLOGICAL APPROACH TO UNDERSTANDING HUMAN BEHAVIOUR

Strengths and limitations: Leinenga and Gotz (2015)

Strengths	Limitations
1. Opens a possibility of a line of research into a condition that has brought a great deal of suffering to elderly people and their families.	1. It is not clear what medical issues might be involved when attempting to enable proteins in the bloodstream to enter the normally inaccessible brain.
2. Ethically justifiable on the utilitarian grounds relieving widespread human suffering.	2. The findings on mice may not be readily generalised to humans. Human beings have much thicker skulls and would not be able to endure the much higher temperatures that an effective ultrasound treatment would involve.

1.8 Ethical Considerations in Animal Research (Higher Level only)

The EU directive of 2010 for any academic research using animals is required to follow 3Rs, first described in 1959 by Russell and Burch. These are:

▶ **Replace**: Use non-animal-based methods where similar results can be obtained. Possibilities today would include using computer simulations, human volunteers and cell cultures.

▶ **Reduce**: Use the minimum number of animals. Where possible, obtain more findings from the same animals rather than introduce new ones.

▶ **Refine**: Ensure that the research is carried out in such a way that the animals suffer as little as possible before, during and after the research.

These guidelines are typical for countries whose laboratories carry out research that is recognised by the international academic community.

Today's standards in humane care and use of animals in research may be exemplified by the guidelines of the American Psychological Association, whose main principles include the importance of researchers:

- Being trained in the care and the handling of species used.
- Minimising the animals' pain and infection, with surgery under anaesthesia.
- Justifying the scientific value of the research to human well-being in order to give a good reason for any stress and pain that the animals might suffer. The benefits of the findings should clearly outweigh the suffering of the animals. This is especially vital where the treatment is biologically invasive.

In other countries professional practice is guided by legislation, for example the Animals Act (1986) in the UK. Similar directives govern animal research in Japan, although there is increased recognition of the need for an effective accreditation system to maintain compliance with those directives.

Despite the above, ethical use of animals remains controversial: between the utilitarian position presented above and the animal rights position that holds that the fact that animals to not have the capacity to consent or withdraw from the study does not take away from the reality that they experience pain and are entitled to our protection rather than exploitation.

1.9 Research Methods, Designs, and Techniques Used in the Biological Approach to Understanding Behaviour

Research methods include the following examples:

1. Laboratory experiments can be used to investigate a possible cause and effect relationship, e.g. Baumgartner et al. (2008) investigating the effect of oxytocin on economic decision-making.
2. Correlations research: for example genetic patterns may be identified and used to explain behaviour patterns. This is detailed in the section on genetics and human behaviour.
3. Case studies (e.g. Milner et al. 1966–2008), particularly where linking an atypical behaviour pattern with atypical biology such a brain damage.

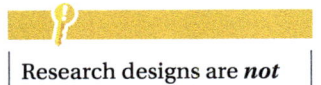

Research designs are *not* research methods.

Research designs include independent measures, repeated measures, and match pairs: twin studies being an example of match pairs. Research designs are exemplified within twin studies, adoptions studies, meta-analyses and longitudinal analyses.

Techniques in research can use biological material, e.g. a saliva sample to detect the level of adrenaline. Techniques also increasingly include brain-imaging technologies (for example, CAT (computerised axial tomography), PET (positron emission tomography), and fMRI (functional magnetic resonance imaging), enabling the study of living brains in action as various tasks are performed. This makes it possible, for example, to correlate specific areas of brain damage with specific changes in a person's personality or cognitive abilities. The key word is correlate. We know relatively little of the actual changes that take place within the brain. We do not have the capacity to view a piece of brain tissue and read the knowledge contained therein.

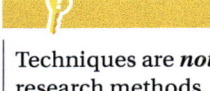

Techniques are *not* research methods.

When answering a question on technique, specify that technique as clearly as possible. For example, specify Harris and Fiske (2006) used the fMRI technique rather than brain scanning.

1.10 Strengths and Limitations: Biological Approach

Strengths of the Biological Approach

- High credibility: scientifically-based subject matter and its experimental methodology.
- Effective practical applications: e.g. the use of medication in treating mental conditions.
- Contributes to an understanding a wide range of phenomena: e.g. why people fall in love.
- Nature based: strong arguments favouring the nature side of the nature/nurture debate.

Limitations of Biological Approach

- Reductionist: could overlook interactions with environmental factors that also affect people's behaviour.
- Determinist: can lead to e.g. explaining criminal behaviour in terms of individual physiology, and genes: "It wasn't me, it was my nervous system."
- Nature based: lacks sufficient recognition of the nurture side of the nature/nurture debate.

1. THE BIOLOGICAL APPROACH TO UNDERSTANDING HUMAN BEHAVIOUR

1.11 Ethical Considerations: Research Methods Used in the Biological Approach

- Informed consent – participants must know the object of the study, that their involvement is voluntary, what the data will be used for, and if necessary be debriefed at the end of the study. In extreme cases, the ethical requirement for informed consent may be waived, when the focus of the study is of public importance and there is no other way to obtain the sought-after information.
- Avoiding deception, except possibly where the research cannot be carried out in any other way (e.g. Hare et al.).
- Protection from harm: particularly important when handling potentially sensitive material such as genetic information (e.g. Caspi et al.)
- Making the participants anonymous to protect them, even at the risk of reducing the authenticity of the research and of preventing any follow-up study. This was carefully observed with H.M. until he gave consent for his anonymity to be waived before his death.
- The right for any participant to withdraw from the study at any point, and communicating that right before the commencement of the study.
- All participants are to be debriefed at the end of the study.
- Avoiding the use of animal participants, as examined in Section 1.7, above. Where not possible, minimising the use and suffering endured by animals involved in the research.
- Bearing in mind that biological research involving associated cultural issues is extremely sensitive with many ethnic groups. Typically, the elders of the society must be consulted for permission to work with members of their group.

 PRACTICE QUESTIONS

Exam-style Practice Questions: The Biological Approach

Short Answer Questions
1. Describe *one* study related to localisation of function in the brain.
2. Explain the role of *one* antagonist with reference to *one* study.

Essay Response Questions
1. With reference to at least one research study, to what extent does genetic inheritance influence behaviour?
2. Discuss ethical considerations in animal research. (HL ONLY)

Chapter 2: The Cognitive Approach to Understanding Human Behaviour

Overview

Our studies in cognitive psychology focus on cognitive processing being shaped by our past experiences that are encoded into memories, and on our cognitive schemas: learning-formed mental representations that process information. As with the computer, the memory functioning of our brain selects what it wishes to store, but as we shall see, the brain does not always store, recall, or enable us to act on information as accurately as a computer.

Though there are many cognitive functions, such as attention, perception, and language learning, we will consider two: memory, and thinking and decision-making. Our journey in cognitive psychology considers how we can model both memory and thinking and decision-making processes, and with what degree of accuracy. We also bear in mind that human beings, unlike computers, experience a range of emotions that may influence cognition.

If you are a Higher Level student, you also look at the computer/human brain analogy in more depth; including how digital technology can influence cognitive processes and human interaction, and how these might be researched.

> Understand that cognitive psychology views thinking and behaviour as coming from the mind acting as an information processor, rather like a computer. Inputs come from people and places, which we contact through our five senses. Processing takes place in our own extremely complex processing unit called the brain. As a cognitive psychologist, you look at the ways that the brain processes incoming information into the outputs, which are thinking and behaviour.

KEY QUESTION

How do we mentally process our experiences into thinking and behaviour?

Learning objectives of this unit include an understanding of:

- The nature of the cognitive processes of memory and schemas (HL and SL)
- The reliability of the cognitive processes of memory and schemas (HL and SL).
- The ways in which emotions might influence cognitive processing (HL and SL).
- Cognitive processing in the digital world (HL only).

2. THE COGNITIVE APPROACH TO UNDERSTANDING HUMAN BEHAVIOUR

2.1 Introduction to the Cognitive Approach

The cognitive approach views behaviour as being a product of the way the human brain processes information. The cognitive approach is defined as focusing on "the processes by which the sensory input (e.g. something we read or hear) is transformed, reduced, elaborated, stored, recovered, and used" (Neisser, 1967).

Cognitive Principles of Interest to Psychologists

- The human being is a vigorous information processor. Like computers, our brains actively organise and manipulate information and cues from the environment. The brain is the hardware, and the schemas (below) are the software
- Cognitive **schemas** (individualised mental representations) guide our behaviour. We tend not to see a reality or situation objectively. Instead, we select and process the inputs from the environment through our personal schemas. These incorporate and apply our stores of related knowledge and experience. Our reactions and behaviour patterns, guided by those schemas, are the outputs.
- The way we mentally process representations that guide our behaviour should be studied scientifically, even though our current understanding of the workings of the brain is elementary.
- Bias and errors in cognitive processes often form patterns and thus tend to be predictable.
- The way we process information is influenced by the emotions that we feel at the time of processing.
- Cognitive processes are influenced by social and cultural inputs, including social norms and societies' values and way of life.
- (HL only) The analogy of the brain being compared to a computer system can serve as a valuable investigative framework to the cognitive psychologist.

Today, cognitive psychologists increasingly work together with neuroscientists, social psychologists and cultural psychologists. They recognise that the cognitive approach interacts in many ways with biological and sociocultural phenomena.

2.2 Cognitive Processing: Models of Memory

Cognitive psychology breaks down the memory process into three separate aspects:

Encoding: entry of information sensed and transformed into the memory system. This can involve the additional cognitive function of **attention**.

Storage: keeping the information in the memory system.

Retrieval: accessing the memory store when the information is needed.

2.2.1 The Multi-Store Memory Model (Atkinson and Shiffrin, 1968)

The Atkinson and Shiffrin multi-store memory model is a model of cognitive processing and retention of information. It presents memory storage and recall as being a **linear process**, with *three separate stores*: **sensory memory**, **short-term memory store (STM)**, and **long-term memory store (LTM)**. There is actually more than one cognitive process involved: attention, and memory: encoding into the memory, and retrieval from the memory.

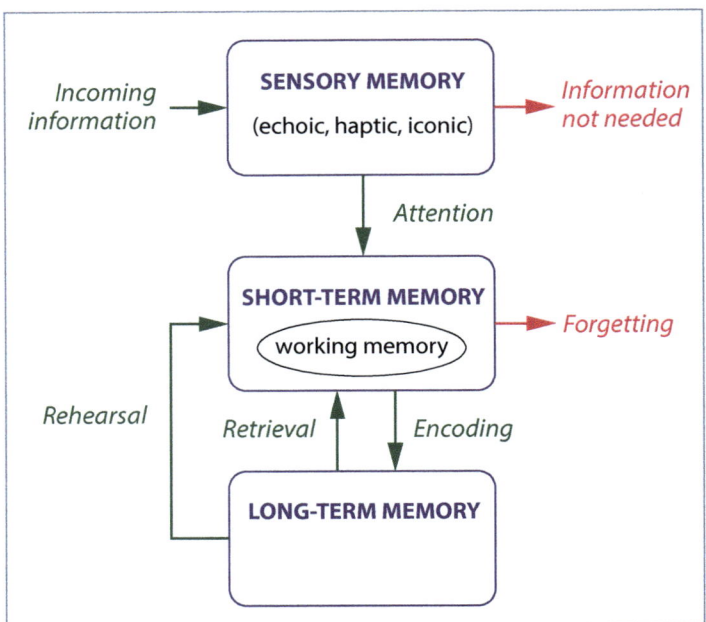

Figure 2.1: **The multi-store memory model**

(i) ***The sensory memory does not process information.*** The sensory memory store's function is to detect information and hold it as it is being attended-to and transferred to the short-term memory, or not attended-to and lost from the system. The attention that is being given can be to information input in any form: sight, sound, smell, taste, or touch. It can be echoic (representing a particular sound), haptic (representing a particular touch or feel), or iconic (representing a particular sight). The information that receives **attention** is then eligible for:

(ii) ***Entry into the STM (short-term memory)*** which temporarily stores a very limited amount of information for up to about 30 seconds). It needs to be processed and rehearsed; otherwise it can be 'displaced' and lost (Think of your straining to remember a seven-figure telephone number). That may further undergo:

(iii) ***Encoding into LTM (long-term memory)***, as the memory trace in the STM becomes consolidated and encoded and enters the LTM, whose capacity appears to be unlimited

In other words, this model regards the memory stores as the structural components of the model. It also incorporates processes, including attention, encoding, and rehearsal, that cause items to enter and leave the memory stores as well as being retrieved from the long-term memory stores.

Support for the STM and the LTM being separate stores in the Multi-Store Memory Model

RESEARCH STUDY

Glanzer and Cunitz (1966)

The aim was to research whether the degree of successful memory encoding from the STM and the LTM depended on the serial position of the information: the **serial position effect**. Would the recall accuracy vary as a function of the item's position on the list?

There were 240 participants. army-enlisted men. In the first condition, the participants heard recordings of 20-word lists, each word being a noun of one syllable. The participants were then given two minutes to recall as many words as possible. The hypothesis was that the recall success rates would depend on the opportunities for rehearsing the words, which would be higher at the beginning (**primacy effect**) and at the end (**recency effect**), but lower in the rehearsal time-lacking middle. In the second condition, a similar list was read out, but at the end the participants were given a count-backwards filler task for 30 seconds and only then went on to recall the words. That was to prevent opportunity for rehearsal to create the recency effect of the last set of words, and a lower success rate of recall was expected.

The results indeed supported the serial position effect, with the words at the beginning and end of the list having the highest frequency of accurate recall evidencing the primacy and recency effects. The results showed that indeed in both conditions the first words had a higher correct recall rate as they had less competition from later words when trying to rehearse them. But the recall rate of the words at the end was significantly higher in the first condition than in the second condition where the recency effect was blocked by the filler task.

As the memory trace seems to have disappeared in the lack of recency effect in the second condition, the researchers concluded that there are two separate systems for storing memory. Rehearsal is vital for the transfer and creation of a memory trace that the LTM, but not the STM, can hold. The first words on the list tend to get repeated and thus rehearsed often enough to enter the LTM. The second condition with the 30-second filler task was designed so that the participants would not have time to rehearse the words at the end of the list, and thus reduced the recency effect by interfering with the STM. This supports the multi-store model by indicating that the STM and LTM have separate memory mechanisms.

Strengths and limitations of Glanzer and Cunitz

Strengths	Limitations
1. Quantitatively supported: large sample that significantly indicated lower rates of recall for the recency effect. 2. Repeated measures design: both the first and second conditions involved the same participants.	1. The task itself was artificial. 2. Low ecological validity as it took place in a laboratory environment.

RESEARCH STUDY

Milner et al. (1966–2008); The Case of HM

The study of HM (Milner et al. 1966–2008, Chapter 1, Section 1.2 – review this study) indicates that amnesia may be caused by damage to the hippocampus and related neural networks that interfere with the formation of permanent new **explicit** (non-procedural) memories. This biologically supports the LTM's having a different memory mechanism to the STM: HM was able to take part in a conversation though he could not recall that conversation afterwards. The strengths are there are biological correlates to HM's patterns of memory recall, and that the HM study's findings been supported by other case studies such as Clive Wearing (below). However, their value as support for the multi-store model is limited by their being single case studies, and that the biological mechanisms supporting long-term memory may well be more complex.

Strengths and Limitations: the Atkinson and Shiffrin Multi-Store Model (1968)

Strengths of the Multi-store Memory Model

1. Studies of anterograde amnesia patients (where brain damage prevents the encoding new items into the LTM) show a good recall of instructions given in the last few seconds (good STM), but a very poor or non-existent recall of those given less recently (poor LTM), suggesting different stores. The brain damage may be caused by brain injury or infection. In behavioural decision-making, this will mean being cut off from past experiences and/or not being able to act with regard to future consequences of the behaviour.

2. The spread of memory functions into different stores explains many STM/LTM deficits shown by brain-damaged patients, as exemplified by the case studies of HM (above) and also of Clive Wearing. In 1985 Clive Wearing, a distinguished English musician and musicologist, suffered a brain infection which interfered with his memory. It reduced the memory span to a few seconds – practically living in the very present only, thus supporting the idea that the STM and LTM are separate stores and his condition prevented transfer from the STM to the LTM. His amnesia was mainly anterograde. He could still perform and conduct the music he knew before the infection. His emotional memory prior to the infection was unaffected: he still loved his wife.

3. In free-recall experiments (e.g. Glanzer and Cunitz, 1966, above) involving memorising lists of words, subjects tend to remember those that are most likely to have been well-rehearsed (in the beginning, before the novelty of taking part in an experiment has worn off – rehearsal in to LTM), and those at the very end of the list (STM, before forgotten through lack of rehearsal).

Limitations of the Multi-store Memory Model

1. Too simple: it focuses on the different stores but does not take into account the different levels and motivations for processing information. It assumes that memory processes are relatively passive. But we more readily succeed in memorising numbers if they are the digits of people we would like to meet again than if they are mere random numbers as we are motivated to give them greater attention and process them more deeply, such as associating the numbers with rhythm or something already familiar

2. The ability to visualise and recall the sound of something at the same time strongly indicates that the STM is not one single store. This is supported by H.M. being able to store **procedural memories** (such as needed for performance of skills), but not **declarative memories** (facts, ideas), This point is attended to by the working memory model, below.

Declarative memory differs from **procedural memory**, which encompasses skills such as the use of objects or movements of the body that are deeply embedded and are performed without being aware. Declarative memory (**explicit**) is memory that recalls 'what', while procedural (**implicit**) memory is memory that recalls 'how'.

2.2.2 The Working Memory Model (Baddeley and Hitch, 1974)

The Baddeley and Hitch **working memory** model (focusing on the parts of short-term memory that immediately work to process information) challenged the multi-store's model short-term memory store. It holds that working memory is a working and active store, designed to hold and manipulate information that is currently being consciously thought about. *Unlike the multi-store model which treats the STM as a single component,* *the working memory model effectively divides the STM into three separate STM components*, each of which operates in parallel at the same time, and all lead to the LTM.

The Central Executive

The central executive (the selective sensory memory component) is a controlling attention mechanism with a limited capacity. It decides which information is picked up, and which of the three STM systems working in parallel the information is passed into.

The Three STM Subsystems

The three STM subsystems are two-way systems between the central executive and the LTM. The central executive selectively directs into those three channels (three separate components) visual and conceptually-based information. These can be operating at the same time: you can visualise and think about a concept simultaneously. (You may claim that when you tell your teacher that you are paying attention while doodling over your notepad.)

Figure 2.2: **The working memory model**

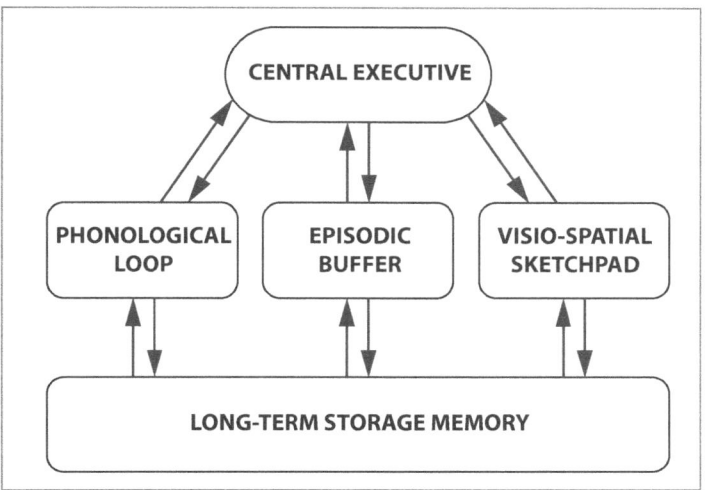

- **The phonological loop** (or 'articulatory loop') as a whole deals with sound or phonological information. It consists of two parts: a **short-term phonological (sound) store** with auditory memory traces that if left alone is quickly lost, but it is supported by an **articulatory rehearsal component** (sometimes called the articulatory loop) that can revive the memory traces. This 'inner voice' repeats the series of words (or other speech elements) on a 'loop' to prevent them from decaying.
- The **visual-spatial sketchpad**—or 'inner eye'—which holds visual and spatial information from either the central executive, or returned and activated from the long-term memory store.
- The **episodic buffer** is a separate complex memory device enabling you to recall an interrelated set of phenomena, such as a personal story, the sound of your favourite pop group, or how you felt as you came off your first-ever roller-coaster ride. It is much like a television recall of an event.

The LTM

The LTM receives from, and releases to, the three STM subsystems above.

Support for the presence and work of the central executive in the Working Memory Model

RESEARCH STUDY

Baddeley (1996)

The aim was to research evidence for the existence and the distributing mechanism of the central executive. One of the claims of the model is that switching system of the central executive slows down multi-tasking when moving from component to component.

The participants were required to carry out a basic task simultaneously with a series of other tasks that would focus on the central executive's role and functioning in directing different information into the different stores in the STM.

In all conditions, the participants had to generate a series of 100 digits that were random, at the rate of one digit per second. In the first condition, the participants were also told to count upwards 1, 2, 3... at the same rate of one number per second. In the second condition it was letters of the alphabet A, B, C... But the third condition asked for the count at the same rhythm to use both letters and numbers: A1, B2, C3...

The results showed that the first two conditions generated the same degree of digit randomness. But the final condition that required the constant switching over from letters to numbers produced series of digits that were mathematically significantly less random than in the first two conditions.

The results had the strengths of indicating the presence and work of the central executive. It showed that its work is slowed down by tasks requiring constant switching of attention. This finding therefore supports both the existence and distributive functioning of the central executive, and the slowing down of the memory function when the central executive is switching from component to component. It also had the strengths of being a controlled, repeated measures study. However, the deduction of the central executive-named specific mechanism for switching from component to component is based on evidence that is correlational. In addition, the decrease in digit randomness may have been due to the temporary information overload in the study rather than the switching of attention mechanism.

Support for the presence and work of the phonological loop in the Working Memory Model

RESEARCH STUDY

Landry and Bartling (2011)

The purpose of this experimental study was to show the presence and role of the phonological loop in memory formation. The study's purpose was to determine whether suppression of the phonological loop would prevent the rehearsal of new information into the memory-forming process.

Independent measures in design, the 34 undergraduate participants were randomly assigned to the test or to the control group. Both those in the test and control group were tested individually. Both were presented with a list of a series of seven letters F, K, L, M, Q, R, and X, letters that were chosen for their lack of similarity. Those in the test group were given a list using those letters that they had to remember whilst saying "1, 2" at the speed of two numbers per second. They viewed that list for five seconds, and were told to wait five seconds – still saying "1, 2" at the same speed. They then had to write down the seven letters in the order that they had been given. This was repeated ten times, each time in a different order. The control group had the same procedure, but without the "1, 2" articulatory suppression.

The results showed a significantly lower score in correct recall in the experimental group than in the control group. That appears to indicate that disrupting the phonological loop by articulatory suppression interferes with accurate memory recall. It is the articulatory suppression that prevents the rehearsal in the phonological loop.

The strengths of this study included its experimental, independent-measures design. Its multi-tasking nature ("1, 2") indicates the presence, and disruption, of the phonological loop, thus supporting the structure of the Working Memory Model. Its limitations are the laboratory setting and nature of the task, and the degree that articulatory suppression used can be generalised to multi-tasking in general.

Strengths and Limitations: the Baddeley and Hitch Working Memory Model (1974)

Strengths of the Working Memory Model
   (a)   In contrast to the multi-store model, this working memory model can accommodate a person's ability to visualise and recall the sound of something at the same time, as it accepts that the STM is not one single store. It explains how people can multi-task.
   (b)   Problems in studying by one method may be put right through studying by another method. For example, those who have difficulties in following a lecture (phonological loop), can master the material with a different means using a different STM such as a series of diagrams (visual sketchpad). This explains why the lecture method can fail where a person is a visual learner rather than an auditory learner.
   (c)   There is support for the central executive and its distributive function (Baddeley, 1996), and for the phonological loop (Landry and Bartling, 2011)

Limitations of the Working Memory Model
   (a)   The nature and role of the central executive is still unclear – and with it, the exact way in which the three elements of the STM interrelate.
   (b)   The need to Incorporate the existence of other stores (the episodic buffer was not in the original 1974 model, but added later) by evidence of brain-damaged patients able to recall anecdotes.

2.3 Cognitive Processing: Schema Theory

Cognitive schemas are networks of knowledge, beliefs, and expectations about particular aspects of the world. Cognitive psychology operates on the assumption that our developing schemas guide our behaviour. If the brain is the hardware, the schemas are the software. Although not identifiable and definable biologically or in modern brain scanning, they are mental representations that organise our knowledge, beliefs, and expectations.

Schemas are built up through our own experiences of life, education, and culture. They are applied to synthesise new inputs from the environment though the mental components that the schemas incorporate. Schema processing tends (but is not always) to be automatic; we apply schemas and process information without necessarily thinking at the same time. That saves cognitive energy, but at the same time it can results in biases in thinking and errors, and inaccuracies in memory processing and memory recall. Examples of schemas are the capacity to communicate in English, pick up on the teacher's mood, drive a car, and stereotyping an individual based on a fixed mental representation of the group that the individual appears to be part of.

Our schemas become more complex through the process of **assimilation**. For example if we already know how to drive a car and then learn to drive a more complex heavy goods vehicle, the assimilation of the new driving-associated techniques results in our schemas in driving becoming more sophisticated.

The wide field of applying the cognitive short cuts of schema processing with varying degrees of accuracy incorporates elements including:

Top-down – Bottom-up Processing

Top-down imposes pre-existing schemas on new, apparently similar, information; bottom-up considers the information first and then applies the schemas where relevant.

Pattern Recognition

Matching a current input to information in the memory that it seems to resemble.

Stereotyping

Attributing to the individual the popularly-believed characteristics of the group that he or she is believed to represent, which can involve the cognitions of bias and prejudice, and the behaviours of positive and negative discrimination. These concepts also form part of social cognition considered in more depth in Chapter 3 and exemplified by the research of Bargh et al. (1996) in the same chapter.

Effort after meaning: the attempt to match unfamiliar ideas into a familiar framework

This cognitive process can result in schema-driven inaccuracies in memory encoding and memory recall, which in turn may be a product of the individual's attempts to fit new information into the existing schemas that cannot fully accommodate it. This is exemplified by the research of Bartlett, below.

2.3.1 Support for Cognitive Schemas

RESEARCH STUDY

Bartlett (1932)

Bartlett sought to investigate whether cultural schemas would affect the level of memory recall of a scenario that was outside their cultural experience. The hypothesis was that memory was reconstructive, and that cultural schemas influence the way that people store and retrieve information.

2. THE COGNITIVE APPROACH TO UNDERSTANDING HUMAN BEHAVIOUR

The participants, all of whom were British, were divided into two groups. The researcher read out a short Native American story to the all participant. The names and concepts were culturally unfamiliar to a British audience. The first group was told to reproduce the story after a 15-minute interval, and then again and again after the passage of days, weeks, months, and years. The second group was told to tell the story to someone else after a 15-minute interval, and then after periods of days, weeks, months, or years. Both groups were required to recall the story in as much detail as possible.

The results showed that the details reproduced, employing effort after meaning, were the ones that British cultural schemas could most easily relate to. Thus unfamiliar ideas tended to be changed to things that were closer to the experiences of British participants. There was no significant difference in the accuracy of narrative recall according to its form: reproduction or telling it so someone else. However, the stories reproduced and recalled did communicate as narratives with a plot, rather than as a list of unconnected details, even though they became progressively shorter over time without losing the main theme of the story. The study concluded that people tend to recall unfamiliar narrative through existing schemas even though they are not necessarily suitable for promoting accurate recall. In wider terms, individuals reconstruct the past though effort after meaning; by trying to fit it into existing schemas even though it can involve imaginative, but inaccurate reconstruction of the experience.

Strengths and limitations: Bartlett (1932)

Strengths	Limitations
1. The story was chosen deliberately as being outside the culture of the audience. The recall supported the idea that the human tendencies to both encode and recall information through existing schemas do not promote accuracy. 2. It illustrates that mind does not necessarily function like a computer, as the participants' recall include elements of imagination that advanced the interpretation rather than the recall of the narrative.	1. Informal design of the research, including the lack of experimental controls. The periods between the recalls were not standardised through the study, resulting in a low reliability. 2. It lacked the control of a native American group participating in the study. 3. Lack of ecological validity: the laboratory situation may have encouraged demand characteristics (participants recalling the information a way they believed would please the investigators), as well as not being perceived by the participants as being important enough to merit their best efforts at recall.

 RESEARCH STUDY

Anderson and Pichert (1978)

The idea that schema processing affects retrieval from the memory store as well as encoding into the memory store been supported by the classic study of Anderson and Pichert.

The participants were two groups of people at the first stage, which became four groups of people at the second stage.

In the first stage, they were divided into two groups: one was to think in the framework, the schema, of a house-purchaser, and the other in the framework of a house-breaker (burglar). Both groups heard a story about two boys who missed school and went to one of their homes, knowing that it was always empty on Thursdays. The story contained a total of 72 points for recall, including that the roof was leaky and the basement was damp. Also, the house contained a colour TV, a ten-geared bicycle, and a valuable coin collection. The groups were given a short distraction task and then each member of the group had to recall as many points as possible.

In the second stage, half the house-buyer sample was given the house-breaker schema, and half the house-breaker sample was given the house-buyer schema. The other halves kept the same schema as in the first stage. There were thus four groups in all.

The two groups that retained the first schema recalled fewer points the second time round. The results showed that on the second recall, participants recalled more information that was important only to the second perspective or schema than they had done on the first recall. Indeed, the two groups that changed schemas the second time round recalled 7% more points in total, with 10% more directly related to their new schemas. Recall in points related to their original first schema declined.

This controlled study indicates that schema processing affects retrieval from the memory store as well as encoding into the memory store, focusing on the finding that those with changed schemas relied entirely on what they heard at the beginning of the first stage. The study may be criticised on its laboratory setting (lacked ecological validity), but it may be supported in that there was a controlled situation that highlighted effective retrieval from the memory store as the sole source of information for recall.

Strengths and limitations: Anderson and Pichert (1978)

These strengths and weaknesses can also be used at a more general level, to evaluate Schema Theory.

Strengths	Limitations
1. Helps to understand social issues such as bias and prejudice. Schema theory explains how a person who witnesses an incident turns it to fit in with what he already believes and feels he knows. 2. Schema interference explains people's failure to remember and report information accurately. The schema lies at the base of people's natural scope to reconstruct memory. It reflects the brain's search for meaningful patterns without checking whether the images produced are correct.	1. Some of the research experiments, such as this study, and Loftus and Palmer (section 2.5.1) have been criticised for lack of ecological validity. This raises the issue of whether 'reconstructive memory' might be distorted by laboratory conditions, such as demand characteristics. 2. Difficulties involved in identifying specific schemas and understanding how and to what degree they interrelate with other schemas. 3. Lack of sufficiently detailed biological support enabling the identification and defining of individual schemas and how they relate with other schemas.

2.3.2 Strengths and Limitations: Schema Theory

Strengths of Schema Theory

- The theory has been tested and found to have statistical support, e.g. Anderson and Pichert (1978).
- Understanding schemas can predict what details are likely to be accurately recalled and inaccurately recalled.
- Schemas help to explained phenomena such as reconstructive memory and patterns of errors in decision-making.

Limitations of Schema Theory
- Much evidence for schemas is based on research of low ecological validity, as in the above studies.
- Schemas cannot be biologically identified in modern brain scanning technology.

2.4 Cognitive Processing: Thinking and Decision-Making

Thinking and decision-making involve the following cognitive stages:

Perception: during which process the mind registers the information.

Memory: where the mind encodes, stores, and retrieves the information.

Thinking: where the mind goes beyond the given information. Thinking modifies the information by analysis (breaking it down into small pieces), synthesis (bringing different elements of information together as a new coherent whole), categorisation (classifying the information under particular headings), inference (using given information to deduce new information) and drawing conclusions (using given information as evidence for a judgment).

Decision-making: where the mind applies the thinking to choose what action to take from possible alternatives.

Thinking and decision making can be **normative**, whereby the thinker uses all the possible resources such as time, mental effort, available information, and **utility-based**: deciding according to the probable costs and benefits of each alternative choice. Not all thinking and decision-making is normative. Psychologists study the patterns of short-cuts and mental energy-saving procedures that people make, and often find shared, involve predictable patterns in thinking that are not always accurate. The reliability of thinking and decision-making processes is considered in more detail in Section 2.7.

The **dual model of thinking and decision-making** (Stanovich, 1999) shows that decision-making processes are not always normative nor do they always maximise utility.

System-1 thinking: where the thinking is quick, automatic, involves little effort, and may be more likely to promote bias in decision-making. It is often influenced by the emotions felt at the time rather than by rational reasoning. It is likely to apply heuristics, mental short-cuts that may or may not be suitable bases for particular decisions.

System-2 thinking: where the thinking involves patience, logic, effort, careful reasoning and application to the particular goal. System-2 thinking aligns with the normative thinking and decision-making in exploring options on the basis of accessible information. It is particularly difficult to apply when feeling tired or under pressure. System-2 thinking is likely to result in a better-informed decision without it necessarily being the optimum one. The tendency is for people to use System-1 thinking for decision-making in perceived familiar situations and System-2 thinking for decisions that are not everyday ones, and are complex and important.

Indeed, modern research into thinking and decision often refers to **intuitive thinking** (automatic) and **rational thinking** (controlled), respectively modelled by System-1 and System-2 thinking.

Intuitive thinking is fast, uses little effort, and open to influence that bias.

Rational thinking is more focused on the specifics of the goal, slower and more demanding, and strives to be objective in seeing the situation for what it is.

RESEARCH STUDY

Alter et al. (2007)

This experimental study aimed to investigate whether individuals employ System-2 rather than System-1 thinking when everyday tasks become unusually difficult. The 40 participating undergraduates read a text and answered questions that measured their degree of understanding the text. The text for those in the control condition was printed in easy-to-read black Myriad Web 12-point font. The text for those in the test condition was printed in a hard-to-read 10% grey italicised Myriad Web 10-point font. Thus the independent variable was the font used, and the dependent variable was the number of errors in the immediately-following standardised cognition test.

The results showed a significantly higher level of accuracy in the test condition, with 65% of the participants correctly answering all the questions in contrast to those with the test condition easy-to-read font whose responses indicated an all-correct rate of only 10%. This indicated that the rational System-2 thinking is likely to achieve more accurate results than the more intuitive and rapid, heuristic and thus cognitive-schema-based, bias-promoting System-1 thinking.

The study has the strengths of being easily replicable, experimental in design, with an easily manipulated independent variable. Its limitations include that it may be the nature of the task rather than the deliberate switch-over from System-1 to System-2 thinking that slowed the reading down resulting in more accurate responses.

RESEARCH STUDY

Dijksterhuis (2004)

This experimental study aimed to consider whether there were situations in which the heuristic-based, schema-driven-with-possibility-of-bias System-1 thinking actually produced more accurate decision-making than the more normative, effort-demanding thinking of System-2. The participants were 63 undergraduates from the University of Amsterdam who were randomly assigned to one of three conditions: conscious-thought decision, immediate decision, and unconscious thought decision. All participants, working in separate cubicles, were given data about four different apartments A, B, C, and D, in Amsterdam (such as on cost, location). All were told to choose the best apartment to rent. They were given eight positive and four negative pieces of information about each apartment. Those who were in the unconscious-thought condition had three minutes to make a choice but were given a distractor activity extending through that time, so that they had no time to think about the choice. Those in the immediate condition had to choose between the four apartments at once. Those in the conscious-thought condition were given three minutes to choose the best apartment without disturbance.

The results showed that a significant number of those in the unconscious-thought condition chose apartment B, which in fact was the best one. Those in the conscious-thought and the immediate-thought conditions took had a significantly greater tendency to choose the less desirable apartments.

This supports the idea that the intuitive and more extreme System-1 thinking when in unconscious mode may actually produce more desirable results than the rational and better-informed System-2 thinking in certain situations. It does suggest that unconscious thinking is not random, but can activate decision-making using schemas that can organise effective thinking when left alone. The study is also easily replicable. However, it is difficult to generalise which decisions are best made in the unconscious-thought decisions, which can also wrongly imply that lazy thinking is a desirable cognitive attribute.

2.5 Reliability of Cognitive Processes: Reconstructive Memory

Section 2.3 on page 37 on schema theory considered that schema interference can help to explain people's failure to remember and report information accurately. It is the schema that lies at the base of people's natural tendency to reconstruct memory. The process of memory encoding, storage, and recall reflects the brain's search for meaningful patterns without necessarily checking whether the images produced are correct. Reconstructive memory can involve **confabulation** (where individual sincerely believes that the recalled information is true even though it is contradicted by evidence and likely to be based on distorted or misinterpreted memory), **selective memory** (being able to recall certain, but not other events and their details), and **false memory** (where the individual recalls something that did not happen). The possibility of memory recall being at least partially reconstructive and inaccurate has been supported by the classic study of Loftus and Palmer.

RESEARCH STUDY

Loftus and Palmer (1974)

This classic study researched the effectiveness of implanting a false memory through the phrasing of a question on the accuracy of memory recall.

The researchers showed a series of video clips featuring traffic accidents of relatively slow-moving vehicles to 45 participating university students. The study was designed to investigate whether the participants' recall of the estimated speed of the colliding vehicles could be influenced by the key verb in the framing of the question.

The students were given follow-up memory-recall questions including the critical: "How fast were the cars going when they ___ each other?" The hypothesis was that the phrasing of the question and prompts designed to elicit incorrect memories would affect the speed the cars were recalled to be moving at the time they contacted one another. With different students, the word 'contacted' was replaced with 'hit', 'bumped', 'collided', or 'smashed'.

The results indicated a significant support for the hypothesis. Those asked using 'smashed', 'collided', 'bumped', or 'hit' recalled significantly faster speed estimates than those where 'contacted' was used. The conclusion was that different words activate different schemas in the memory, so that hearing the word 'smashed' influenced the memory to reconstruct a memory of faster speed than hearing the word 'contacted'.

Loftus and Palmer conducted a second experiment with 150 university students. All were shown a one-minute video of a car crash. The researchers asked 50 students to estimate the speed of the cars that 'smashed' one another, 50 students the speed the cars 'hit' one another, and the other 50 (the control group) were not required to estimate the speed. All students were given a series of questions a week later that included whether they saw any broken glass, even though there had been no broken glass in the video.

The results showed that the previous week's use of the verb 'smashed' elicited 16 responses of seeing broken glass, more than twice that of 'hit' (7) or the control (6).

The researchers concluded from both experiments that different words activate different memory schemas, that they can interfere with the accuracy of recall, and in the case of the broken glass, prompt false memories.

The study had the strengths of the formal independent measures experimental design in a laboratory setting. It is easily replicable. It can also be used to support schema theory, the independent variables eliciting different schemas. The findings can have serious consequences in police and court procedures when assessing the accuracy of statements of the accused and of testimony. Its limitations include the highly artificial environment: the video rather than real life, and also that some of the respondents may have responded with demand characteristics (giving the answers they thought the researchers wanted).

RESEARCH STUDY

Yuille and Cutshall (1986)

This study aimed to investigate whether inaccurate memory prompts would promote inaccurate recall in a real life situation. Would they be similar or different to the laboratory set-up of Loftus and Palmer?

The study followed a real-life robbery of a gun shop, whereby the attacker immobilised the owner who managed to break free. The thief shot twice, but the owner discharged six shots from his revolver and killed the attacker. Following police interviewing the witnesses, 13 out of 21 agreed to work with the researchers and take part in the study, whose questions included two key items similar to those used by Loftus and Palmer (e.g. was there a broken lamp on the getaway vehicle?) They also rated their level of stress for that day so that variable could be taken into account. The results were more accurate than in the laboratory conditions of Loftus and Palmer, with the researchers concluding that false memory prompts are less likely to work in real-life than in laboratory situations.

The strengths of the study included its real-life environment, and the participants not knowing that they were in a study at the time they witnessed the event. It is limited by its details and circumstances being practically non-replicable, and the possibility that the researchers knew more about the event from media reports.

2.6 Reliability of Cognitive Processes: Biases in Thinking and Decision-Making

Section 2.4 on the cognitive functions of thinking and decision-making contrasted the energy-saving heuristic System-1 thinking typical of everyday decision making with the more grounded and thoughtful, but generally less-frequently used System-2 thinking. The work of the school of Amos Twersky and Daniel Kahneman highlighted that cognitive biases and errors in decision-making are predictable in the way they interfere with optimum decision-making. These suggest that System-1 thinking is likely to be frequently unreliable. Types of biases include:

Availability heuristic: the more we know about a particular danger, the more we think it might happen to us. Per kilometre, a person is in greater mortal danger travelling to and from the airport than on the flight, but far more people fear flying than a ride in a taxi.

Anchoring bias: over-reliance on the first piece of information at the time of the decision (considered the "anchor", irrespective of its accuracy or its relevance). For example, you

2. THE COGNITIVE APPROACH TO UNDERSTANDING HUMAN BEHAVIOUR

overhear that the going rate for a taxi ride is $2 per kilometre, and you agree on your negotiated price at $1.80, only to find that on the meter it would have cost only $1.25. But if you had casually overheard in the conversation that people paid $1 per kilometre, your initial offer might have been enough to bargain the rate down even further to $1.20.

Peak-end rule: memories of a good or bad extended experience focus on best or worst thing that happened, and how it finished. For example, an ex-patient in hospital might remember the feelings on waking up from the operation and days later the feelings on being finally discharged, forgetting the general daily routine at the hospital even though that filled nearly all the time there.

Confirmation bias: focusing on information and interpretations that support pre-existing opinions and expectations whilst disregarding those that contradict them. See Lord et al. (1979), below.

Framing effects: where the decision is likely to be biased by the way the information is given. See Rahman and Crouch (2015), below.

RESEARCH STUDY

Lord et al. (1979)

This study aimed to determine the degree that cognitive **confirmation bias** could interfere with assessing evidence. The study participants were 48 undergraduate psychology students, 24 who supported the use of the death penalty and 24 who did not. They were all placed into groups and given cards with stimulus material and detailed studies on the death penalty. Both during and at the end of the procedures, they filled out questionnaires that were designed to highlight any change in attitude as a result of working through the materials.

The overall results indicated polarisation rather than moderation in attitude, even though some had warily moved a little distance towards the opposite view in the earlier stages of the study. However, their initial views whether for or against the death penalty survived the discussion and the persuasion, and actually tended to become more extreme, convinced that the materials examined supported their position. The research thus indicated that even academics with experience in critical analysis can apply schema-biased system-1-type thinking to the degree of placing different weights on supporting and contradicting evidence.

The study had the strengths of using the academically able as participants whose training included critical analysis and assessment of evidence. It used a purposive sample, selecting on the basis of those who were definitely for and definitely against the death penalty. Its limitations include the problems in generalising the prevalence of confirmation bias in the laboratory setting to real-life decision-making. Additional issues in generalising the study may arise from the material being presented in writing rather than by higher-impact auditory or visual means, and that the emotive nature for subject made it far more prone to confirmation bias than day-to-day decision-making.

RESEARCH STUDY

Rahman and Crouch (2015)

The study aimed to investigate how the cognitive bias of **framing** may influence decision-making; how the way the question is asked can influence the choice of a plan of action.

There were 179 participants mostly aged 20–50 and with international travel experience, who were divided into two conditions. The exercise involved booking a flight.

The first condition was gain-framed. They had the choice of either paying two months in advance and saving $300 off the price, or waiting one week in advance and saving nothing off the full price if the demand for the flight was high, or getting a $600 discount if the demand for the flight was low.

The second condition was loss-framed. They had the choice of either paying two months in advance and losing $300 of the possible discount, or waiting until a week before the flight and losing the entire discount if the demand was high or losing nothing of the $600 discount if the demand was low.

In both cases the chances of a high or low demand for the flight were each placed at 50%.

The results showed that nearly three-quarters of the gain-frame group chose the two-months in advance option, but that fell to less than half in the loss-frame group.

The study indicates that framing of the question influences the decision-making process. It used a large sample, with a high proportion of travellers with experience in making similar travel decisions. It is easily replicable.

The research of Alter et al. (2007) and Dijksterhuis (2004) are also relevant in studying possible factors that may lead to bias in decision-making. Both these studies investigated the possible influence of intuitive rather than rational thinking in influencing schemas promoting cognitive bias.

However, not all evidence indicates that System-1 thinking by itself in necessarily inaccurate (e.g. Dijksterhuis 2004, in Section 2.5). There is also evidence that real life situations are less likely to invoke unreliable schema processing than in the laboratory setting (e.g. Yuille and Cutshall 1986, in Section 2.6)

2.7 Emotion and Cognition: The Influence of Emotion on Cognitive Processes

Emotions, a state of mind determined by one's mood, are a combination of biological and cognitive factors. They involve:

- **Physiological changes**: involuntary arousing the autonomic nervous system and endocrine system.

- **Feeling of an emotion**: e.g. anger, surprise, happiness.

- **Associated behaviour**: such a smiling or running away.

It is argued that emotions have evolved as an adaptive mechanism for survival: in hunter-gatherer societies, showing the most effective emotional and behavioural responses in life-and-death situations were the ones that survived to pass on their genes.

Also, memories that are emotionally charged tend to be more easily retrieved, although not necessarily accurately.

This section considers one aspect of the very wide field of emotion and cognition: flashbulb memories.

2.7.1 Flashbulb Memories

Flashbulb memories are a special type of emotional memory that relate to specific events: "memories for the circumstances in which one first learned of a very surprising and consequential (or emotionally arousing) event" (Brown and Kulik, 1977).

2. THE COGNITIVE APPROACH TO UNDERSTANDING HUMAN BEHAVIOUR

This theory suggests that some memories are remembered distinctly, even after time had passed, because the events incited highly emotional responses at the time. The emotional events are recorded in the brain as if by the flash of a camera. They not only recall the event, but also bring up the emotions that went with the event, and the more mundane things happening at the time of the event: the multi-dimensional experience being incorporated as with a flash picture on a camera. It is extremely vivid, but not necessarily completely accurate in details.

Flashbulb memories tend to have the following five components:

1. Where you were at the time of learning of the emotional event (e.g. witnessing it, hearing about it, viewing it on television), and what your surroundings looked like.
2. What you were doing at the time of the event.
3. The person who told you about the event.
4. How you felt when you first heard about it.
5. What happened afterwards, e.g. an immediate family gathering, a special assembly at school.

The basis of this concept is supported by the work of Brown and Kulik (1977).

RESEARCH STUDY

Brown and Kulik (1977)

Brown and Kulik aimed to investigate whether events that shocked or evoked deep emotions could create flashbulb memories as described above.

The study included 80 adult male participants: 40 black and 40 white. They were given a series of questions on the death or attempted assassination of nine well-known American personalities including JF Kennedy, Martin Luther King, and, in addition, one personally significant event. Their questionnaires were designed to elicit information along the lines of the above: at the time of the event where they were, with whom they were, what they were doing at the time of the event, how they first felt on hearing the events, how important these events were in their lives, and how often they had since talked about them. The latter used to factor in the frequency of memory rehearsal.

The results indicated that 90% of the participants recalled a great deal of such detail about the deceased close relative, but less about public figures: 75% of black participants and only 33% of white participants had memories of the flashbulb character of Martin Luther King.

The study concluded that the flashbulb memory cognitive mechanism was determined by two elements: event importance and event emotionality.

This study indicated at it is the emotional arousal experienced during the time of the event that makes flashbulb memories so strong. For example, when a person first learns about the death of a loved one, the sadness felt at that moment is so strong that the memory gets etched in a little deeper than other memories and are stored in the mind forever.

Brown and Kulik suggest that there may be a specialised neural mechanism that sets off an emotional arousal because of the very deep impression made by the event. Indeed, emotional events are better remembered than less emotional events because of the crucial role of the emotional part of the brain, the amygdala, something that was only found years after this study. In other words, the emotions and events are registered in the same 'flashbulb memory package' and a recollection of the event recalls your personal situations surrounding it and the way you felt, as in the five components above.

The study had the strengths of a large sample and was divided into the black and white participants as the assassination of Martin Luther King was hypothesised to be of especial emotional importance to the black community. It is also biologically supported by the later work of Sharot et al. (2007). This study was designed to investigate the biological aspect of flashbulb memory. It used scanned evidence of increased amygdala action as suggesting that there are indeed specific neural structures involved in flashbulb memory.

However, flashbulb memory has been questioned by the work of Neisser and Harsch (1992).

They argue that flashbulb memory may be a narrative, where people take later events and put them back into the memory, mixing them with 'flashbulb event'. It may be that there is still a special memory mechanism for the 'flashbulb memory package', but if there is, is the memory recalled with the details of the flashbulb memories, rather than less-emotionally grounded memories?

Indeed, Neisser and Harsch's investigation followed the 1986 Challenger Space Shuttle Disaster (using questionnaires to 106 participants) indicated that some 40% of the participants who recalled the event showed distinct memory distortion, which they argued was based on information found out sometime after the event that was being fed into the memory of the actual event. On the day after the disaster, they responded to questions on their circumstances when they heard the news including what they were doing. The participants responded to the same questions three years later. Although they expressed confidence about their memory accuracy (83%), on average participants only accurately responded to just under 3 questions out of the 7.

The study had the strength of using the same participants, and it used a real-life event. Its limitations included its scope: one incident only, which by itself may not have incited the flashbulb mechanisms to the same degree in all the participants. In addition, as in Brown and Kulik, it was non-experimental: neither study included control conditions that distinguish between 'normal' memories and flashbulb memories.

2.8 Cognitive Processing in the Digital World (Higher Level only)

The interest that cognitive psychology has in the digital world follows the concept that the brain is the hardware and the cognitive schemas are the software. In addition, access to online storage has enabled **transactional memory**, meaning that it is possible to delegate the task of memorising information to storing it on a digital device, with human memory functions being restricted to how to encode it and the where to find it on the device or in cyberspace when it is needed. Our studies of cognitive processes in the digital word consider two interacted areas:

1. The influence (positive and negative) of technologies (digital and modern) on cognitive processes.
2. Methods used to study the interaction between digital technology and cognitive processes.

2.8.1 Positive and Negative Effects of Computer Technology

Public and professional debate on the positive and negative effects of computer technology on cognitive processes and human interactions include the following commonly-cited arguments.

Computer gaming promotes **brain plasticity**), and positive neurological growth (Haier et al., 1992), with other studies indicating that they enhance visual attention quality, ability to think quickly, and skills in making inferences from statistical information.

However, digital processes have been linked with **digital amnesia** (Kaspersky laboratory international survey, 2015, based on self-reporting) indicating that people tend to forget information stored on a computer (transactional memory) more quickly than that memorised information. It drew attention to the widespread participant reporting of digital memory replacing autobiographical memory. Other arguments challenging the use of computer technology include the argument that the precise skills learnt in computer gaming have very limited application in the real world (e.g. in air traffic control), that the spatial skills learnt online do not put the players at any advantage over the non-players in real-life situations requiring navigational skills, that the speed of such games promotes inattention in real life where person-to-person information is delivered at a slower pace and the reward that stimulates the dopamine-rush is not immediate, and the possibility that playing computers with violent content might desensitise the players to human suffering in the real world.

In addition, the validity of research methodologies in researching the effects of computer technology on cognition tends to elicit severe criticism. Research on gaming comparing skills of participants to non-participants frequently raises the possibility that those with high skills in a particular field who attribute them to their gaming actually reached their performance levels through natural aptitude rather than their long hours on the computer. There are similar problems when comparing the academic performances of students studying conventionally and those learning online, for example the amount of online support that the online company provides. This may be addressed by conducting a **meta-study**, surveying the general trends within a sample of existing studies in the same field: for example the meta-study of study of Liao (2007) that compared the efficacy of computer-assisted instruction versus traditional learning encompassed 29 relevant studies on Taiwanese students. Its consensus indicated that computer-assisted learning was more effective, but also found that to be more significant when students worked in small groups (with the possibilities of deeper mental processing through discussion) than as individuals.

Research into Effects of Modern Technology on Cognitive Processes and Human Interaction

The following four research items of focus on the positive and negative effects of modern technology on cognitive processes and human interaction.

- Sanchez (2012) on the degree that computer gaming affected learning in science subjects. May be used for the following areas prescribed by the syllabus: the influence (positive and negative) of technologies (digital and modern) on cognitive processes, and (experimental) methods used to study the interaction between digital technology and cognitive processes.
- Mueller and Oppenheimer (2014) on the relative impact of digital and non-digital taking of notes on the understanding of the material attended to. May be used for the following areas prescribed by the syllabus: the influence (positive and negative) of technologies (digital and modern) on cognitive processes, and (experimental) methods used to study the interaction between digital technology and cognitive processes.
- Sparrow et al. (2011) on the use of transactional memory on human memory systems. May be used for the following areas prescribed by the syllabus: the influence (positive and negative) of technologies (digital and modern) on cognitive

processes, and (experimental) methods used to study the interaction between digital technology and cognitive processes.

- Shakya and Chistakis (2017) on the relationship between social media and personal well-being, including its cognitive effects on promoting real-life human interaction. May be used for the following areas prescribed by the syllabus: the influence (positive and negative) of technologies (digital and modern) on cognitive processes, and (self-reporting and quantitative) methods used to study the interaction between digital technology and cognitive processes.

RESEARCH STUDY

Sanchez (2012)

The aim of this study was to investigate the degree that playing computer games that develop spatial training can assist science learning.

The study with 60 university-student participants was experimental in design. The test group played computer game "Halo: Combat Evolved", an activity that demanded use of spatial skills. The control group played computer game "Word Whomp", an activity that, though engaging, made no demand on spatial skills. All participants were then given a 3,500-word scientific-text focusing on the geophysical forces (particularly plate tectonics) contributing to volcanic eruptions in general. They were then given an exercise where they had to apply that material to explain the real life volcanic eruption of Mount St. Helens, Washington State, USA.

The results indicated that those who had the computer game spatial training performed significantly better than those in the control group who had not. The research concluded that spatial-skill video games have the potential of enhancing real-life spatial skills and understanding spatial phenomena.

Thus the findings of this study support: (a) the potential of suitable digital-based training for development of specialised cognitive skills, (b) the potentially positive effects of such training on understanding natural phenomena that impact human interactions of those affected by them, (c) that modern technology can have positive effects on cognitive processes, and (d) the use of experimental methods in studying the interaction between digital technology and cognitive processes can be effective.

The study has the strength of being experimental in design, with the independent variable (input of spatial training) effectively manipulated. It is also easily replicable. However, it may be criticised as the volcanic eruptions spatial exercise took place very soon after the spatial training, creating problems in generalising the long-term effects of computer gaming. Also, the study needed to take into account the participants' spatial skills prior to the computer training exercise.

RESEARCH STUDY

Mueller and Oppenheimer (2014)

Is the pen mightier than the keyboard? Is taking notes by hand more effective than typing them into the computer?

The participants were 65 college students who in small groups watched one of five TED talks that were interesting, but not common knowledge. Each group was subdivided into those issued with laptops, or notebooks; thus the design was independent measures. The participants were told to use whatever strategy they wished to take notes. Immediately afterwards, they completed three distractor tasks. Half an hour later, they answered a series of question on the TED talk they had seen without use of their notes. Those tested both factual recall and conceptual understanding.

The results showed that both groups scored similarly on factual recall, but those who made notes by hand performed significantly better on conceptual understanding than the others that used the computer. On retesting one week later, the longhand note-takers again scored higher than those with the laptops, even though on that occasion all participants were allowed to review their notes before the session.

The researchers concluded that students taking notes on their laptops appeared to be cognitively processing the information at a shallower level than those recording the information by hand. They argued that the students using the computer were making notes verbatim rather than reframing them in the words that would be most meaningful to them.

Thus the findings of this study suggest: (a) that (in contrast with the context of Sanchez et al.) digital technology can adversely influence cognitive-based tasks such as note-taking, with the possibility that the use of IT instead of hand-writing suggests the application of shallower mental processing, and (b) the use of experimental methods in studying the interaction between digital technology and cognitive processes can be effective.

This study had the strengths of being experimental in design, and used a variety of TED talks to avoid the possibility that any pre-existing knowledge of subject material in one particular topic might have affected the different methods of taking notes on the memory. It is also easily replicable. Its limitations include the researchers' laboratory conditions with its implications for low ecological validity, and the need for biological support on the relative depth of processing in long-hand and electronic-device note-making.

RESEARCH STUDY

Sparrow et al. (2011)

This study used an experimental design to research whether the use of transactional memory can negatively affect human memory. The objectives were to test whether (a) being told to remember the information, and (b) being told that the information would be stored by the device, would influence the accuracy of memory recall.

The experimenters used four conditions, and the study was independent measures in design, with each participant being assigned to one of the four groups. There were 140 participants, all of whom were university undergraduates. All participants typed 40 trivial facts into the computer, following which:

Condition 1: the computer would store all the information, but their task was to remember it.

Condition 2: the computer would not store the information, and their task was to remember it.

Condition 3: the computer would store the information. Participants were not specifically asked to remember it.

Condition 4: the computer would not store the information, and the participants were not asked to remember it.

The results showed that when told that the computer would save the information (conditions 1 and 3), there was no difference in memory recall, whether the participants were told to remember the information (condition 1) or not (condition 3). However, memory recall rates improved by 50% when told that the computer would not save what they typed into it (conditions 2 and 4). It made little difference whether or not they had been told to store the information. Even more significantly, memory recall rates were 50% more accurate in condition 4 (not asked to remember, but told that the computer would not save the information) than in condition 1 (asked to remember, and told that the computer would save the information).

The researchers concluded that the study seemed to indicate that transactional memory has an adverse effect on memory, which could be at both the encoding and recall stages. The study may well support the idea that the use of computer and Internet storage reduces the motivation for the effort required to encode sensory information into LTM and effectively recall it from the LTM. This in turn can adversely affect the cognitive process of memory as its functions are outsourced to the computer as transactional memory, leading to digital amnesia (Kaspersky at al. 2015), forgetting information entrusted to a digital device for press-button storage and recall.

The research had the strength of being experimental, and replicable. The sample base was relatively large. Its limitations were its laboratory setup, and not being able to explain why it appears that the more people use transactional memory, the less they appear to try to remember.

RESEARCH STUDY

Shakya and Christakis (2017)

This study investigated the relationship between social media use and personal well-being, including the quality of human interaction. This study aimed to investigate the degree of similarity between the personal benefits of online and real-life friendships. It was a longitudinal study, using Facebook data between 2013 and 2015.

The participants were a total of 5208 adult Facebook users, from a national panel in the USA. All gave permission for the use of their Facebook accounts in the research. The research obtained data and classified each participant's well-being under four criteria: life satisfaction, self-reported mental health, self-reported physical health and body-mass index. Data from each person's Facebook accounts included number of likes given for other posts and number of clicks on links. In addition, each participant disclosed data on real-life social relationships: naming up to four friends with whom they discussed important matters, and up to four friends with whom they shared their leisure time.

The results showed that the number of real-life friends correlated positively with the measures of personal well-being. The number of clicks 'liking' other posts and also the number of Facebook links clicked-on, actually correlated negatively with most of the measures of personal well-being: life satisfaction, physical health and particularly mental health.

The researchers concluded that Facebook relationships did not replace the real-life relationships needed for social well-being. The results seemed to imply that the cognitive effects of Facebook use reduced, rather than enhanced the overall development of a quality social life. They also seemed to support the possibility that other people's selection of what and what not to display on Facebook might cognitively lead to negative self-comparisons. Moreover, the cognitive effort of keeping up with the torrent of Facebook postings might adversely affect the skills needed to develop more rewarding and meaningful deeper relationships.

2. THE COGNITIVE APPROACH TO UNDERSTANDING HUMAN BEHAVIOUR

The findings of this study are based on the use of self-reporting as well as quantitative data in studying the influence of digital technology on cognitive processes and human interaction. They indicate that digital technology can have a negative effect on cognitive process and human interaction when compared with traditional, non-digital social interaction.

The study had the strengths of being monitored over a two-year period. This timeframe made it possible for the researchers to observe the trend of increasing Facebook use correlating with poorer reported levels of well-being. In addition, evidence was taken from the Facebook accounts rather than relying entirely on self-reporting. Its limitations were the need to factor in the overall importance of social media in each participant's life, and that the study was confined to those who gave permission to individuals who allowed the researchers to access their Facebook accounts.

2.9 Research Methods Used in the Cognitive Approach to Understanding Behaviour

- Quantitative, experimental methods (e.g. Anderson and Pichert 1978), whose findings tend to support theory rather than identify specific mental processing patterns in the brain.
- Self-reporting, such as used in Brown and Kulik in flashbulb memory, and Shakya and Christakis in the effect of digital technology and personal well-being, including the quality of human interaction (HL)
- Case studies: such as those on brain-damaged patients that examine the effect of their condition on their cognitive processes (e.g. Milner et al. 1966–2008, Chapter 1, Section 1.2).

2.10 Strengths and Limitations: Cognitive Approach

Strengths of the Cognitive Approach

1. A substantial advance on behavioural psychology that it tends to have replaced, as it does not avoid considering the workings of the brain in studying how stimuli from the environment influence behaviour.
2. Becoming increasingly scientific credible as brain-scanning research produces data that correlates with cognitive theory, e.g. on flashbulb memory, thus having biological support.
3. Cognitive theory is adaptable to the capacity to model cognitive functioning, e.g. memory.
4. Contributes to an understanding a wide range of phenomena – e.g. why memories are not always accurate, and why errors in thinking and decision-making are sometimes predictable.

Limitations of Cognitive Approach

1. Reductionist: could underemphasise the biological, sociocultural, and psychodynamic elements that also affect people's behaviour, and that cognitive process work with.

2. Need to exercise care in applying cognitive models that may be too simple and general to explain the realities of individuals.
3. Cognitive research relying on brain scanning tends to yield data that shows the presence or absence of localised brain engagement rather than what the brain is actually engaged in.

2.11 Ethical Considerations: Research Methods Used in the Cognitive Approach

Similar to those in the biological approach, including:

- Informed consent – participants must know the object of the study, that their involvement is voluntary, what the data will be used for, and if necessary be debriefed at the end of the study. In extreme cases, the ethical requirement for informed consent may be waived, when the focus of the study is of public importance and there is no other way to obtain the sought-after information.
- Avoiding deception, except possibly where the research cannot be carried out in any other way (e.g. Loftus and Palmer).
- Protection from harm: particularly important when handling potentially sensitive information such as Facebook accounts even when given permission (e.g. Shakya and Christakis – HL section)
- Making the participants anonymous to protect them, even at the risk of reducing the authenticity of the research and of preventing any follow-up study. This was carefully observed with HM until he gave consent for his anonymity to be waived before his death.
- The right for any participant to withdraw from the study at any point, and communicating that right before the commencement of the study.
- All participants are to be debriefed at the end of the study.
- Bearing in mind that cognitive research involving associated cultural issues is extremely sensitive with many ethnic groups. Typically, the elders of the society must be consulted for permission to work with members of their group.

2. THE COGNITIVE APPROACH TO UNDERSTANDING HUMAN BEHAVIOUR

Exam-style Practice Questions: The Cognitive Approach

Short Answer Questions

1. Outline *one* bias in thinking and decision-making.
2. Describe *one* study showing the effect of emotion on one cognitive process.

Essay Response Question(s)

1. Discuss the reliability of any *two* cognitive processes.
2. Evaluate the influence of digital technology on memory. (HL only)

Chapter 3: The Sociocultural Approach to Understanding Human Behaviour

Overview

Our studies in sociocultural psychology focus on the contribution of groups and cultures to individual thinking and behaviour patterns. This approach considers social identity theory: the way individuals view themselves in terms of the groups they see themselves as part of and also the groups and types of people they avoid, which could be based on stereotyping. It also brings in social cognitive theory: the idea that children and adults model their behaviour on other people.

> Understand that sociocultural psychology views thinking and behaviour as being strongly influenced by our environment and the people that we come in contact with, both in real life and through different types of media.

The cultural side examines the cultural roots of thinking and behaviour, and how differing cultural values are expressed in particular environments, such as in the workplace. It also looks at cultural influences on individual attitudes, identities, and behaviours through the concepts of enculturation, acculturation, and other elements underlying cultural change.

If you are a Higher Level student, you will also be paying attention to how globalisation may influence local attitudes, identities, and behaviours.

KEY QUESTION

How do social and cultural influences shape thinking and behaviour?

Learning objectives of this unit include an understanding of:

- The individual and the group (HL and SL)
- Cultural origins of behaviour (HL and SL).
- Cultural influences on individual attitudes, identity, and behaviours (HL and SL).
- The influence of globalisation on individual attitudes, identities, and behaviour (HL only).

3. THE SOCIOCULTURAL APPROACH TO UNDERSTANDING HUMAN BEHAVIOUR

3.1 Introduction to the Sociocultural Approach

Sociocultural psychology recognises that the behaviour of the individual may be better understood when the social and cultural contexts are taken into account.

The sociocultural perspective emphasises how the presence and behaviour of individuals and communities affect the behaviors and attitudes of a person.

It also provides a broader framework for exploring topics such as aggression, which is often regarded as an individual personality trait.

As social psychologists continue to integrate the biological and cultural contributions into social behaviour, there is a general consensus that a synthesis of the biological, cognitive and sociocultural levels of psychological analysis brings us closer to understanding the complex interacting systems that make up the human being.

Sociocultural principles of interest to psychologists include:

- Social and cultural environments influence people's behaviour. For example, eleven-year-old students know exactly how to handle the classroom routines of speaking to the teacher in the correct mode, interacting appropriately with a group of other students when working together, and handling conflicts in the classroom and the playground (SL and HL).
- People want to feel connected, and identify with groups of people. That can mean going through persistent and tough qualifying to be accepted by the group of one's choice (SL and HL).
- People have a social self through engagement with others: for example a person's behaviour patterns may be very different with a group of friends than at home (SL and HL).
- Increasing contact with other societies on different scales can influence individual attitudes, identities, and behaviours (HL only).

Today, sociocultural psychologists increasingly work together with neuroscientists and cognitive psychologists. They recognise that the sociocultural approach interacts in many ways with biological and cognitive phenomena.

3.2 The Individual and the Group: Social Identity Theory

Social identity theory holds that people's sense of who they are is based on their feeling part of certain social groups and not feeling part of other social groups.

These groups can develop on the basis of nationality, religion, family, school, age group, sports teams, and leisure interests.

Developed by Tajfel and Turner (1979), social identity theory can help to explain behaviours whereby individuals strive to improve and adapt their self image towards being accepted in groups that express their ideals, identity, and dreams. If you are 'in' with the group you choose to be part of, you tend to develop the image of that group. For example, if you aspire to be the "cool rebel without a cause" you might grab the back seat of the bus, together with the other troublemakers.

Tajfel and Turner proposed that people use three mental processes in evaluating others as "our type" or "not our type": the in-group or the out-group. These are:

▶ **Social categorisation**: the first stage, that divides the social environment into those who "belong" and those who do not "belong", for example political parties, leisure, social class, or nationality.

- **Social identification**: where individuals adopt the identity and behavioural norms and standards of the group they identify with. For example, a teenager wanting to be a professional sportsperson will try to follow the behaviours and routines of those in that sport. Social identification can extend to the sociocultural cognitions of bias and prejudice, and to the behaviours of positive and negative discrimination.

- **Social comparison**: where individuals consider where their group stands relative to rival out-groups, emphasising the positive distinctiveness of their in-group and why they are happy to belong to it. It is the final stage of social identity theory; once we have categorised ourselves as part of a group and identified with the group, we compare our group to other groups.

Social identity theory may be applied to explain the cognitions of bias and prejudice, the behaviours of positive and negative discrimination, and other phenomena such as hostility between groups, for example in competitive team sports.

3.2.1 Research in social identity theory

RESEARCH STUDY

Tajfel et al. (1971)

This classic study aimed to demonstrate that people show bias to individuals in in-groups and prejudice to individuals in out-groups, even where there is nothing of objective importance that distinguishes the in-group from the out-group.

The study was experimental, the participants being 48 14–15 year schoolboys living in Bristol, UK. They were placed into two groups, supposedly on the basis of whether they preferred the paintings of artist Kandinsky or artist Klee. The key word in both studies is "supposedly". In fact, the grouping was completely random as the experimenters wanted, irrespective of Kandinsky and Klee.

The purpose was to find out whether members of groups that formed on a completely random basis would show favouritism to in-group members and discrimination to out-group members. The boys participated in a series of activities organised by the research program, and were told to allocate points to those who deserved them according to the criteria of the researchers. Those who won the small sums of money supplied by the research study for this purpose were told that they would be allowed to keep the money.

The results showed that for most part, boys were inconsistent in applying the criteria when awarding points. They were more generous to those in their in-group than to those in their out-group. Those who observed the boys agreed that they were trying to judge as fairly as they could.

The study concluded that the research indicated that individuals can develop biases and prejudices once groups form, even if they are on a random basis.

3. THE SOCIOCULTURAL APPROACH TO UNDERSTANDING HUMAN BEHAVIOUR

Strengths and limitations: Tajfel et al. (1971)

Strengths	Limitations
1. Repeats of this easily replicable study have indicated similar patterns of bias and discrimination. 2. It supports the view that bias and discriminatory behaviours can be explained by social identity theory, even where the in-groups and out-groups form on a random basis.	1. Difficulties in generalising the study from early teenage UK schoolboys to the other populations and environments. 2. Greater bias and discrimination may have been shown due to the winners being allowed to keep the money they won in the activities.

RESEARCH STUDY

Abrams et al. (1990)

This study was based on the classic study of Asch (1951) on social conformity to group norms, detailed later in this chapter (Section 3.3). Its purpose was to investigate whether people's judgements are more likely to conform to the other participants if they are in their in-group rather than their out-group. The hypothesis was that the participants would be significantly more likely to socially categorise those in their in-group as being correct than those in the out-group, and follow accordingly.

50 beginner male and female psychology students participated in this study which was initially presented to them as an investigation of visual accuracy. There were three confederates unknown to the individual participants who were introduced as students studying psychology (in-group), or as students studying ancient history (out-group).

Each student in turn had a similar task to the Asch study: they were given a stimulus line and three other lines, and had to decide which of those lines was the same length as the stimulus line. This was repeated, making a total of 18 times. The confederates were instructed to give the correct response nine times and unanimously the incorrect response nine times.

The results showed that the rate of conformity to incorrect answers was over 5 in the in-group condition, and under 1 in the out-group condition. The researchers concluded that social categorisation can influence deciding whether or not to conform.

Strengths and limitations: Abrams et al. (1990)

Strengths	Limitations
1. The study design enabled the simulation of an in-group situation and an out-group situation. 2. It supports the view that people are more likely to conform to those they socially categorise as being members of their in-group than of the out-group. An immediate follow-up with the participants revealed that it was their being fellow-psychology students that influenced them to sway towards error even when doubting their judgments. 3. No gender bias as there was a similar number of male and female participants.	1. Difficulties in generalising the findings on social categorisation from this study using university students to other populations and environments. 2. As with social identity theory generally, people's decision on whom and whom not to follow can be influenced by factors other than social categorisation, such as the influence of a particularly charismatic personality who may belong to the out-group.

3.3 The Individual and the Group: Social Cognitive Theory

Social cognitive theory as a whole holds that both learning and behaviour develop through observing other people. Social cognitive theory considers the ways in which individuals process information about other people in various environments. In addition, our decision whether or not to imitate depends on the consequences of that behaviour.

Sociocultural cognition, how we understand and think about people and social situations, is based on principles including the following:

- Individuals learn social norms and skills by observing and imitating others.
- Individuals' social cognition includes and applies schema development, attribution (explain to ourselves why people behave in particular way; trying to make sense of the world), and stereotyping.
- Interacting with others can communicate beliefs and behaviours that lead to compliance and conformity with perceived norms and accepted behaviours.
- Individuals can influence the behaviour of society by communicating new norms to society.
- The individual's self-efficacy influences the extent he or she can participate in society.

3.3.1 Individuals Learn Social Norms and Skills by Observing and Imitating Others

Social cognitive theory suggests that much behaviour, including aggression, is learnt in a sociocultural context from the environment and in the process of **modelling**, as well as by direct instruction. Modelling involves learning through observation of other people (models), which may lead to **imitation** if the behaviour to be copied appears to lead to desirable consequences. Over time, individuals internalise the social and cultural norms of their environment and use them to guide their interactions with other people.

Social cognitive theory suggests behaviour is modelled by other members of a group and acquired through observation or imitation based on consequences of a behaviour.

Social learning involves paying attention to the person modelled, remembering the behaviour that was observed, subsequently replicating the action, and feeling good about demonstrating what has been learnt. Social learning is distinguished from conditioning, in that the learning is indirect (not stimulus/response/reward). It models the behaviour of others (vicarious learning) and gets reinforced according to the results of following that behaviour, which in turn can influence the individual's motivation and **self-efficacy**. Self-efficacy theory holds that "people who believe they have the power to exercise some measure of control over their lives are healthier, more effective, and more successful than those who lack faith in their ability to effect changes in their lives" (Bandura, 1997).

For example, many believed that the human being could not run a four-minute mile before Roger Bannister succeeded in 1954. Within the next few months that record had been broken several times as leading athletes had learnt by his example that it could be done.

Models may be categorised under two headings: **positional models** (e.g. cartoon figures, famous people) and **personal models** (role models – parents, teachers, peers, and community leaders). The latter models are more likely to be sources of long-term developments of social behaviour.

3. THE SOCIOCULTURAL APPROACH TO UNDERSTANDING HUMAN BEHAVIOUR

RESEARCH STUDIES

Bandura's (1961) study in social cognitive theory aimed to demonstrate that learning can occur through mere observation of a model, and that imitation can take place in the absence of the model.

His team investigated whether children would imitate the aggression modelled by an adult, and also whether children were more likely to imitate same-gender models.

The participants were 36 boys and 36 girls aged 3–6, who were divided into similar groups. Group 1 was exposed to adult models who showed aggression by bashing an inflatable 'Bobo' doll. Group 2 observed a non-aggressive adult who assembled toys for 10 minutes. Group 3 was the control and did not see any model. In groups 1 and 2, some watched same-sex models and others watched opposite-sex models. All groups were then placed in a room with toys. As their play was becoming more involved, the toys were removed and the participants were told that they were for other children. This was the provocation to possible aggression. They were then left with the Bobo doll.

The results showed that those exposed to aggression at the earlier stage showed significantly higher levels of aggression towards the Bobo doll than those who had not been exposed to aggression. The conclusion was that aggression is learnt; it is not part of the child's nature. Also, boys were more likely to imitate the physical aggression that they had seen from men, and the girls were more likely to imitate the verbal aggression that they had seen from women.

In evaluation, the study does appear to support social cognitive theory, i.e. that we copy the behaviour learnt from others. Indeed, the models did perform aggressive acts that were not likely to be within the children's behaviour repertoires. It also highlighted the role of same-sex gender as a motivator for following the modelled behaviour.

However, the study was in a laboratory setting: low ecological validity. The children may well have not related beating a doll that bounced back with a smile to actual aggression. Also they were likely to be frustrated when the toys were taken away, whether they witnessed the aggressive scenes or not. There was a very brief encounter with the model, which contrasted, for example, with the long hours that children view aggressive scenes on television. There was no follow-up study to assess how long-lasting the violence learning experience was. Finally, there was an issue of demand characteristics: the children might have acted aggressively in order to please the researchers.

By today's ethical standards, there would be the issue of the merits of provoking very young children and exposing them to violence for research purposes.

The study of Bandura contrasts with the St Helena study (**Charlton et al. 2002**), which was based on observing the degree of violence in the school playground environment before and after the introduction of television on that island in 1995. A content analysis of TV programs showed a similar level of violence as TV in the UK. However, the observations showed no significant change in the pre-television-day low degree of violence after the introduction of TV on St. Helena. This study therefore downplays the importance of social cognitive theory.

Unlike Bandura, the study took place in the ecologically-valid school playground setup, by covert observations. It may be criticised as pre-1995 St. Helena children might have experienced violent-behaviour learning experiences from media other than television (books, comics, movies) that might have served the same function as television in the UK, and were in a cultural environment that was less inclined to tolerate similar conduct.

It may also be argued that the television-based violent characters in the St. Helena study were positional models. They were less likely to be models of violence for children, as they were personally unknown them, and for much part were not close to them. In contrast, the very young children in Bandura, who saw and trusted the researchers as associates of their parent/school environment, might well have viewed the researchers as personal models, as extensions of their parents and teachers. Consequently, the children identified more closely with the researcher, and would have more readily modelled the violent behaviour.

3.3.2 Individuals' Social Cognition Includes and Applies Schema Development, Attribution, and Stereotyping

Stereotyping is assuming that an individual or individuals have the behavioural characteristics that are commonly attributed to the group that they belong to. The actual judgments that are based on stereotyping vary from person to person and can be influenced by personal as well as second-hand experience of individuals from those groups, which can be in-groups and out-groups. They can influence both the way that people behave to others, and the way that they think about themselves.

In short, stereotyping involves a generalised and rather inflexible way about thinking about a group of people.

Stereotypes can be based on gender, nationality (Shih et al. 1999, below), religion, means of earning a living, and choice of leisure activity. They can be automatically activated, without the person being aware of it (Bargh et al. 1996, below). The degree that stereotyping resembles reality can vary from situation to situation.

RESEARCH STUDY

Shih et al. (1999)

This study aimed to determine whether stereotyping could affect one's own performance at a particular task.

This was an experimental, laboratory-conducted, study. The participants were 46 Asian-American female undergraduates. The procedures for each participant in the test group were designed to activate a particular stereotype in the individual and then give a mathematical task immediately afterwards. Their performance was compared to a similar group that carried out the mathematical task without any stereotype priming before the test.

In the first condition, the participants responded to a questionnaire that activated the gender stereotype (women were poorer than men in mathematics), being asked questions such as whether they preferred to be placed on single-sex or co-ed floors when living on campus. They were then given the mathematical task. In the second condition, the participants responded to a questionnaire that activated the ethnic stereotype (Asian students are clever), being asked whether their parents spoke any languages other than English and which languages they spoke at home and on campus. They were then given the mathematical task.

The results indicated that the women in the test group performed significantly better than those in the non-primed group when the ethnic stereotype was activated, but significantly poorer that those in the non-primed group when the gender stereotype was

3. THE SOCIOCULTURAL APPROACH TO UNDERSTANDING HUMAN BEHAVIOUR

activated. The researchers concluded that stereotyping, including self-stereotyping, can affect performance. Stereotypes may be internalised as templates and affect individual behaviour such as intellectual performance.

Strengths and limitations: Shih et al. (1999)

Strengths	Limitations
1. Indicates that stereotyping can influence performance, both positively and negatively. 2. It was experimental in design, with both conditions showing differences from the control population.	1. The sample was a relatively small one, with 46 taking part. 2. Those who took part were university undergraduates, raising the question of the degree that its findings can be generalised to wider populations.

RESEARCH STUDY

Bargh et al. (1996)

In this study, the researchers performed a series of experimental studies to consider whether stereotyping can activate cues that in turn influence behaviour. One of them induced stereotypes of the behaviour of elderly people in the test group.

The participants were divided into two groups, one of which was subtly primed with old-age stereotypes, and the other was primed with a series of words that were not related to that age-group. The priming took place with each group by providing them with a series of words to unscramble, with the test group's including words such as 'wrinkled'. Participants were instructed that on finishing the task they were to walk a short distance along a corridor to the elevator.

The researchers found that that those primed with the 'elderly' words took significantly more time to get to the elevator; they were timed as walking more slowly. They concluded that activating stereotypes can influence the individual to behave in accordance with the stereotype, even without the individual knowing it.

Strengths and limitations: Bargh et al. (1996)

Strengths	Limitations
1. It showed that stereotyping can influence the behaviour of an individual without the individual necessarily being aware of it. 2. It was experimental in design, with the independent variable being manipulated for the priming of the elderly person stereotype.	1. The sample was a relatively small one, with 14 taking part in the gender stereotype condition, and 16 in the ethnic stereotype condition. 2. There may be differences between the individuals in the degree that the experimenters' priming activated the participants' stereotypes.

3.3.3 Interacting with Others Can Communicate Beliefs and Behaviours That Lead to Compliance and Conformity with Perceived Norms and Accepted Behaviours

Both compliance and conformity involve changes in behaviour with cues from environment.

Compliance is where a person carries out a request to do something under direct pressure, even though the pressure may not necessarily be perceived by that person (e.g. in advertising). This contrasts with **conformity**, which is where the situation does not use direct pressure, but pressure is often perceived by individuals as influencing their behaviour change.

Compliance techniques include:

▶ **Reciprocity**: people comply out of feeling that they need to return a favour. People feel they must repay what another person has provided. For example **Lynn and McCall (1998)** found that restaurant diners leave a bigger tip when the bill comes together with a candy.

▶ **Door-in-the-face technique**: make a request which is turned down, because it is obviously too big. Then make a second smaller request, which might well be accepted – as the person will feel that the request has been reduced to accommodate them. **Cialdini (1975)** and his team tried to persuade one group of university students to chaperone a group of juvenile delinquents on a trip to the zoo. Nearly all refused. Then the same people stopped another group of students and firstly asked them if they would sign on as volunteer counsellors for two hours weekly for two years. They said no. Then afterwards, they asked them to chaperone a same day trip to the zoo. Half said yes.

▶ **Foot-in-the-door technique**: for example the study of **Dickerson (1992)**, where the team wanted students to conserve water by taking shorter showers (in Santa Cruz, California, where water is in short supply). To do so, they asked students to sign a poster that said: "Take shorter showers. If I can do it, so can you." That was the foot in the door. Then later on, they asked them to time the period they took for a shower. Overall, it turned out to be much shorter than the average time for students as a whole.

▶ **Low-balling**: for example the study of **Cialdini (1974)** on a group of enthusiastic first-year university psychology students. The first group of enthusiasts was asked to take part in a study on cognition and that they were to be there at 7:00 a.m. Less than one quarter agreed. In the second group, they were asked the same thing, but not told a time. More than half agreed to take part. When the 7:00 a.m. time was revealed, nearly all turned up on time.

▶ **Hazing**: this involves a series of initiation rites required to join a group perceived as exclusive, such as a college fraternity or sorority. In deciding to join, the individual complies with the often dramatic and stringent ceremonies. This initial degree of compliance leads to a greater degree of compliance later on, within the group activities. The study of **Aronson and Mills (1959)** involved asking female students to join a sex discussion-group. They were placed into two groups. The first had to go through an embarrassing initiation procedure to join. The second was allowed in straight away. Once both groups were in the meeting, the activity involved accomplices who were instructed to conduct an extremely boring program. Those who went through the initiation commented on the meeting being valuable and instructive. Those who were admitted straight away found the meeting to be a waste of time. Thus early compliance demanding initial sacrifices appears to lead to a greater commitment to comply subsequently.

Conformity to group norms is exemplified by the theory and research of Asch, known as the Asch Paradigm, whereby individuals may show a tendency to follow the counsel of the majority of the group (majority influence) even where they feel that they are wrong.

RESEARCH STUDY

Asch (1951)

The study aimed to determine whether participants would **conform to majority influence**, which promoted the giving of incorrect answers in a situation where the correct answers were clearly evident.

Each target participant entered a room where there were six other participants, dressed formally in business suits. Participants were told that they were going to take part in "a psychological experiment on visual judgment." Unknown to the target participant, the six others were accomplices of the experimenter.

All participants went through a series of exercises, involving a series of single lines on individual cards, and three comparison lines of different lengths on a second card. Participants had to say, in turn and out loud, which line on the second cards was the same as the one on the first cards. The target participant was placed towards the end of the group. Accomplices, dressed formally in businesses suits, gave the same wrong answers on 12 of the 18 trials.

Participants conformed to the unanimous majority on a third of the critical trials. Nearly three quarters conformed at least once, but just over one quarter never conformed. In follow-up, some conforming participants claimed to have seen the same as the majority. Others conformed because they did not want to be ridiculed by the group. The majority who conformed did so because they thought that their perception of the lines must be inaccurate, and the majority's must be accurate.

Thus it seems that even in unambiguous situations, there is still pressure to conform to a unanimous majority. Asch concluded that some people experience social influence and conform to avoid rejection. Others experience informational influence and conform because they doubt their own judgments. Follow-up experiments indicated that a majority of three with no accomplice dissenters was more effective in producing conformity than a majority of eight with one accomplice dissenter.

Strengths and limitations: Asch (1951)

Strengths	Limitations
1. The formal and serious atmosphere confronting the target participants did seem to have created an environment where conformity was expected. 2. Asch repeated the experiment during the 1950s, with similar results.	1. The time and the place that the research was carried out might have affected the findings. In the 1950s, the USA was very conservative and in the grip of McCarthyism, an anti-communist witch-hunt. That placed greater pressure on people to conform, and not 'rock the boat'. 2. The work of Perrin and Spencer (1981) led to the conclusion that cultural change over 30 years in the USA led to a reduction in the tendency of students to conform. The study repeated the Asch experiment using mathematics, science, and engineering students as target participants. Only one out of the 396 tested conformed. The researchers concluded that the Asch paradigm was far less significant in American society in the 1980s, which took questioning of 'authority figures' for granted. It may also be argued that the students in the above disciplines were less likely to let themselves be deceived. 3. Bond and Smith (1996) concluded from a meta-analysis of over 100 studies that conformity was more evident in collectivist cultures (valuing group loyalty) than in individualist cultures (valuing individual initiative). People would be more likely to conform in Fiji, Hong-Kong, and Brazil, that in North America and Western Europe. 4. Ethical considerations: the original Asch experiment would, by today's standards, have raised the issue of the participants being deceived and made to feel anxious about their performances.

3.3.4 Individuals Can Influence the Behaviour of Society By, In Turn, Communicating New Norms to Society

This includes the theory of **reciprocal determinism**, which holds that both the environment and the individual can influence each other. For example, a student finds art difficult. The teacher tends to overlook her, giving time and effort to the more talented students. She then makes a special effort to improve. The teacher then notices her changed attitude and responds by giving her a more central position in the class. That student continues to improve as a result, and the cycle repeats itself as both the student feels fulfilled through her new levels of achievement, and the teacher takes pride in her progress.

Reciprocal determinism can take place on a large scale, for example a perceived injustice in society influences movements for social change that in turn succeed in changing public opinion.

3.3.5 The Individual's Self-Efficacy Influences the Extent He or She Can Participate in Society

As already introduced, self-efficacy theory holds that "people who believe they have the power to exercise some measure of control over their lives are healthier, more effective, and more successful than those who lack faith in their ability to effect changes in their lives" (Bandura, 1997). Bandura identifies four sources of self-efficacy: past personal success in a similar task, seeing other people successfully carry out the task, support and expressed confidence from others, and cognitive ability to interpret the situation that minimises the stress and raises the confidence.

RESEARCH STUDY

Hochstetler et al. (1985)

This study focused on manipulating self-efficacy to improve performance in sporting activities.

There were 40 female participants, divided into two groups. The first was shown a video of a woman tackling a cycling challenge with great difficulty. The second was shown a video of a woman tackling the identical challenge with ease. Both groups were then given the same cycling task. The researchers observed that the first group found the cycling task significantly more difficult than the second group. The researchers concluded that modelling, in this case seeing others successfully carrying out the task with ease, can be a crucial element in sporting success. This conclusion is supported by anecdotal evidence of sporting celebrities, as well as the evidence from this and similar studies in how the example of one person can influence the self-efficacy and thus performance of many people. However, the self-efficacy in this study was limited to one aspect only: sporting performance, with the problem of generalising it to other activities. In addition, there are other situations, such as shyness, which are influenced by psychological factors other than self-efficacy.

3.4 Cultural Origins of Behaviour and Cognition

Psychology's interest in culture extends to how it affects the behaviour of individuals and societies.

The key areas of study in cultural origins of behaviour and cognition are the influence of culture on behaviour and cognition, cultural dimensions and behaviour, and etic and emic principles, as explained below.

Culture in psychological terms has been defined by **Hofstede (2002)** as the mental software common to the members of the sociocultural group. This includes ideas and ideals that are shared by those in the sociocultural group, which in turn are likely to influence the behaviour of those in the group. Members of the group learn the cultural norms through daily interactions, and from feedback from other members of the group.

In order to apply culture to psychology, it is necessary to find how specific factors in culture relate to behaviours, include cultural extremes such as initiation rites, witch doctors, infanticides, and honour-killings.

These factors reflect the ways that these people have survived in their environment, how they have organised life in social groups, and the resulting beliefs, attitudes, and norms that can influence their specific behaviours.

Perspectives of culture vary between cultural psychologists. A **universalist** perspective takes the position that psychological mechanisms are fundamentally the same in all cultures, but the behaviours and experiences vary from culture to culture. A **relativist** perspective takes the position that the behaviours and psychological processes between cultures are so different that they cannot be compared across cultural groups.

Cultural norms and conventions are behaviour patterns that are typical of specific groups. They are passed down from generation to generation by observational (and reinforcement) learning by the group's "gatekeepers" (guardians of culture): parents, teachers, religious leaders, and peers. Cultural norms include such things as how marriage partners are chosen, attitudes towards the rights of animals, physical punishment of children, and alcohol consumption.

Culture and cultural norms can be classified into **surface culture**; easily observed behaviours specific to a particular culture, and **deep culture**; the beliefs, values, and assumptions that are part of the thinking of those inside the culture, but hard to access for those outside the culture. For example, it is common in Western societies for children to study at a university far away from their families, which may reflect those cultures' fundamental emphasis on individual choice and independence.

3.4.1 Cultural Dimensions

Cultural dimensions are means of describing the values held by individuals living within a particular culture. For example, some cultures encourage risk taking, and others lean towards conservatism and practices that traditionally have been working for them. Knowledge of cultural dimensions can be vital for cross-cultural communications in international diplomacy, business, and tourism.

RESEARCH STUDY

Hofstede (1967)

Hofstede is a study on cultural dimensions that began in 1967 with a focus on the IBM workplace in 53 different countries and has since been continuing, incorporating other companies within the research. Using questionnaire surveys issued to individual workers, the trends were analysed. The findings were used to identify the existence of the following cultural dimensions, along each one of which the culture of each country or society may be placed.

Individualism/collectivism: describes the relative importance of individual interests versus group interests. Individualistic cultures focus on uniqueness, individual achievement, freedom and self-actualisation. Collectivistic cultures focus on social harmony, interdependence, modesty and group memberships and norms. The US is an example of an individualist culture, which can be expressed in work ethics: in the US one can typically leave a job as soon as one with better prospects and benefits is on offer. In Japan, there is group and company loyalty; you stay with the company you are part of. In the US, a mistake costing the company millions of dollars means instant dismissal for the employee concerned. In Japan, the company may well take the error in its stride, covering up for the employee, especially if he has established himself as trustworthy and "one of the company".

Uncertainty avoidance: describes the span of a society's comfort zones, and willingness to stray out its comfort zones to reap the potential rewards. Argentina and Chile rate high on uncertainty avoidance. In contrast, North America's culture (and the IB's culture) is that constructive risk-taking is a necessity for developing maturity, and that learning from mistakes is a positive experience. It is low on uncertainly avoidance. Going bankrupt, as long as the business has been run in good faith, can be expected as part of the learning experience for a first-time businessperson. In some European countries it can have serious consequences, such as great difficulties in obtaining credit for future ventures. Such a situation may well reflect a culture of higher uncertainty avoidance.

Power Distance: describes the social distance between those in different positions in the organisation. It expresses the beliefs about the suitable distribution of power in society. The greater the power distance, the greater formality and deference that exists between people at different levels in the organisation. Where the power distance is greater, those at the upper levels of the organisation are involved in the key decision-making, with those lower down accepting it as part of the work reality. Power/distance tends to be higher in Arab countries and in China, and lower in Western European countries such as Denmark and Austria.

Masculinity/Femininity: describes the degree that behaviours traditionally associated with each of the two genders underpin the culture. The Masculine end of this dimension focuses on competition, achievements, heroism, and material rewards of success, whereas the Feminine end includes cooperation, consensus, all-inclusivity, and quality of life. Countries that emphasise conflict resolution by negotiation, work-family balance, and a pleasant and congenial working environment lean towards femininity, whereas those placing more emphasis on hard-bargaining, competition, and money, tend to be more masculine in culture. Japan is considered masculine, Sweden feminine.

Long term/short-term (added in 2001): describes the degree that the company's goals prioritise short-term results with immediate benefits as opposed to the long-term. Long term is more prevalent in countries such as those in East Asian countries, which emphasises persistence and resilience and self-sacrifice for long-term and long lasting progress and achievements. Short term is more typical of countries that place more emphasis on immediate gratification and dazzling, but not necessarily long-lasting achievements.

Indulgence/restraint (added in 2010): describes the degree that society expects its human drives to be gratified instantly, or is prepared to forgo the immediate pleasures in favour of a more restrained and conservative route towards personal pleasure. Latin America and Western Europe tend towards indulgence; East Asian countries and Middle Eastern cultures prefer to postpone gratification.

RESEARCH STUDY

Berry (1967)

This study had similarities to the study of Asch (1951) on social conformity to group norms, detailed earlier in this chapter (Section 3.3.3). Its purpose was to investigate whether people's judgements are more likely to conform to a hinted-at norm if they are in a conformist culture and less likely in an individualist culture. The cultural dimension considered by this study would be **individualism/collectivism**.

There were three groups, with each approximately 120 participants:

1. Inuit, from Baffin Island, Canada, an individualist culture based on hunting and fishing. Only one quarter had significant contact with Western culture
2. Temne people, from Sierra Leone, a more collective culture based on settled agriculture. Again, only one quarter had significant contact with Western culture
3. Scots (as a control group): half from rural and half from urban environments.

Each participant was tested without any others present, and in native language. For the test, each was given a series of six questions, every one having a stimulus line and a total of 8 other lines, and had to decide with one matched the stimulus line. They did the first two questions unaided. On question 3, the participant was told by the researcher that most members of his/her group thought that a particular line matched the stimulus line. That was correct. On questions 4, 5, and 6, they were given similar information, which was always incorrect.

The results showed that the Temne people paid the greatest attention to "most members of your group think", and the Inuit the least. The Scots were in the middle, but closer to the Inuit. There were no signficant differences within each culture of those exposed to Western culture. This indicates that factors influencing decision-making include the individualism/collectivism cultural dimension.

Strengths and limitations: Berry (1967)

Strengths	Limitations
1. Indicates that cultural dimensions can contribute to explain the decision-making process. 2. The experiment used a control, and also took into account potential linguistic and exposure to Western culture issues.	1. Low ecological validity due to the task's artificial nature and laboratory setting. 2. The study is dated, raising the question of whether the growing influence of media and other globalisation influences could affect the rates of culture-based erroneous collectivism-based conformity.

RESEARCH STUDY

Lamm et al. (2017)

This study also considers enculturation: the process whereby people learn the norms and skills of their own culture.

This study can be related to two dimensions: **individualism/collectivism**, and **indulgence/restraint**. Its aim is to determine the extent that culture issued the degree that young children were prepared to delay immediate gratification in favour of the prospects of greater rewards in the future (indulgence/restraint). It could also be said to determine the degree that culture promotes individual freedom or following the restrictions of group norms (individualism/collectivism).

The participants were 201 4-year old children, 76 from Cameroon (sub-Saharan Africa), and 125 from Germany. The two sets of children were from contrasting cultures. Those from Cameroon were brought in a strictly traditional and controlling style, with closer physical closeness, restraint, and conformity to group norms. Those from Germany had grown up in an atmosphere that responded more quickly to the child's mood and present situation, and encouraged proactive and influential interaction with the environment.

Each participating child was left in a room with one tasty item at the table: a marshmallow, a cookie, or a pretzel. The child was told that he or she had a choice: either eat it now and get no more, or wait until later and there will be more of the same.

3. THE SOCIOCULTURAL APPROACH TO UNDERSTANDING HUMAN BEHAVIOUR

The results shows than nearly 70% of the Cameroon children, but less than 30% of the German children chose and succeeded to forgo immediate gratification, favouring considerably more gratification later on. The research team concluded that the cultural dimension of indulgence/restraint influences parenting styles, with the Cameroon children being more prepared to wait as the parental style tended to be more delayed in reacting to the child's mood than with children brought up in Germany. This reflects contrasting enculturation processes in Cameroon and Germany. It could also be concluded that the cultural dimension of individualism/collectivism was reflected in the relative individualistic freedom shown by the German children and the modesty and group norms more prevalent with the Cameroon children.

Strengths and limitations: Lamm et al. (2017)

Strengths	Limitations
1. Indicates that cultural dimensions can contribute to explain the decision making process with children even as young as 4 years. 2. The design for the delaying-gratification experience was standard for the children of both cultures.	1. Not all children and for that matter adults are affected by cultural dimension influences to the same degree, making the findings difficult to generalise to particular individuals. 2. Despite standardisation, some children (of whatever culture) are likely to be more attracted to the "reward" than others, resulting in delayed gratification and conformity to collective social norms being a more severe ordeal.

3.5 Cultural Attitudes on Individual Attitudes, Identity, and Behaviours: Enculturation and Acculturation

From pre-school age onwards, individuals continue to develop their behaviours within the boundaries of social cultural norms. This process also helps them to form a sense of social identity, as they acquire the skills and habits that enable them to participate and be socially accepted within that society. This process is **socialisation**.

Socialisation leads to **enculturation**, the way in which individuals learn and adopt the norms, ways and manners of the culture. The cultural dimensions explored in the previous section, and the differences in Cameroon and German 4-year olds in their capacity to postpone immediate enjoyment with the prospect of substantial gains later on demonstrated in Lamm et al. (Section 3.4) express and exemplify the enculturation differences in the cultural norms acquired in the socialisation process.

Socialisation can also extend to **acculturation**, which may happen where people change or at least adapt due to contact with another culture, in order to **assimilate** with that culture. This can happen through voluntary or forced migration from one country to another, or though the influences of globalisation (Section 3.7; Higher Level only), travel, and the media. These factors can also cause cultures to change, as can education and modernisation.

Enculturation may be described as the product of first culture learning. Acculturation may be described as the product of second culture learning.

Both enculturation and acculturation develop at the **surface culture**, behavioural level (such as gender roles and ways of spending leisure time) and at the deep culture,

cognitive level, (such as in beliefs, attitudes, and ideals). Cultures are also dynamic, on both the surface and the deep levels. For example, Western culture has moved towards both the practice (surface culture) and belief (deep culture) in equal opportunities for both genders in education, work, and leisure activities.

Berry (1974) identified four types of acculturation strategies that individuals and communities may choose to use when facing interaction with another, population-wise dominant community:

Assimilation: where an individual or minority community strives to adopt the attitudes and behaviours of the majority culture and exits the original culture in the process.

Integration: where the individual or minority community fits in with the majority culture, but still maintains the original culture.

Separation: where the individual or minority community minimises contact with the majority culture, but strives to maintain the original culture.

Marginalisation: where the individual or minority community is excluded from the majority culture and cannot maintain the original culture.

Barriers in acculturation can occur for reasons including acculturation stress, the psychological strain of trying to come to terms with a different culture, which can be especially severe where:

- There are language barriers with the majority community: particularly for the older generation who tend to find it challenging to learn a new language.
- The individuals or community left their first culture surroundings because they had no choice.
- Migrants being unable to build strong social support networks within their own expatriate community in their new surroundings.
- Experience of substantial discriminatory attitudes and behaviours in their new surroundings, from the host community.

RESEARCH STUDY

See also Lamm et al., 2017 (Section 3.4), a study that considers enculturation.

Greenfield (2006)

The aim of this study in **enculturation** was to find out how the distinctly Mayan (in Mexico) cultural practices of weaving were transmitted from mothers to daughters. Passing cultural norms from parents to children is **vertical transmission**, in contrast to horizontal transmission (between people of the same generation, such as friends), and oblique transmission (between people of different generations outside the family, such as teachers).

This is a longitudinal study. Greenfield researched as a locally-dressed participant-observer (where the researcher becomes part of the group studied), through (i) regularly visiting and observing over the 40-year length of the study (ii) obtaining data through studying, interviewing, and later videoing the 14 mother and daughter pairs in their native language.

The study found that although the mothers denied that they were consciously teaching that craft to daughters, Greenfield observed they were involved in their daughters' progress by showing them what to do and giving feedback as necessary. It drew attention to the importance of traditional local weaving skills within the culture. The observations of the vertical transmissions of the technical weaving skills pointed to the underlying

3. THE SOCIOCULTURAL APPROACH TO UNDERSTANDING HUMAN BEHAVIOUR

cultural values of respecting maternal authority, contributing to the family income from a young age, and progressing in skills to qualify for, in due course, a quality husband.

Strengths and limitations: Greenfield (2006)

Strengths	Limitations
1. Longitudinal and qualitative nature of the study: enabling the researcher to observe the culture-defined vertical transmission process at close range for an extended period.	1. Possibility of researcher bias in interpreting the observations, interviews, transcripts, and video information: especially when inferring cultural norms.
2. Validity of the study: the researcher's integration into Mayan society through learning the local language (Tzotzil), culture, and following their dress code earned her the trust of the people she was studying over an extended period. That gave them the comfort to open out to her at a level not easily accessed by questionnaires, for example. It may be classified as an emic (researched by an insider) study.	2. Possibility that the mothers and daughters were on their best behaviour in the researcher's presence.
	3. Possible limits in the study's transferability to other situations in vertical transmission of cultural skills, norms, and values, given the nature of Mayan culture and the small number of participants.

 RESEARCH STUDY

Lueck and Wilson (2010)

The aim of this study on **acculturation** was to find out which factors could predict **acculturative stress** in Hispanic migrants to the USA.

The study involved a total of 2057 people of Hispanic migrants. 946 were first generation and grew up in their Spanish-speaking countries of origin, and the rest had lived in the USA since their childhoods.

Using semi-structured interviews face-to-face or over the Internet, the researchers determined the levels of acculturation for each participant under the following criteria: native language proficiency, English language proficiency, language preference, experience of discrimination from the host community, family cohesion, social networks, socioeconomic status, reason for migrating to the USA, and levels of acculturative stress. Those conducting the interviews were of similar cultural and linguistic backgrounds to the participants, which would make it an emic rather than an etic study (see below, in this section).

The study found the following factors to be significant predictors of acculturation stress:

- Language barriers with the majority community: particularly for older migrants.
- Having had no choice but to leave their country of origin.
- Lack of support from their expatriate community.
- Experiencing incidents of discrimination in their new surroundings.

Strengths and limitations: Lueck and Wilson (2010)

Strengths	Limitations
1. Large sample of 2000 people took part, which generated a considerable volume of data. Each interview lasted on average 2.4 hours. 2. The interviews were conducted by people who were familiar with both the Hispanic culture and the context of the investigation. 3. The semi-structured interviews gave the interviewer the opportunity to enable each participant to supply more detailed information where necessary.	1. The results were correlation, with difficulties in identifying cause and effect despite the semi-structured nature of the interviews. 2. It was not always easy to determine which stresses were non-acculturation in origin.

RESEARCH STUDY

Pantiru and Barley (2014)

The aim of this study on **acculturation** was to find out the relationship between two variables: **acculturation strategies** used and the degree that they **assisted the process** of acculturation in order to assimilate with a new culture. The focus of the study was Romanian immigrants in the UK.

The study involved a total of 245 participants. This study used a **mixed-method** approach: quantitative by using an online survey questionnaire, followed up by qualitative using detailed semi-structured interviews of three participants. This mixed-methods approach had a **triangulatory** function: the two methods were designed to support the study's credibility, and also give a deeper explanation of the findings that would have been beyond the reach of the standard questionnaire.

The study found that the Romanian immigrants to the UK were predominantly using the integration (rather than the separation or marginalisation) strategy in acculturating to the UK, fitting in with its culture while at the same time maintaining its own. The migrants tended to be well-educated, competent in use of English, and had migrated there in search of a higher quality of life. Major factors that seemed to further assist the acculturation process, acculturation strategies, were the hours spent in the UK working community, involvement in the lives of their children going through the school system, and relatively low use of Romanian written and media material. In addition, the study found that the immigrants' expat prior networks of friends were also relatively well acculturated within the host community.

3. THE SOCIOCULTURAL APPROACH TO UNDERSTANDING HUMAN BEHAVIOUR

Strengths and limitations: Pantiru and Barley (2014)

Strengths	Limitations
1. The mixed methods approach supported the study's validity and credibility. The use of semi-structured interviews enabled the investigators to access explanations for trends indicated by the quantitative survey. 2. The questionnaire considered a wide range of possible acculturation factors that could assist, and restrict, the process of acculturation.	1. Possible underrepresentation of less educated migrants who might have been harder to reach through the online questionnaire. 2. Difficulties in generalising findings on the Romanian community to other newly-migrated groups in the UK and similar countries, as the Romanians were relatively well-educated, without appearances and practices that might arouse prejudice and discrimination in the host society.

3.5.1 Etic and Emic Approaches

Cultures are studied in different ways by researchers. When studied by an outsider, the approach is **etic**, tending to explore universal behaviours and assuming that they would apply to human beings worldwide. When studied by an insider, the study is **emic**. An emic study is likely to view the cultural meanings that people attach to their experiences, and the meaning of social actions within the context that people live.

Etic studies

Etic studies to the study of depression – for example, the **WHO (World Health Organization) (1983)** investigation of the diagnosis and classification of depression in Switzerland, Canada, Japan, and Iran. The study identified the symptoms reported by most of the over-500 patients studied in those four countries. These included sadness, joylessness, anxiety, and a sense of insufficiency.

The etic approach of that study (and its consequent limitations) was underlined when further investigation of the sample showed that nearly half of the patients displayed symptoms of somatic complaints and obsessions that were not within the scope of the symptoms measured by the study. Thus the meaning of 'depression' has different connotations to different cultures. Depressive symptoms are not experienced the same way in all cultures. Indeed, the Chinese often tend to report depression in terms of somatic symptoms, such as body pains and upsets (Draguns and Tanaka-Matsumi, 2003).

Emic studies

One example of an emic study is **Greenfield (2006)**, above. Another is **Manson et al., (1985)**, on depressive illness amongst the Hopi tribe of American Indians. Most Hopi participants could not identify a Hopi word that translated into depression. But they were all familiar with the Hopi mind-disturbance categories, including worry sickness, unhappiness, heartbroken, drunken-like craziness, and disappointment. Some of those characteristics identified by the Hopi followed the Western perception. Others, for example "heartbroken", on investigation were very different to the Western understanding. Heartbroken to the Hopi meant weight-loss, fatigue, loss of sexual appetite, trouble thinking clearly, and feelings of not being likeable.

Thus although depression appears to be a universal phenomenon, its development and expression are culturally determined. Indeed, the work of **Marsella et al. (2002)** suggests that depression is expressed differently according to whether the culture is individualist or collective. In individualist societies, it comes out in feelings of loneliness and isolation. In collective societies, it comes out in somatic symptoms such as headaches and dizziness.

Both the studies of Lueck and Wilson (above) and Parker et al. (Chapter 4) have emic dimensions. A further example is **Zhang et al (1998)** on mood disorders in different regions of China, using suitably adapted local criteria. Mood disorders in China are very hard to identify using Western criteria, as the Chinese tend to frame them in somatic terms due to the cultural stigma of mental illness in China.

3.6 The Influence of Globalisation on Behaviours (Higher Level only)

The IB program uses the International Monetary Fund (IMF) definition of globalisation: "The growing interdependence of countries worldwide through the increasing volume and variety of cross-border transactions in goods and services and of international capital flows, and through the more rapid and widespread diffusion in technology". Globalisation can involve you as a student: you are following a program identical to some 3,000 schools in more than 130 countries, and might well be involved in trans-national CAS project.

Our studies of the influence of globalisation on individual attributes, identities, and behaviours consider two interacted areas:

1. The effect of the interaction of local and global influences on behaviour.
2. Methods used to study the influence of globalisation on behaviour.

3.6.1 The effect of the interaction of local and global influences on behaviour

Individual reactions to globalisation may fall into the following positions, depending on the nature of the globalisation influence. For example, there are individuals and societies that are happy to consume Western fast-food, but do not accept young people choosing spouses that have not been screened by the elders of the family. Globalisation's influences on behaviour may be placed under the following headings:

Integrative accommodation of globalisation

This position accepts global inputs as being non-threatening to traditional local culture, and at the same time feeling comfortable as citizens of the world. There is a local-global accommodation in personal identity formation, without any perception of cultural intrusion. For example, **Richard Condon's (1988)** investigation of Inuit communities in Northern Canada found that they were able to live according to their traditional values of deep family ties and shyness and at the same time feel part of the wider, modern Canadian society such as in identifying with Canadian hockey teams and obtaining their higher education and training in other parts of the country.

Global citizen

Individuals move towards reducing or even rejecting their identity with traditional, local culture, choosing instead to assimilate into global culture. Such culture shedding is exemplified by the work of **Saraswathi and Larson (2002)**, which investigated the lifestyles of the growing urbanised middle-class population of young people in India and South-East Asia. It highlighted the practice of postponing and even avoiding the traditional marriage and family-centred way of life, assuming increasingly modern and secular identities with education and training continuing well into the 20s.

Exclusionary responses to globalisation

Putting globalised influences into second place, or even rejecting them as threatening and unwelcome materialistic and hedonistic forces. Their non-acceptance of globalised values can intensify their respect for local cultural icons, and for greater involvement in perpetuating the traditional culture of the local community. It may include promoting fundamentalist and extremist religious ideals that emphasise eternal truths and exclude non-like-minded people. For example, the study of **Wu et al. (2014)** highlights exclusionary trends among individual Hui-Muslims in China, who increased their commitment to fundamentalism and especially separatist dietary practices in their endeavours to exclude Han-Chinese influences. Though nervous of outside influences, such groups typically handle outsider encounters with pro-social behaviour, terrorists striking at representations of global culture (e.g. the attacks on the World Trade Center in New York, 2001) being exceptions.

Marginalisation, or disorientation

Such individuals find the conflicts between traditional local culture and global inputs hard to resolve. They feel at home in neither society, constantly asking themselves where they belong. The study of **Norasakkunkit and Uchida (2011)** focused on the situation of disorientated young adults in Japan. They found that the traditional company-dominated lifestyle with long hours and job security was less available and desirable. At the same time, they found the increasing trends of globalised integration in the Japanese corporate world as a vague challenge to the vitality of their society. The study indicated that these individuals felt marginalised and disorientated, with confused identities and lack of long-term goals influencing their shift to the margins of both their own communities and the wider global communities.

People facing issues whereby local and global influences prompt different behaviours are likely to act somewhere along the glocalisation (global/local) spectrum. For example their weekly diet may include items that are associated with both the fast-food and the local cuisine. Areas of interest to psychology include:

- The individual experiences a simultaneous interaction with global and native culture. Will attitudes and behaviour be integrative or exclusionary?
- The individual reads novels and listens to music from both local, and more global culture. How may that affect thinking and behaviour?
- The individual experiences globalisation through foreign travel. How may that affect the level of trust shown towards strangers?
- The individual and society experiences Western ideals of the ideal body shape through the media for the first time. How may that affect their behaviour?

The two studies below researched the first question and the last question.

RESEARCH STUDY

Torelli et al. (2011)

Torelli et al. conducted an **independent measures, experimental study** aimed to find how people would react when valued icons of their local culture were challenged by global elements.

This study focuses on (i) the effect of the interaction of local and global influences on behaviour, as well as (ii) how globalisation may influence attitudes, identities, and behaviour. Its use of quantitative, laboratory experimental methods also exemplifies (iii) methods to study the influence of globalisation on behaviour.

The participants were 125 American students of European origin. They were placed in a simultaneous two-culture situation, with the hypothesis being that the participants would identify far more intensely with their national icon when it was set in the background of a very different culture. They would protect their icon with exclusionary attitudes and behaviour.

The first group (the test) was culturally primed by being shown three iconic items that were strongly associated with the USA: running shoes, jeans and breakfast cereals. The second group (the control) was also primed, but with items that were less iconic of the USA: table lamps, bread toasters and umbrellas. These created the psychological conditions in the first group in which national identity and global identity would be both strongly represented in a conflicting situation.

Half of the first group was told that the strongly-iconic running shoes, jeans, and breakfast cultures were made by local companies in China; the companies being 'Qinjin' for the running shoes, 'Xenshi' for the jeans and 'Chenxiao' for the breakfast cereals. The other half of this group were given the American-sounding names of 'Aspire', 'Nine-Zero' and 'Uncle Bob' for the running shoes, jeans and breakfast cereals respectively.

Half of the second group was told that the less-iconic table lamps, bread toasters and umbrellas were made by Chinese companies; 'Zhongyan' for the table lamps, 'Beihua' for the toasters and 'Wufeng' for the umbrellas. The other half of the group were given American-sounding names for the same products: 'Schonbek', 'Robin' and 'Murray' for the table lamps, toasters and umbrellas respectively. All participants rated their assigned products using three criteria, on a 1–9 scale: bad-good, unappealing-appealing and unfavourable-favourable.

The results showed significantly lower ratings for products that were Chinese-made brands of highly iconic American products than for any other type of products. The researchers concluded that individuals tend towards exclusionary reactions to a foreign culture when it conflicts with a cherished icon associated with their native culture.

Strengths and limitations: Torelli et al. (2011)

Strengths	Limitations
1. The use of quantitative, experimental method, with the independent variable of cultural priming/conflict suitably controlled. 2. The relatively large size of the sample.	1. The questionable validity in transferring a laboratory experience of global/local discord to a similar situation in real life, when, for example making a purchasing choice between locally-iconic goods or imported-similar goods. 2. The use of specifically Chinese-sounding names for native culture icons may not elicit the same reactions in other languages. 3. Difficulties in generalising attitudes towards globalisation from a study whose participants were exclusively students.

3. THE SOCIOCULTURAL APPROACH TO UNDERSTANDING HUMAN BEHAVIOUR

RESEARCH STUDY

Becker et al (2002)

The globalisation of culture has used to explain changes in the prevalence of bulimia nervosa. It has involved imposing Western ideals on the ideal body shape, being socially reinforced worldwide through slim female figures on globalised television, movies, and women's magazines. That puts social pressure on women worldwide to conform to the model of the 'affluent and successful Western society'.

This study focuses on (i) the effect of the interaction of local and global influences on behaviour, as well as (ii) how globalisation may influence attitudes, identities, and behaviour. Its use of quantitative, natural experimental methods also exemplifies (iii) methods to study the influence of globalisation on behaviour.

This is emphasised by the work of Becker et al on the prevalence of bulimia in adolescent girls in a remote area of the Fiji Islands before the then introduction of TV (1995), and three years after the introduction of TV (1998). It thus used natural experimental methods, as the independent variable the introduction of Western norms through the TV, was out of the control of the researchers.

This study used a questionnaire and follow-up semi-structured interviews on 17-year girls' eating patterns from two secondary schools: a mixed methods approach. It was independent measures in design: 63 students participated in the 1995 phase, and another 65 from the same schools and of the same age in the 1998 phase.

The results indicated that there had been a significant change in the ideal body profile from fairly round and robust before television introduction, to the slim Western model afterwards. There was no dieting before the introduction of TV. Three years later, more than 10% of the girls reported dieting and self-induced vomiting as a means of working towards the Western-idealised body shape. The researchers concluded that television indeed promoted a new social norm by setting an ideal Western-style body image.

Strengths and limitations: Becker et al. (2002)

Strengths	Limitations
1. The use of the natural experimental method. The participants were restricted to Fijian girls only who in the first stage had no experience of Western TV, in contrast with the second stage where it was available to all. 2. The relatively large size of the sample, and the consistency in recruiting the 17-year-old participants from the same two schools in both phases.	1. The questionable validity in generalising from Fijian girls to other cultures as Fiji has a strong culture of both eating and idealised body shape. 2. Becker observed that the participants were naïve in their veneration of Western TV, allowing their vision of Western norms to be based on soap operas and similar materials.

3.6.2 Methods Used to Study the Influence of Globalisation on Behaviour

Methods of studying globalisation are exemplified by the laboratory experimental method in Torelli et al (2011), and by the natural experimental research of Becker et al (2002), both in this section.

In addition, the following factors need to be taken into account when researching how globalisation might influence behaviour:

1. Language issues: questionnaires have to be adapted to fit in with local cultures, so that they communicate in the same way as in the home culture. It can involve a series of demanding and time consuming procedures in order to avoid cultural bias at the points where the participants receive the questions, and where they communicate their answers for translation into the language of research. This is exemplified in Parker et al. (Chapter 6).

2. Construct issues: for example the nature of depression is understood and communicated differently in Western and East Asian cultures. This is also exemplified in Parker et al. (Chapter 6)

3. Response bias: for example the interpreting of quantitative data from Likert scales. For example, on a five-point scale, a midpoint response in South Korea tends to mean mild agreement, whereas in the UK it is likely to communicate being unable to decide. It tends to be avoided in Southern Europe as that culture values the quality of being decisive in one way or the other.

3.7 Research Methods Used in the Sociocultural Approach to Understanding Behaviour

- Quantitative, such as experimental methods (e.g. Bandura, 1965), designed to establish a cause and effect relationship.
- Quantitative and correlational methods (e.g. Lueck and Wilson, 2011), investigating the relationship between two sets of values already in existence.
- Qualitative methods, including interviews, focus groups (when several people are interviewed together, as in a panel), and case studies. These can access depths and details about individuals that are hard to access in large quantitative studies.
- Observations methods, such as those used by Charlton et al. (2002) on the influence of aggressive scenes on television promoting violent behaviour in real life, and Greenfield (2006) on the vertical transmission of cultural values.
- Mixed methods, e.g. Pantiru and Barley, where qualitative semi-structured interviews are used to provide in-depth information on acculturation experiences that could not easily be accessed by that study's questionnaire.

3.8 Strengths and Limitations: Sociocultural Approach to Understanding Behaviour

Strengths of the Sociocultural Approach to Understanding Behaviour

1. Wide scope of application: in all issues requiring an understanding of how aspects of society and culture influence behaviour. For example, how they modify the behaviour of individuals when in different social contexts and groups.

2. Contributes to giving further dimensions to the biological and cognitive approaches. For example, an individual may have the genetic tendency towards depression, but those genes can be switched on or off by the individual's surroundings and nature of social interactions.

3. THE SOCIOCULTURAL APPROACH TO UNDERSTANDING HUMAN BEHAVIOUR

Limitations of the Sociocultural Approach to Understanding Behaviour

1. Reductionist when used by itself: could underemphasise the biological, cognitive, and psychodynamic elements that also affect people's behaviour.
2. Need to exercise care in applying sociocultural models that may be too simple and general to explain the realities of individuals.

3.9 Ethical Considerations: Sociocultural research to Understanding Behaviour

Similar to those in the biological and cognitive approach, including:

- Informed consent – participants must know the object of the study, that their involvement is voluntary, what the data will be used for, and if necessary be debriefed at the end of the study. In extreme cases, the ethical requirement for informed consent may be waived, when the focus of the study is of public importance and there is no other way to obtain the sought-after information.
- Avoiding deception, except possibly where the research cannot be carried out in any other way.
- Protection from harm: particularly important when handling potentially sensitive information such as the experience of immigrants in acculturation (e.g. Pantiru and Barley, 2014), and the prevalence of changed eating habits following the introduction of Western television (e.g. Becker et al., 2012 – HL section).
- Making the participants anonymous to protect them, even at the risk of reducing the authenticity of the research and of preventing any follow-up study.
- The right for any participant to withdraw from the study at any point, and communicating that right before the commencement of the study.
- All participants are to be debriefed at the end of the study.
- Bearing in mind that socio-cultural research involving associated cultural issues is extremely sensitive with many ethnic groups. The study of Greenfield (2006) in Section 3.5 exemplifies this issue strongly being taken into account. Typically, the elders of the society must be consulted for permission to work with members of their group.

Exam-style Practice Questions: The Sociocultural Approach

Short Answer Questions
1. Explain *one* study of social identity theory.
2. Describe *one* research study relating to acculturation.

Essay Response Question[s]
1. Discuss how stereotyping influences behaviour.
2. Evaluate the ways in which globalisation can influence behaviour. (HL only)

Chapter 4: Approaches To Researching Behaviour (HL)

Overview

This part of the syllabus enables you to apply critical thinking skills in evaluating the strengths and limitations of the research studies by challenging their assumptions, designs, methodologies, findings, and conclusions. Though methodology and critical analysis underlie the entire syllabus, they are formally examined in their own right at HL only.

Approaches to researching behaviour form this final chapter. This position is due to their being directly examined in Paper 3, the last examination paper. Paper 3 is taken by HL students only, and forms 20% of the HL final IB assessment.

This topic underpins the entire syllabus. All students should be thoroughly familiar with it, even though it is directly examined at Higher Level only.

As stated above, this final chapter, directly examined at HL only, is short. Do not be deceived by its brevity. The tools that are commonly used by researchers in psychology form its content. The chapter exemplifies their application, making references to studies already encountered. It draws together the methods used (which should be mostly familiar), adding to them where necessary, and presenting the whole as a coherent framework for investigation in psychology.

Approaches to researching behaviour form a vital, integral part of the course, without which psychology would have little or no credibility. Methods used to study behaviour including the design of the investigation, the methods of analysis, the drawing of conclusions and the critical analysis of the results. These are essential elements within the theories and research studies occurring throughout the chapter's text. Suitable responses to exam questions in Papers 1 and 2, as well as 3 will tend to incorporate research methods and their critical analysis of their use in various depths. This applies equally to HL and SL students. For this reason, SL students as well as HL students will need to be familiar with the content of this chapter. Its purpose is to place and present the methods mostly already encountered into a systematic framework that is coherent, logical, all-embracing, and easy to review.

Indeed, every essay response question in Papers 1 and 2 (HL and SL) allocates 12 marks out of 22 for the method-related issues: Criterion C use of research to support answer (6 marks), and Criterion D critical thinking (6 marks).

As a student, you will find yourself constantly dealing with methods as you progress through the course. You will have also grappled with research designs, hypotheses, methods of analysis, and evaluation of evidence in the experimental investigation that forms your internal assessment. You should also find yourself revisiting earlier theories and research studies in the light of your growing understanding of the methods through your progress in this unit.

Our integrated framework for researching behaviour includes

1. The types of quantitative and qualitative research methods used in psychology.
2. The elements of researching behaviour, including research designs, hypotheses, independent and dependent variables, sampling techniques, and ethical considerations.
3. Analysing quantitative data, and qualitative data.
4. Drawing conclusions: causation, replication, generalisation for quantitative research, transferability for qualitative research,
5. Evaluating research, assessing its reliability and validity, credibility, biases, and any use of triangulation.

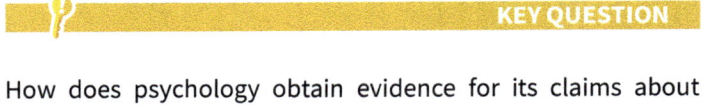

How does psychology obtain evidence for its claims about human behaviour?

Learning objectives of this unit include an understanding of:

- Which methods are suitable for investigating phenomena in psychology?
- In which ways may the evidence for claims made by theory and research studies in psychology be assessed?
- What are the scopes and limitations of quantitative and qualitative approaches to researching behaviour?
- How may the research process be designed to optimise validity and reliability?
- What criteria determine a research study's ethical acceptability?

4. APPROACHES TO RESEARCHING BEHAVIOUR (HL)

4.1 Introduction to Research Methods in Psychology

4.1.1 Quantitative research methods used in psychology

The five quantitative methods in the table below are commonly used to investigate psychological phenomena. These are laboratory experiments, field experiments, quasi-experiments, natural experiments, and correlations research.

Description	Strengths	Limitations	Research example
Laboratory experiments			
Uses similar samples in the control condition and in the test condition(s). The IV (independent variable) is manipulated entirely by the researcher.	Allows researcher to determine cause and effect. Laboratory environment is easier to replicate than natural environment.	Needs to take into account possible extraneous variables that if not suitably controlled can become confounding variables which may negate the validity of the study.	Loftus and Palmer (1974, Chapter 2)
Field experiments			
Similar to laboratory experiments, but the researcher manipulates the IV in a natural, real-life rather than laboratory setting	Allows researcher to determine cause and effect. Ecological validity; natural setting	May be difficult to control extraneous variables in a natural environment. May be harder to find similar conditions for replication	Draganski et al. (2004, Chapter 1)
Quasi-experiments			
The IV is pre-existing; it occurs naturally, e.g. gender, age group, nationality. It is not manipulated by the researcher	Ecological validity; natural setting.	Experimenter cannot manipulate the IV.	Baron-Cohen (1985, Chapter 5)
Natural experiments			
All variables occur naturally. The IV cannot be manipulated by the researcher	Likely to have ecological validity.	Extraneously variables could be difficult to control. May be hard to find similar conditions for replication	Charlton et al. (2002, Chapter 3)
Correlations research			
Non-experimental: no test and control populations, no IV and DV (dependent variable). Focus on two or more variables that may be related to each other, the degree of the relationship being shown in the statistical degree that the variables appear to be related.	Allows the use of quantitative data that might be difficult or impossible to manipulate experimentally, e.g. genotypes. Can accommodate the collection of data over a longer period of time.	Cannot not demonstrate cause and effect: variables A and B which appear to be correlated may have both been influenced by not-studied variable C. At best, can only indicate a statistically significant relationship.	Bouchard et al. (1990, Chapter 1)

85

4.1.2 Qualitative methods used in psychology

The three qualitative methods in the table below are commonly used to investigate psychological phenomena. These are interviews, observations, and case studies.

These methods can elicit in-depth information that cannot always be obtained by quantitative research. Qualitative research can also explore in depth relationships that have been indicated by previous quantitative studies.

Description	Strengths	Limitations	Research example
Interviews Interviews in qualitative research are typically **semi-structured** or **unstructured**. They become **focus groups** where several respondents are being interviewed at the same time.			
Semi-structured interviews include both closed and open-ended questions that enable the participant to expand in detail and the researcher to use prompts to keep the responses within the framework of the research objectives. They tend to be informal and conversational in style. **Unstructured** interviews tend to be narrative in content: typically, "tell me what you thought, how you acted, and how you would act now when in that situation". They tend to be flexible: the participant can be asked to expand on the parts of the narrative of importance to the researcher. **Focus groups** typically consist of about 6 respondents where the researcher, presents the areas of investigation and keeps the group discussion on focus. It can enable participants to react to one another as they would in real life.	Interviews and focus groups enable the researcher to pursue themes of importance that arise during the interview that until then may have not been considered by the researcher. They also enable participant(s) to communicate an in-depth experience from their own viewpoint though which the researcher can explore how they construct meaning in their lives. As long as focus groups are well-structured, and skilfully managed, they can respond to issues raised by others and enable the interviewer to access the spectrum of opinion. The participant is likely to feel less pressure from the interviewer when being one of a few than when being the only one.	May be time consuming and demanding to analyse. Lack of investigator reflexivity (where the data's accuracy may be influenced by the viewpoint of the researcher) could affect the objectivity of the research. Possibility of the participants' responses being affected by demand characteristics (the participant responds according to what he or she thinks that the researcher wants to hear), especially when not feeling relaxed and secure. Lack of structure can elicit a great deal of irrelevant information and can often be difficult to manage. Focus groups may face clashes in personalities, dominant personalities over-presenting and shy participants unable to make their contributions heard.	Greenfield (2006, Chapter 3)

4. APPROACHES TO RESEARCHING BEHAVIOUR (HL)

Description	Strengths	Limitations	Research example
Observations Naturalistic observations include **participant observation** (where the researcher(s) act as part of the group studied) or **non-participant observation**; and **overt observation** (where participants know that they are being watched) or **covert observation** (where participants do not know that they are being watched).			
Naturalistic observations in qualitative (as well as in quantitative) research involve measuring naturally-occurring behaviour with as much precision as possible. Likely to produce field-notes, record frequencies of behaviour, and intensities of the behaviour (e.g. displays of aggression) as judged by the observing researcher.	Likely to have high ecological validity as it takes place in the natural environment, and in the usual routines of those being watched. Can supply a relatively large amount of detailed data. Observation can more easily build up trust between participant and researcher than in the laboratory environment, with less likelihood of participants' behaviours being influenced by demand characteristics – particularly true in covert observations. Using several observers with standardised procedures and comparing notes afterwards reduces possible individual researcher bias.	Difficulties in assessing how far naturalistic observation-based findings may be transferable to environments that are not the same as the one observed. Problems with recording data accurately and objectively in the field, particularly if only one researcher is involved. Possibility of interference from extraneously variables: atypical behaviour may be erroneously generalised as being the norm. Ethical issues involved in covert observations that have to be justified, as this method invariably involves deception. Possibilities of the **Hawthorne Effect**: where the behaviour of those observed differs from the norm as they perceive they are being watched. Possible difficulties in finding similar environments in which to replicate the research.	Greenfield (2006) (Chapter 3) Rosenhan et al. (1973) (Chapter 4) "On being sane in insane places".

Description	Strengths	Limitations	Research example
Case studies Focus is on one individual or a small group, usually over a period.			
Data collection could use both periodic observations and semi-structured interviews with the student and teacher. For example, a researcher focuses on a single immigrant teenager in investigating the efficacy of a particular approach for learning English for the first time. It can be used to investigate sensitive issues, such as team issues and conflicts within a group,	Likely to elicit highly level of detail. Also, the only way of studying people in unique circumstances (for example a single survivor of a particular sensory deprivation). Likely to share the advantages common to observations and semi-structured interviews (above).	Likely to share the same difficulties common to observations and semi-structured interviews (above). Possible hazard of the **interviewer effect**, where the interviewer's attitude and demeanour could influence respondent inaccuracy, for example giving a sudden frown that could prompt a demand-characteristics-influenced response (applies also to interviews in general). The respondent may exercise the right to withdraw information later regarded as sensitive, leaving the investigator with no recourse to continue the study.	HM (Chapter 1)

4.2 Elements of Researching Behaviour

Once the methods are chosen, the study has to choose the best **research design** for the task, set **hypotheses**, (if experimental) specifying the **independent variable(s)** and **dependent variable(s)**, select the participants using a suitable **sampling technique**, and demonstrate that the study is **ethically acceptable**.

4.2.1 Research Designs

Experimental research may be **independent measures design** or **repeated measures design**.

Independent measures design

The **independent measures design** uses two or more separate groups of participants, whereby one forms the control group and one or more forms the test group(s), e.g. Loftus and Palmer (1974, Chapter 2). In the test group(s), the independent variable is manipulated in at least one way. *Each participant is involved in one condition only*. It may set up the groups to be as similar as possible, such as by using a **matched pair design** whereby the researchers will deliberately assign different but similar participants to a different condition, for example Bandura (1961, Chapter 3). Care must be done in matching the pairs to avoid the possibility of different results between each group resulting from differences between the groups rather than the manipulation of the independent variable.

4. APPROACHES TO RESEARCHING BEHAVIOUR (HL)

Repeated measures design

The **repeated measures design** in contrast uses the same participants in both the control and test condition(s) of the experiment. There is one group of participants only. That removes the need to ensure similar characteristics between the test and control groups, but could have problem of the order effect: that the answers given in the first stage being likely to influence those given in the second stage. In addition, in that later stage, the participants could be less alert, but at the same time more aware of the scope of the study, for example Fisher et al (2005, Chapter 1).

4.2.2 Hypotheses

Statements that may be tested and falsified in view of the data obtained by the investigator. The **null hypothesis (H0)** proposes that the researcher's intervention will have no effect on the phenomenon being studied, for example human behaviour. If the data supports the null hypothesis, it will not be rejected. If the data significantly does not support the null hypothesis, the null hypothesis may be rejected. The relationship stated in the **alternative hypothesis (H1)** is that what the investigator thought might exist will have been supported. An example is used in Asch (1961) (Chapter 3), where the null hypothesis is that people do not conform to majority influence when they have evidence that the majority are not correct. The alternative hypothesis (H1) is that people do conform to majority influence even when they have evidence that the majority are not correct.

A hypothesis can be a **one-tailed hypothesis** or a **two-tailed hypothesis**. Both state the possibility that a relationship might exist between the variables. A one-tailed hypothesis predicts that the relationship may exist and specifies whether it will be direct or whether it will be inverse. A two-tailed hypothesis predicts that a relationship may exist, and that it could be *either* direct *or* inverse.

4.2.3 Independent and Dependent Variables

Independent and **Dependent Variables** are components of the experimental method, which is designed to demonstrate cause and effect. The researchers manipulate the independent variable in the test sample only. The variables need to be **operationalised**: they need to be measurable, e.g. on an arithmetical scale or on a rank-order scale. The investigator needs to control for **extraneous variables**, other elements that might influence the data patterns.

4.2.4 Sampling Technique

Sampling technique is the basis on which participants are selected for the investigation. There are several methods as tabulated below:

Sampling technique	Description	Strengths	Limitations
Random sampling	Each member of the target population has an equal probability of being selected by, for example, a computer program that generates a list of random participants from a target population.	Numerically representative of the target population. Easily generalised to the target population.	Smaller samples may not be large enough to adequately represent the diversity within the target population.

PSYCHOLOGY SL & HL

Sampling technique	Description	Strengths	Limitations
Stratified sampling	The target population is divided up into sections such as age or gender. This sampling method is designed to ensure equal representation of the different groups. Participants do not have an equal chance of being selected. For example, if the population is 55% male and 45% and the study requires an equal number of both genders, each male has a lower opportunity of being selected than each female.	Sampling method reaches the diverse elements within the population.	Not numerically representative of the target population. May therefore be more difficult to generalise findings to the target population. Researchers may have insufficient knowledge of the target population to stratify the sample effectively.
Opportunity sampling, a.k.a. convenience sampling	The sample is composed of participants that are easily available, such as university researchers working with first-degree psychology students.	Less effort is needed to find eligible participants in suitable quantities.	There are possibilities of bias in the sample. For example, 19-year-old psychology students may not represent 19-year-olds in general.
Volunteer sampling, a.k.a. self-selected sampling	Participants are not selected by the researchers, but volunteer themselves, for example through a social media advertisement. May become a **snowball sample** were participants in turn recruit new participants, e.g. by word of mouth or through social media.	Less effort to find eligible participants in suitable quantities.	Possibility of the sample's composition of those volunteering being unrepresentative of the target population.
Purposive sample	Eligibility for participation is determined by possessing the characteristics of what is being researched: a study on adoption may be limited to people who have been adopted. May become a snowball sample were participants with a particular condition in turn recruit new participants with the same condition.	Excludes participants without the characteristic of what is being researched. Allows the use of quantitative data that may be difficult to manipulate experimentally, e.g. genotypes.	Where, for example, the determinant of participation is being diagnosed with a particular condition (e.g. bipolar disorder), some participants may be less severely affected than others.

4.2.5 Ethical Considerations in Psychology

Ethical considerations in psychology are primarily for the protection of the well-being and dignity of the participants.

4. APPROACHES TO RESEARCHING BEHAVIOUR (HL)

Their importance may be exemplified by the US Federal **Belmont Report (1978)**, which addressed ethical practices in both biomedical and behavioural research. Its main principles are:

- **Respect for participants**: with additional protection for those who are too young or otherwise unable to give an informed decision on whether or not to voluntarily participate.

- **Beneficence**: where the research is designed to minimise risk to participants and maximise benefits to society.

- **Justice**: where the improved welfare of one group in society does not happen at the expense of another group, for example those legally, economically, or psychologically unable to rationally decide on whether or not to participate in the research.

In essence, these principles are common to the professional and academic psychology community worldwide. Their main purpose is to protect the well-being and dignity of the participants, which may be delicately balanced with the alternative – or lack of alternative – research methods available, together with the investigation's benefit to society. They apply whether the study is quantitative or qualitative. Qualitative studies require additional precautions, as they tend to involve a longer association with the researcher that can extend to more than one meeting. The need to guarantee anonymity can be harder to implement where there is more researcher interaction with the same, few, participants.

Also, additional guidelines apply where research takes place on non-human subjects. These are detailed in Chapter 1.

It is standard practice that a professionally-conducted research project receives the approval of an academic ethics committee at the early stages, particularly if any deception may be involved.

The main areas of ethical concern that have to be satisfied before the research may proceed are **informed consent**, the **avoidance of deception**, the **protection of participants**, **debriefing** at the end of the study, the **right to withdrawal**, and a guarantee of **confidentiality/anonymity**.

Informed consent

Participants should be clearly briefed about the study's purpose, their roles within it, and that involvement is completely voluntary. Willingness is normally indicated by the participants (parent/legal guardian with children) signing a consent form prior to the study. The consent should be fully informed. The issue of informed consent becomes harder to deal with when the data has to be covert in order to be ecologically valid: an ethics board is only likely to approve such an investigation where the information from the study is likely to be of value to society and in no way threatens the well-being of the participants.

Avoidance of deception

Deception on the true purpose of the study at any stage is normally unacceptable, except when stating the true purpose would interfere with the validity of the study. In such a case, deception may be permitted as long as the research is of benefit to society, cannot suitably be done in any other way, does not harm the participants, and full debriefing occurs at the end of the study.

Protection of participants

This includes anonymity, confidentiality, protection of privacy, and anything that might cause distress during the study. Typically, written data needs to be kept locked in a safe, electronic data has to be password-protected or encrypted. All data should be destroyed at the end of the study. Access to the data by researchers not directly involved with study needs to follow ethical research practice.

Debriefing

Researchers must inform the participants about the results of the study, and reinforce that the study will not have harmed them in any way. Any necessary deception that had taken place needs to be explained at this stage. Participants should be offered access to the research when completed. However, this can be waived where the reading of the final report might affect the participant's well-being.

Right of withdrawal

The researchers have to communicate the right of withdrawal to the participants at the beginning of the study. Participants have the right to opt out at any stage and to withhold permission for the investigator to use the information contributed prior to the withdrawal.

Confidentiality

Researchers are responsible for ensuring that all data remains anonymous and cannot in any way be traced back to the participants.

In addition, the analysis must be conducted with integrity and in good faith, and with special attention where participants belong to the more vulnerable sections of society. Due attention is required for possibilities of researcher bias and reflexivity.

4.3 Analysing Data

This is the stage where the researcher processes the data to discover possible trends. The data can be in qualitative form (e.g. interview transcripts) or quantitative form (numerical values). This section considers **inductive content analysis** as an example of a method of analysing qualitative data, and **statistical analysis** in analysing quantitative data.

4.3.1 Inductive Content Analysis: Qualitative Research

The purpose of this method is to generate new meanings and theory that emerge from the data provided by the interviewee(s). It uses classification and/or colour codes to turn interview transcripts or field notes into a more manageable form for analysis, and for facilitating the finding of relationships between the data items. There is no pre-existing theoretical framework. If there is, it is likely to be deductive content analysis rather than inductive content analysis.

There are different ways in which inductive content analysis may be carried out. One method is **thematic analysis**, which involves working through and coding the data, identifying emergent themes, placing them in clusters and hierarchies, and using the frameworks for summarising the data and showing the links between data items.

Inductive content analysis has the strength of being flexible, enabling the researcher to identify and explore relationships that had not been contemplated at the time of the research. It can also accommodate the post-modern transcript, which also contains the participant's changes of tone of voice, hesitations, and fillers such as "er" and "um". Its

4. APPROACHES TO RESEARCHING BEHAVIOUR (HL)

limitations include possibilities of bias: how objective has the investigator been in avoiding overemphasising material supporting the research objective(s) and underemphasising material not supporting the research objective(s).

4.3.2 Statistics: Quantitative Research

There are two categories of statistics, **descriptive** and **inferential**.

This section is designed to serve as summary rather than a guide of the use of statistics in psychological research.

Descriptive statistics

Descriptive statistics are used with numerical data. They aim to present – within the bell-shaped **normal distribution** – both the degree of **central tendency** and the **measure of dispersion** around the mean. Their purpose is to summarise the data. The central tendency is shown by calculating the **mean** (average score), **median** (score at the midpoint of the rank-ordered data) and **mode** (most frequently occurring score).

Dispersion can be showed using **quartiles**: which divides the rank-ordered data into four equal parts: Q1, Q2, Q3, and Q4. These embrace every item in the data set. The **inter-quartile range** is a measure of variability, showing the range of scores within each quartile, as well as any outliers. This statistic can identify any asymmetrical tendencies that are present in the distribution of data. Dispersion statistics also show the degree that the variance differs from the mean; the **standard deviation from the mean** being commonly used, which is found by calculating the square root of the variance.

Descriptive statistical data can be presented as **data tables** (rows for the individual participants, columns for the different variables), **pie charts** (show the frequencies of categories as percentages), and **graphs**. The type of graph will depend on the variable. Where it is a **continuous variable** (no restriction to precision of the measurement: for example number of heartbeats per minute could be 50, 50.5, 50.45 etc) it can use a **histogram** (where the bars are joined together). Where it is **discrete variable** (a limited number of possible values, such as values 1 to 5 representing strongly disagree/disagree/neither agree nor disagree/agree/strongly agree) it can use a **bar chart** (where there is a space between each bar on the chart).

Inferential statistics

Inferential statistics present values from correlation studies and experimental studies. The **correlational coefficient** indicates the degree that two or more variables appear to relate to one another and the likelihood of the found distribution having occurred by chance. Data from correlational studies can be analysed by calculating the correlation coefficient, typically by using the Spearman's ρ (rho) or Pearson product moment statistical tests. The closer the correlation to 1.0, the stronger the correlation; the closer to 0.0 the weaker the correlation. A value above 0.7 indicates a strong correlation.

Experimental studies use two (or more) sets of quantitative data; from the control group and from the test group(s). Inferential testing is applied to determine whether there is a mathematically determinable significant difference between the data generated from the control group, and from the test group(s). It is on that basis that the researcher can make an informed judgment on whether the data indicates significant differences between the groups or not.

The researcher (i) sets a hypothesis (ii) selects an inferential statistical test (see below) (iii) uses the data and test's formula to calculate a value and (iv) looks up the value in a distribution table for that particular test to see whether differences do have or do not have the mathematical support of being significant. The **significance level** α (alpha) is the amount of tolerated error. The significance level of 0.05 is commonly used, meaning that

PSYCHOLOGY SL & HL

there is a 5% chance that such a relationship might have occurred by chance. The lower the significance level, the greater the chance that a real difference exists between the two samples. The researcher needs to judge where precisely to set the hypothesis rejection level: if too low, there can be a type 1 error (where differences between the data sets can wrongly described as being significant). If too high, there can be a type 2 error (where the differences between the data sets can wrongly be described as not being significant).

The correct choice of the inferential statistic to be calculated and applied depends on the nature of the data, the research design, and whether the hypothesis proposes a difference between two or more data samples or a correlation between two or more data samples. The criteria for choice are shown in the following table.

Inferential statistic	Criteria for selection		
	Experimental or correlation	Design (if experimental)	Nature of the data
Independent *t*-test	Experimental	Independent measures	Interval form (where the distance between the values is known)
Repeated *t*-test	Experimental	Repeated measures	Interval form
Mann-Whitney *U* test	Experimental	Independent measures	Ordinal form (where the data is ranked, without knowing the distance between the values)
Wilcoxon (signed-matched ranks) test	Experimental	Repeated measures	Ordinal form
Chi-square test	Experimental	Independent measures	Nominal form (non-numerical quantitative variables), such as named favourite colours
Sign test	Experimental	Repeated measures	Nominal form
Spearman's rho	Correlational	Not applicable	Interval or ordinal form. Data is in the form of paired scores for each participant.
Pearson's product movement	Correlational	Not applicable	Interval form. Data is in the form of paired scores for each participant.

4.4 Evaluating Research

The findings of a research study in psychology tend to support rather than prove theory about human behaviour. There will invariably be questions on the study's **validity**, **reliability**, **credibility**, and the possibility of **bias**.

In quantitative studies, **validity** judges the degree that the investigation measures what it set out to measure. **Internal validity** is assessed according to the degree that test and control samples are similar, all variables other than the independent variable are controlled, and **investigator effects** (where the behaviour of the researcher might influence the responses given) have been minimised by maximum **reflexivity** (where the researcher bears in mind possibilities of personal-viewpoint bias at every stage of the investigation). **External validity** is judged according to the degree that the study can be **generalised** (quantitative) or **transferred** (qualitative) to a different environment or population. It is particularly important when estimating the degree that a study conducted in a laboratory-type setting may be ecologically valid.

In qualitative studies, **credibility** replaces internal validity. Factors maximising the research's credibility include evidence of maximum researcher reflexivity (as with internal validity in quantitative studies) and statements of the various stages of the investigation. These are evidenced in records that leave clear documentation through the research process, as well as giving insight into the research's viewpoints and perceptions.

Reliability is the extent that the study produces the same results in repeated trials that use the same methods, design, and measurements. Reliability may be assessed by:

- **The test-retest method**: the investigation is conducted twice with the same participants. The stronger the correlation between the two sets of scores, the greater the reliability.

- **Inter-observer reliability (in an observation-based study)**: several researchers carrying out the standardised procedures for the investigation. Again, the stronger the correlation between the two sets of scores, the greater the reliability.

Possibilities of Bias

Bias can influence the researcher to view the data in a non-objective manner. Bias may include **researcher bias**, **participant bias**, and **sampling bias**.

Researcher bias

Where the findings could be influenced by the investigator's beliefs, culture, and hoped-for findings. This can include **confirmation bias**, where the researcher places a greater emphasis on supportive evidence than non-supporting evidence. Good practice involves reflexivity, as explained above.

Participant bias

Where the participant alters the information to be more socially desirable, and fit in with (or possibly make life difficult for) the researcher and the participating group.

Sampling bias

Where the sampling method does not represent the population being studied. In quantitative studies, it can happen in opportunity samples where the sampling procedure selects people who together do not typify the target population, but who happens to be available at the time. It can also happen in a qualitative study where those making up the characteristically short number of participants are all individuals that are previously known to the researcher.

4.5 Drawing Conclusions

If the study is experimental, it may conclude that the research hypothesis is supported if the quantitative data does support the researchers' hypothesis, resulting in the null hypothesis being rejected. A non-experimental study may also conclude that there exists a statistically-supported correlation between two or more variables.

PSYCHOLOGY SL & HL

As well-supported as the findings of the study may be, the researcher will still have to consider the degree that the study is **replicable** (in different environments and time periods), and may be **generalised** (quantitative data) or **transferred** (qualitative data: both terms indicating the degree that the study's findings indeed apply to the target population, and possibly a wider population). In addition, it may follow-up the same phenomenon by other methods: for example a questionnaire survey-based study may then use observation methods or a series of one-to-one semi-structured interviews on a smaller sample. This enables the study's validity and credibility to be improved if supported by the second or further methods: a practice called **triangulation**.

4.6 Your Paper 3 Examination (Higher Level only)

The 1-hour examination is based on an unseen passage describing a piece of research in psychology. You as a student have to apply your understanding of research methods within the following question-response framework below. Though the field of possible research methods in psychology is a big one, the range of questions that may be asked in Paper 3 is limited by the syllabus to the 8 questions below.

Question 1 is always the same, dividing into three parts:

- Identify the method used and outline two characteristics of the method (3 marks).
- Describe the sampling method used in the study (3 marks).
- Suggest an alternative or additional method giving one reason for your choice (3 marks)

The question is assessed by a simple analytical markscheme.

Question 2 will be any *one* of the two following questions:

- Describe the ethical considerations that were applied in the study and explain if further ethical considerations could be applied.
- Describe the ethical considerations in reporting the results and explain ethical considerations that could be taken into account when applying the findings of the study. (6 marks)

The question is assessed by a simple analytical markscheme.

Question 3 will be any *one* of the three following questions:

- Discuss the possibility of generalising the results of the study.
- Discuss how the researcher could ensure that the results of the study are credible.
- Discuss how the research in the study could avoid bias. (9 marks)

A high-quality response will meet the command term requirements, make effective use of the stimulus material, apply accurate arguments that are fully focused on the question, and assess the strengths and limitations of the research involved. A typical high-quality response would be 350–400 words.

PRACTICE QUESTION

Stimulus Response Practice Question: Paper 3

The stimulus material below is a study on teacher intervention to stop bullying

4. APPROACHES TO RESEARCHING BEHAVIOUR (HL)

Bullying is where a person is repeatedly exposed to intentional negative actions from one or more people. It may be physical, verbal, or psychological. Not all bullying is overt, but can build up through a series of separate incidents. It is traditionally associated with schools, but may also happen wherever people regularly gather together, including the workplace.

The research of Mishna et al (2005) recognised from previous studies that schoolteachers do not consistently intervene to stop bullying. The study aimed to determine the extent that teachers understand the nature of bullying in their schools, what factors might influence their recognition of bullying, and their response to it.

The research team interviewed 17 early-teenage children from two city public schools who had suffered bullying as reported by the school's social worker. All participating children indicated their consent by signing a form that was countersigned by their parents and the school principal. The researchers informed each student about the purpose and scope of their research.

At interview, all 17 children reported details of their school lives which confirmed the social workers' reports of their being frequently bullied. A total of 9 teachers were interviewed about those 17 children in their classrooms. The semi-structured interviews lasted from one hour to two-and-half hours, depending on how many bullied children were in a particular teacher's class. Teachers were asked about the incidence of bullying in their classes, their response to a child reporting being bullied, their general pattern of interactions with the child (and parent, if applicable), and the school's capacity to respond to bullying.

The teacher responses showed that they did not know that 10 of the 17 children had been bullied. Of the seven children – less than half the total - whom the teachers knew about, five had been helped by a teacher in a variety of ways.

These interviews highlighted how teachers identified and handled incidents of bullying. Whilst there was agreement over physical aggression, some tended to take verbal and psychological bullying less seriously. Some teachers also considered the behaviour of individual bullied children as responsible for their being bullied.

The findings of this study showed most of the teachers had neither been trained on dealing with bullying, nor had expressed the desire for such training. It also showed that teachers who would express empathy for others would be more likely to report and follow through with incidents of bullying.

Answer all the following three questions

1. (a) Identify the method used and outline two characteristics of the method. [3 marks]
   (b) Describe the sampling method used in the study. [3 marks]
   (c) Suggest an alternative or additional method, giving one reason for your choice. [3 marks]
2. Describe the ethical considerations that were applied in the study and explain if further ethical considerations could be applied. [6 marks]
3. Discuss how the research in the study could avoid bias. [9 marks]

PSYCHOLOGY SL & HL

Chapter 5: Paper 2 Option – Developmental Psychology

Overview

Development psychology in the IB curriculum looks at three areas: factors influencing cognitive and social development, developing an identity, and developing as a learner.

 **KEY CONCEPT**

The goal of developmental psychology is to understand the processes in human development that are normative (common to humanity), and to know how and where to proactively intervene to enable the individual to get the best experiences from those changes.

Remember that you are applying the biological, cognitive, and sociocultural perspectives to specific issues within the field of developmental psychology. This involves how and why people's thinking and behaviour change over time

Learning objectives of this unit include an understanding of:

- The roles of diet and human interaction on brain development.
- How childhood trauma and resilience may affect young people's social development to various degrees.
- How childhood attachments may affect the subsequent forming of human relationships.
- The different cognitive theories of child development as a learner.
- The sociocultural theories of factors influencing personal identity.

5. PAPER 2 OPTION – DEVELOPMENTAL PSYCHOLOGY

5.1 Influences on Cognitive and Social Development

Influences on cognitive and social development are examined under three headings:
- The role of peers and play
- Childhood trauma and resilience
- Poverty and socio-economic status.

5.1.1 The role of peers and play

Play involves activities that are enjoyable, and that are unrelated to survival or profit.

Peer influence tends to be important as soon as children join playgroups and nursery-school settings. Play, which tended to be seen as frivolous and time-wasting until the 1950s, is now regarded much more positively, as a means of assisting a child's cognitive development which is very different from an adult's (Piaget, see under Development as a learner in this chapter). For example, in the Piaget pre-operational stages (ages 2–7), the child that imitates an adult behaviour or uses toy bricks to build a castle is exploring and developing previously encountered ideas in an enjoyable and memorable way, which with age become increasingly complex and accurate resemblances of the real thing. Such play enables children to learn by building an increasingly complex world that they can master. Such activities frequently involve peers, enabling them to interact with others and at the same time speak up for themselves and maintain their own space where necessary. In addition, the presence of others can form a rich zone of proximal development (Vygotsky, see under Development as a learner in this chapter): their interaction with other children some of whom are more experienced can consolidate and promote cognitive and social development.

Today, psychologists believe that play helps the development of young children's motor skills (biological), sense of fairness (cognitive skills), and theory of mind: ability to see things from other people's point of view.

Psychologists are uncertain whether play reflects and consolidates children's existing skills, whether it actually promotes new ones, or whether each one promotes the other. Does, for example, play assist development in communication, or is use of language consolidated by play?

The role of peers and play on cognitive development: convergent and divergent problem solving

A **convergent problem** has one solution only, for example a jigsaw puzzle. A **divergent problem** has many equally good solutions, for example the range of different items that can be constructed with the same toy building bricks.

RESEARCH STUDY

Russ et al. (2010)

The work of Russ et al. was designed to investigate the relationship between the types of play that children engage in and the degree of divergent thinking that they brought to situations that offered a wide range of actions and solutions.

The aim of the study was to investigate how far the level of pretend play shown by first and second grade (6–7 year old) children would be reflected in the degree of their divergent thinking shown four years later. 31 children took part throughout this four-year longitudinal study.

The researchers assessed the levels of complexity of each child's pretend play by observing them, and then giving them a standardised play task. They were revisited four years later, and were given an age-adjusted tests to assess the level of development of their divergent thinking.

The results indicated a positive correlation between the degree of imagination in their early year play, and their current level of divergent thinking. This indicated a possible role of lets-pretend games in promoting divergent thinking to complex problems later in life.

Strengths and limitations: Russ et al. (2010)

Strengths	Limitations
1. It had the ecological validity of the participants being initially (in the first or second grade) observed within their usual play routines. 2. The researchers controlled for the participants' IQ.	1. The correlational nature of the data indicating the level of lets-pretend play. 2. The reliability of the age-adjusted task given four years later to assess the degree of divergent of thinking. 3. The relatively small size of the sample.

The role of peers and play on social development

The roles of peers and play have interested some individual psychologists long before their value in child development became widely accepted in the 1950s. For example, **Parten (1932)** classified young children's play modes and activities on the basis of observing American pre-school age children, on a 1–6 scale: the higher number involving better-developed peer-interactive involvement, reflecting both cognitive and social development.

1. Unoccupied, but watching peers nearby.
2. Solitary, but occupied: unaware of, or indifferent to peers. More common below age four.
3. Onlooker: observes and talks to peers rather than actively joining in the activities.
4. Parallel play: actively involved in similar activities, played separately, mimicking rather than participating with others.
5. Associative play: attempts interaction between the individual and the peer group, but not completely integrated as part of the group.
6. Co-operative play: where the individual plays as an integrated participant in the group.

Though this classification indicates the levels of social development on basis of the level of play and peer interaction, it does not show the degree that peer and play influence social development, social development influences levels of interactions with peers and play, or whether each assists the other.

5. PAPER 2 OPTION – DEVELOPMENTAL PSYCHOLOGY

> **RESEARCH STUDY**

Ladd (1990)

The study of Ladd aimed to assess how far the quality of children's peer relationships affects their adjustment to school at kindergarten level. It was a **longitudinal study** focusing on the same 125 children over a period of time. Each child's peer relationship level was assessed three times: at the start, in the middle, and at the end of the school year. The child's level of adjustment in terms of performance level, anxieties, and overall feelings about the kindergarten were also assessed through their teachers during and at the end of the school year.

The results indicated a positive correlation between the number/quality of peer connections, and enjoyment and performance at school. It concluded that positive peer relationships, tending to develop in playtime activities, influence both cognitive and social development at school.

The study had the strengths of its longitudinal structure, a relatively large sample, and its being controlled for gender, mental age, and previous pre-school interactions. Its limitations were the correlational nature of the study: whether peer relationships influenced kindergarten progress, or the other way round, or whether each assisted the other.

5.1.2 Child Trauma and Resilience

Optimal child development tends to be influenced by social and environmental factors, such as suitable parenting, being within proximal zones of positive stimulation, ideal diet, and relationships with a positive style of attachment.

A child is in a condition of deprivation where he or she is not having even basic needs taken care of – whether physical, emotional, or social.

A child suffers trauma where there is a powerful shock: death of parents, divorce, serious abuse, or war and refugee status. Deprivation experiences can also create trauma for the child.

Deprivation and trauma can impair the child's development. However, not all children suffer permanent damage. Some eventually develop normally.

Resilience is where the individual can maintain adaptive functioning despite suffering or having suffered adverse factors.

> **RESEARCH STUDY**

Rutter et al. (2007)

This study sought to investigate the long-term effects of severe deprivation in childhood on (a) cognitive development, and (b) attachment disorder.

The study investigated a sample of 144 adopted children aged six years old. They were in two groups. The first were from UK institutions who had subsequently been adopted. The second were severely-deprived children from Romanian institutions, who had been subsequently adopted in the UK. That second group had suffered deprivation and trauma. In some cases, the children had spent their first three-and-a-half years in such Romanian child-care facilities.

> This study can be used in discussing both childhood trauma and resilience

It was the long-term effects of their deprivation on reaching the age of six that was the focus of the study. By that time, they had already spent more than two years (at least) in their adoptive families in the UK.

Information from the adoptive parents on the family and the child's behaviour patterns was obtained by parent interviews and questionnaires. Three months later, the researchers observed the adopted children and gave them standard tests for cognitive impairment and attachment disorder.

For attachment disorder, the research focus was on the behaviour of the children towards the adoptive parents in both familiar and 'strange' situations (Ainsworth-type scenarios). (see Section 5.2: Developing an Identity). The attachment disorders found by this study included:

- no special preference for the adoptive parent over any other adults;
- not turning to the adoptive parent for help in an anxiety situation.

With **cognitive impairment**, the results showed no significant trends with children that suffered less than six months deprivation in Romanian institutions. There was significant cognitive impairment in 12% of the children who had been there from between six months and two years. That figure went up to 36% for those between two years and three-and-a-half years. That was particularly significant for those who had additionally suffered severe malnutrition before adoption. In addition, children who had remained a long time in the deprived Romanian orphanages had a significantly smaller head circumference, suggesting neural damage.

With **attachment disorder**, the results were fairly similar. Again, no significant trend of cognitive impairment was found with children having been less than six months in Romanian institutions. There was significant attachment disorder in 16% of the children who had been there from between six months and two years. That figure went up to 33% for those between two years and three-and-a-half years. This suggests that lack of suitable, individualised child rearing puts the child's cognitive and social development at risk.

However, by the age of six, most children showed neither cognitive impairments nor attachment disorders. This indicates that the effects of severe-deprived child-rearing are not necessarily irreversible, indicating some degree of resilience, as below.

The study's strength included the sample being relatively large, and that the database included inputs from two independent sources: the adoptive parents, and the testing of the children. Its limitations include the partial reliance on parental reports which may contain elements of bias, and that the measures of cognitive development depended on validity of the tools devised for the testing.

Resilience involves the person's capacity to 'bounce back' from past traumatic events and situations. As **Rutter (1990)** explains, the child typically shows capacity to adapt despite past exposure to risk factors, maintaining adaptive functioning in spite of having been exposed to risk factors.

Risk factors include poverty, family breakdown, and death of a close relative. These may be offset by protective factors, such as individual care-giving, and opportunities to develop feelings of self-worth.

5. PAPER 2 OPTION – DEVELOPMENTAL PSYCHOLOGY

RESEARCH STUDY

Felitti et al. (1998): the ACE (adverse childhood experiences) study

This was a large-scale study conducted in the previous three years, with a total of 13,494 adults. It was designed to research the effect of trauma suffered in childhood on long-term effects suffered as an adult. Using a questionnaire, the participants were asked to recall any adverse childhood experiences under seven categories: psychological abuse, physical abuse, sexual abuse, violence against mother, and living in a household shared by individuals that were mentally ill, substance abusers, or imprisoned. They were also asked to report on current levels of health, health lifestyles, health risk factors, and incidence of disease.

The findings indicated that those who reported at least one traumatic childhood situation (over 50% of the total) were statistically significantly more likely to be (a) less likely to exercise regularly (b) practise risky levels of alcoholism, drugs, and turnover of sexual partners (c) suffer depression, and (d) attempt suicide, than those who did not report any traumatic childhood situation.

The researchers concluded that there was indeed a correlation between the degree and range of ACE suffered in childhood, and the level of physically and mentally unhealthy lifestyles in adulthood.

The study had the strength of using a very large sample, and was one of the first to indicate a relationship between childhood trauma and adult at-risk cognitions and behaviours. It is limited by being based wholly on self-reporting, and the relationships claimed were correlationally based: not showing cause and effect.

> This study can be used in discussing childhood trauma

Strategies to build resilience

The environment can create optimum conditions for the development of resilience-building capacities. These include inputs from schools, peer counselling, individual counselling, play counselling, home-visit programs, and after-school programs in high-risk communities.

Schools have the capacity to develop resilience capacities given that they accept the ideal that they are not just dispensers of academic information, but sources of personal values, development of aspirations, contact with ideal role models, and creators of realisable expectations beyond the walls of the classroom. Not all schools meet that ideal, or even have the resources to achieve that ideal.

Strategies for enhancing resilience development

The work of **Sagor (1996)** and **Wang et al. (1994)** indicates that schools may indeed support resilience-development with high-risk children through programs that enable them to feel that they are able to succeed at a task. Schools also need to communicate to those children that they 'belong', that they are valued in the school community, and that they can indeed make a difference. The school should exercise the capacity to create/maintain a general atmosphere of forward-looking optimism.

In practice, struggling schools in deprived areas will have greater difficulties in being able to create such an atmosphere. There is also the issue of being able to exercise suitable supervision where already at-risk children are most likely to face further adversity, such as during movements between lessons, and in the playground.

Strategies for enhancing coping skills

Children at risk cannot be expected to develop coping skills for themselves. The New York Center for Children emphasises that children's improved coping skills may be developed by enabling parents to progress in their child-rearing skills, including:

- Home-visits programs – to enhance the level of attachment between mother and baby, helping the mother to cope with her own issues of poverty, lack of access to healthcare, and maternal depression.
- Teenage parent support and training – to empower such mothers to cope with the reality of child rearing, reaching out to members of the extended family for childcare, and enabling where possible for the mother to complete her high-school studies and graduate. Such programs also involve group therapy, where teenage mothers give support to each other, therefore reducing their feelings of loneliness and helplessness.
- Early Head Start programs for all children and families – involving parental-skills training programs. The work of Love et al. (2005) indicates that those parents who participated in those programs progressed substantially in stimulating their children's language development and improved their emotional-support skills.
- After-school programs in high-risk communities – supported by the work of Mahoney (2005) whose longitudinal study showed that children who had attended those programs for as little as one year showed substantial improvement in motivation, reading skills, and test results.

The difficulties involved include the additional expense of providing services to the child rather than just information to the parents, and to the schools. In addition, New York City is a very multi-racial society. Not all minority groups feel comfortable at having their communities being entered with those objectives.

RESEARCH STUDY

The High/Scope Perry Preschool project

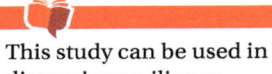
This study can be used in discussing resilience

A longitudinal study of African-American students that started in 1962 was designed to measure the extent that promoting early-age resilience can prevent juvenile delinquency in a high-risk population. The test population within a 123-child sample (aged 3–4) received a special active-learning pre-school program, supported with home visits and a series of follow-up visits to monitor their educational, social, and economic progress. The study found higher degrees of resilience in the face of the factors that put them at high risk in the test group than in the control group: as young adults, there were higher educational achievements, higher incomes, and fewer teenage pregnancies and criminal convictions. The study demonstrated that such early interventions supported by parents positively influence levels of resilience to the realities of their relatively harsh conditions. As evaluation: though the study used a relatively large sample, was longitudinal, and regularly monitored, the findings were correlational rather than causal. There may also be problems generalising the findings to similar situations in communities other than the one studied.

5. PAPER 2 OPTION – DEVELOPMENTAL PSYCHOLOGY

5.1.3 Poverty and Socio-Economic Status

Parenting involves giving a child physical, emotional, social, and intellectual support, although in some societies this role may be partly given to older siblings. The lack of good parenting is often (though not always) a result of poverty and lack of time for the children.

RESEARCH STUDY

The effect of lack of good parenting: Perry and Pollard (1997)

The work of Perry and Pollard showed that good parenting enhanced cognition in terms of better physical brain development – **neuroplasticity** (see also Chapter 1). The study compared the scans of brains of three-year-olds with normal degrees of human (very much including parental) interaction with cases of those suffering extreme poverty and neglect, having had little experience of contact and interaction with other humans (such as observed in the infants adopted from Romanian orphanages in the 1990s).

Their findings were that:

- on the whole, the brains of severely neglected children tended to be smaller than those who had been normally nurtured;
- there were large ventricular spaces in the brains of the neglected children, which would negatively impact sleep, regulation of mood, and regulation of anxiety.

They concluded that as a child grows, the brain absorbs all kinds of experiences. So, if a child is not held, touched, talked to, and interacted with, the neurons will cease to make enough connections to remain functional, and will simply die.

The strengths of the study are that it is supported by biological correlates indicating neurological levels of development in the brain. Its taking place after the period of child neglect unrelated to the study was both ethically acceptable and ecologically valid. However, its conclusions are limited by the need to take into account the child's resilience in recovering in the following years, and also the variations in the amount of time the participating children were neglected in the Romanian orphanages.

RESEARCH STUDY

The effect of poor nutrition: Bhoomika (2008)

The work of Bhoomika studied the effects of malnourishment on the cognitive performance of two age-groups of Indian children: 5–7 and 8–10. Their data of cognitive achievement was compared with a control group of those who ate a regular diet. Those aged 5–7 showed less capacity to process information, in terms of processing information, memorising, and visual-spatial tasks. Those aged 8–10 showed a smaller gap with the control group in these three areas, raising the possibility that poor diet delays rather than impairs cognitive development when other factors (such as an enriched zone of proximal development; see Section 5.3.1) are present.

The strengths of the study are that it is supported by empirical evidence indicating the effect of quality of diet with observed cognitive achievement. Its design also used two distinct age groups whose results were similar in principle, and gave the students a variety of tasks to determine cognitive development rather than just one. However, there was the need to distinguish between the level of deficiencies in the diet of those participants whose diets were classified as inadequate: not all those in the poor diet category were on the same diet. In addition, those from deprived backgrounds may have underperformed for reasons other than nutrition, such as lack of time with the parents.

The importance of eating breakfast on cognitive tasks at school was studied at the USA-based **Food Research Action Center (2010)**, with those missing breakfast more likely to show poorer memory recall (don't forget breakfast before your exam), increased likelihood to make careless mistakes, and poorer results in cognitive tests. Indeed, as evidenced by the work of Raloff (1989) who studied 1023 sixth-grade students over one year, those given free school breakfasts substantially improved their scores for mathematics and sciences.

RESEARCH STUDY

Pollitt et al. (1995)

Pollitt et al. (1995) was an experimental and longitudinal study designed to investigate the relationship between children's diet in early life and their level of progress in language, numeracy, and information-processing skills. Based in four economically-deprived villages in Guatemala, the researchers hypothesised that the lack of protein in the local diet would adversely affect the children's learning progress compared to those receiving an adequate input of protein (generally the most expensive components of the diet). Over an 8-year period, the children of two villages who were the test group were given regular diet supplements of high-protein Atole, and those in the two villages in the control group were given non-protein diet supplement Fresco. All were psychologically and educationally tested 11 years after the diet-supplement program The results showed that the test group receiving Atole performed significantly better the control group on Fresco, but both performed more poorly than middle income groups, indicating that diet was not the only contributor to positively enhancing child psychological and educational development. The study used a large sample and was ecologically valid as it was conducted in the participants' natural environment, but is limited when applied to other communities with protein deficiencies where they have different other nutrients in their diet. In addition, those from deprived backgrounds may have underperformed for reasons other than nutrition, such as lack of time with the parents.

5.2 Developing an Identity

This section considers three aspects of developing an identity:

- Development of attachment
- Development of gender identity and social roles
- Development of empathy and theory of mind.

5.2.1 Development of Attachment

Attachment is a long-lasting, strong, and close emotional bond between two people. Separation causes suffering. The actual bond of attachment can be observed from the age of seven months. By that age infants become attached to specific people and show distress when separated. Attachment theory is used to understand the social and emotional development of children, as well as adult relationships.

5. PAPER 2 OPTION – DEVELOPMENTAL PSYCHOLOGY

RESEARCH STUDY

Ainsworth et al. (1978)

The presence of attachment or lack of attachment is the subject of the work of Ainsworth et al. Here, the research team tested how far a small child had been making an attachment by use of the 'Strange Situation' method. In this laboratory observation study (carried out twice in different cultural environments, with 29 families in Uganda in 1969, and 26 families in the USA in 1971), the mother and child were in an unfamiliar room and subjected to the 'strange situations' of a range of timed and increasingly stressful (for an attached child) set of scenarios such as:

- A stranger is introduced to the child in the presence of the mother
- The mother leaves the infant with the stranger
- After the mother returns and re-settles the infant, it is left alone
- A stranger enters and interacts with the lone infant
- The mother returns again and picks up the infant.

Ainsworth discovered three main types of infant attachment using the Strange Situation.

Type A: Detached or anxious-avoidant (20% of the sample of American infants) – the infant ignores the mother, is not affected by her parting, and although distressed when alone, is easily comforted by strangers.

Type B: Securely attached (70% of the sample of American infants) – the infant plays contentedly when the mother is present, is distressed by her parting and although not adverse to stranger contact, treats them differently from the mother.

Type C: Anxious-resistant or ambivalent (10% of the sample of American infants) – infant disconnected whilst with mother, playing less, is distressed with her parting, is not easily comforted on her return, and may resist contact by both the mother and the stranger.

The study concluded that there is a significant relationship between degree of maternal sensitivities towards the child, and the nature of the child's attachment behaviour: secure (Type B), ambivalent (Type A), and avoidant (Type C).

The study is replicable; it has been widely replicated in different cultures (e.g. Van Ijzendoorn and Kroonenberg, 1998) with results indicating the high frequency of Type B evidenced in the original study. As the mothers and children were observed in their own environments, this study had a high ecological validity. However, there have been exceptions, for example the study of Grossman et al. (1985) on children with German parents that indicated a higher proportion of Type C avoidance patterns – possibly reflecting a culture-bound greater interpersonal distance. The study also was not designed to take into account genetic factors which might have influenced the children's behaviour in the strange situation.

RESEARCH STUDY

Bowlby (1973)

Bowlby claims that there is development continuity. Early attachments with parents continue in later relationships, as the early attachments create an **internal working model**. That is a mental representation – a **schema** – about how one thinks about oneself, about how one thinks about the attachment figure, and about how others react. Where the child feels loved and secure, he or she will tend to grow up with feelings of security and will indeed feel worthy of love and attention. Where the child feels that the attachment figure is continually inaccessible, attachment-based disorders could be a problem later in life. Indeed, it is these early schemas that set the pattern for further attachments during infancy, childhood, adolescence, and finally adulthood.

RESEARCH STUDY

Hazan and Shaver (1987, 1988)

The work of Hazan and Shaver sought to investigate the continuity theorised by Bowlby: that later relationships are influenced by attachments earlier in life. The study investigated how far attachment patterns in childhood were reflected in attachment styles in adulthood. Could 'different' attachment styles in adulthood be linked with the same 'different' attachment styles in childhood?

The investigation involved 620 participants responding to questionnaires. These were designed to elicit information about childhood relationship with parents (attachment history), and the nature of their most important adult relationship. The results were translated into an adaption of Ainsworth's categories of attachment, into adult styles of romantic love. These were:

- **secure lovers** (56%) who described their relationships as happy, trusting, and friendly
- **avoidant lovers** (25%), who referred to their fears of intimacy, jealousies, and emotional roller coasters
- **ambivalent lovers** (19%), with periods of extreme sexual attraction, obsessions, and emotional roller coasters.

The results supported the Bowlby development continuity theory – that the child attachments highlighted in the 'strange situation' model do strongly influence attachment styles in adult personal relationships. The Hazan and Shaver study bridges the theories of infant attachment, and the theories of adult romantic love. It also indicates the importance of the main attachment figure (typically the mother) giving a great deal of her time and attention to interacting with the child in infancy in order to maximise good relationship-building capacities later in life. Indeed, this seems to indicate that receiving love in childhood creates the foundation and capacity for giving love in adulthood. A person loved a child would tend to have more to give to a loving partner in a relationship.

The study has been criticised as the participants were a mostly female opportunist sample, recruited from responses volunteered in a newspaper survey. These people might well not have been representative of the general population. Also, there might have been genetic as well as environmental factors influencing the styles the participants brought to their relationships.

5.2.2 Development of Gender Identity and Social Roles

Gender identity is the person's identifying oneself as male or female. **Gender roles** characterise activities as being male or female. Gender roles are sets of behaviours associated with being male or female and set the ways males and females behave in specific situations and sociocultural settings. A gender role is a type of **social role**.

5. PAPER 2 OPTION – DEVELOPMENTAL PSYCHOLOGY

Psychologists debate the degree that the differences between males and females are due to innate biological differences on one hand and socialisation differences on the other. Specifically, does a boy follow the masculine stereotype because that is within his hormonal structure, or because he was brought up that way?

Biologically-based theories of gender role

Biologically-based theories of gender role include evolutionary theory, and hormone-based psychosexual differentiation theory.

Evolutionary theory

Evolutionary theory explains gender roles having formed and developed out of the needs of early societies. Men were required to be tough and competitive: in attracting a female partner, and in due course being able to obtain the scarce resources for their children. Women focused on nurturing themselves in order to attract a quality male. They continued as nurturers of the children, leaving the men to continue to compete in bringing home quality resources.

Hormone-based psychosexual differentiation theory

Hormone-based psychosexual differentiation theory focuses on gender roles being formed and developed by biological determination. Androgens such as testosterone are what make a male feel male. They are seen as having a masculinising effect on the way the developing male mentally processes information. Socialisation is only of secondary importance. According to this theory, children are *not* born psychologically-gender-neutral and then socialised into their gender role.

 RESEARCH STUDY

Case study: David Reimer

This study can be used in considering gender identity and social roles

Hormone-based psychosexual differentiation theory, that gender differences are influenced by testosterone levels in the womb, is supported by findings from the **David Reimer** case (**Money, 1974**). This is a longitudinal case study which appears to have supported the biological school. The facts of the case were that Bruce Reimer, an identical twin, had his penis accidentally damaged beyond surgical repair at the age of 8 months during a routine circumcision. Psychologist John Money successfully persuaded the parents to change Bruce's gender through surgery and hormone-replacement. The child was renamed Brenda and raised as a girl. This was a unique opportunity for Money to test his belief that children were gender neutral and could be raised according to the norms of either gender. Brenda's twin brother was an ideal control. Money published articles showing that gender roles could be bio-socially determined, but he left out the evidence that went against his theory. Brenda had become increasingly unhappy with other girls and also at her sessions with Money. At age 15, Brenda's parents told her the truth. Brenda decided to become a male again and went through the appropriate surgery to restore his gender, renaming himself David. He subsequently married at age 22. The study thus supports the view that fundamental gender roles cannot readily be bio-socially changed as they are influenced by testosterone levels in the womb.

This case study appears to support hormone-based psychosexual differentiation influences gender identity and social roles. Its longitudinal design enabled the researcher to observe the changes at different stages. It has the limitations inherent to transferring findings based on a single case study. It was also ethically questionable, as Money could have had an agenda that might have persuaded him to persuade David's parents to change his name and raise him as a female.

Cognitive-based theories of gender role

Cognitive-based theories of gender role include gender schema theory.

Gender schemas are rooted in society's beliefs about how boys and girls are expected to behave. Children form and develop their gender roles as they receive affirming and disapproving feedback to the degree that they tend to conform to the behaviour accepted of their gender: boys to action-men, girls to dolls – not the other way round. These schemas influence the way the child processes subsequent information. They also influence the child's self-esteem, where behaviour consistent with the schema-generated gender role receives the approval of those around the child.

Gender schemas can determine what will and will not be of interest to the child: boys to football, girls to caring activities. The work of Sroufe et al. (1993) found that those that did not behave according to their gender-stereotype were the least popular. Such studies indicate that peer pressure (social element) reinforces the gender-stereotype, and thus the gender schema (cognitive element).

RESEARCH STUDY

Martin and Halvorson (1983)

> This study can be used in considering gender identity and social roles

Martin and Halvorson investigated how gender schemas can determine how boys and girls process the same information.

This research showed a group of 5–6 year-old some pictures of children's activities. Some were in line with the gender role (e.g. a boy playing with a gun), and some went against the gender role (e.g. a girl playing with a gun). The children's recall was tested a week later. Those scenes with out-of-gender roles tended to be remembered incorrectly (for example the picture of a girl playing with a gun was recalled as a boy playing with a gun), for that example was outside the framework of the gender schema which was rooted in gender identity, which in turn influenced the resulting memory distortion.

This study had the strength of being controlled and experimental in design in focusing on the gender schema. The activities shown were based on widely-held gender stereotypes. However, the gender schemas have the limitations of tending to look at the individual experience, and not the more general socialisation processes and cultural issues. The study was also conducted in a laboratory setting, with the lower ecological validity as being outside the participating children's natural environment.

Sociocultural Theories of Gender Role

Sociocultural theories of gender role include social cognitive theory (**Bandura, 1977**).

Social cognitive theory suggests that gender roles are learnt and developed out of interactions with the environment and modelling those of the same gender. This involves the observation of same-sex people, which may lead to **imitation**, meaning that the behaviour to be copied appears to lead to desirable consequences.

It involves paying attention to the person modelled, remembering the behaviour that was observed, subsequently replicating the action, and feeling good about demonstrating what has been learnt. It is distinguished from conditioning, in that the learning is indirect (not stimulus/response/reward). It models the behaviour of others (vicarious learning) and gets reinforcement according to the results of following that behaviour.

Indeed, social learning theory in the form of **peer-socialisation** may well explain the finding of Fagot (1985, below) which indicated that at the age of two, boys made fun of boys who played with dolls, or with girls. And even at that age, girls were not too happy with the girls who played with boys. This was also the case with the older 10–11 year-old age group. As previously mentioned, the work of Sroufe et al. (1993) found that those that did not behave according to their gender-stereotype were the least popular. In addition, social learning theory does not explain why there is a considerable variation in conformity to gender stereotypes among boys and girls.

RESEARCH STUDY

Fagot (1985)

This study investigated the role of adult feedback on children's behaviour in terms of gender-appropriateness. It was carried out by a series of naturalistic observations of parent–children interactions, the observers using standardised check lists. The researchers observed parents giving positive feedback to gender-appropriate behaviour without the parents being aware of what they were doing. They also observed parents giving negative feedback to gender-inappropriate behaviour without the parents being aware of what they were doing. They concluded that it was this feedback that was helping the child learn their social role.

The study had the advantage of using naturalistic observations with several observers so that they could compare their checklists for accuracy. It took place in the participants' natural environment, giving it ecological validity. However, the amount of time the researchers observed was limited, and it was correlational in nature when comparing parental feedback with gender role establishment, thus unable to establish cause and effect.

Cultural Variations in Gender Roles

Cultural elements refer to distinctive beliefs, values, and practices within a specific group that are passed down from one generation to the next.

Cultural differences appear to modify the biological determinism view, which would make gender roles and behaviours universal, which is not the case in all cultures.

RESEARCH STUDY

Margaret Mead (1935)

The work of anthropologist **Margaret Mead (1935)** compared the gender-based social roles in three tribes in New Guinea, in each case by spending some time living among them and observing them.

> This study can be used in considering social roles

The Arapesh Tribe	Both genders cooperated in work and child-rearing, in a peaceful manner.
The Mundugumor Tribe	Both genders followed the male stereotype of being aggressive, arrogant, and competitive. Women were not interested in child rearing and the child who left parental care at the earliest possible opportunity was a status symbol.
The Tchambuli Tribe	Women did the hard work to sustain the family, whilst men idled trying to look good, and chat to other men.

Her argument, based on the differences between the three tribes below, is that gender-based social roles are culturally-based rather than biologically-based. The study has the strength of being ecologically valid, as the behaviours were observed in the natural environment, and was longitudinal in designed, as the behaviours were observed over a period. However, it could be argued that as an outside researcher the tribal members wished to demonstrate their culturally ideal behaviour rather than what was practiced behind the scenes. There was a possible susceptibility to bias due to the findings coming from a single, rather than a team of observers.

Echoes of Mead's argument have been found in the study of **Reinicke (2005)**, which found that young fathers in Denmark actually view their fathering, child-rearing roles as part of their personal identity. Indeed, it may be argued that this may become closer to the norm in individualist, Western society as social equality is increasingly taken for granted. It can also be linked with women's greater control over wealth and resources.

5.2.3 Development of Empathy and Theory of Mind

Theory of mind is the ability to attribute thoughts, feelings, beliefs to other people that are different from our own. This extends to false belief: ability to accept that the other person has a different viewpoint even when certain that the viewpoint is wrong.

Empathy involves putting oneself in the position of someone else: being able to realistically relate to the positions of other people. Empathy also involves being able to identify the mindset of someone else and feel the experience of another individual.

Theory of mind helps children in a wide variety of tasks such as in play and in reading. In "Let's pretend" games, the child puts him/herself in the position of another person or role. In reading, the child gets into the personality of the people in the story and can see things from their perspectives and viewpoints.

Theory of mind develops in a number of stages. A child under 18 months old tends to see things from own point of view only. At around that age, the child begins to develop an increasing awareness of the needs of other people, although until age 3 they can only interpret other people's behaviour in terms of their own needs and beliefs. By that age the child has reached the belief-desire stage of theory of mind: able to grasp what is going on around them, and that others can have different understandings and ways of doing things. On reaching age 4, as the roles of peers and play become more important, they are generally able to identify other people's beliefs as true or false, and which things they know that other people don't know. That final stage is the representational stage of theory of mind.

The mountain experiments of Jean Piaget indicated that theory of mind begins to develop between 4 and 6 in normal children: that the child can correctly place a series of model mountains in the order seen by the viewer positioned on the other side of the table.

It is not clear how a child learns to know how someone else thinks. Piaget claims that children are active scientists. By constantly experimenting with how their environment works, they discover by trial and error how other people are likely to think and react in particular situations. However, it has also been argued that our nervous system is activated in sympathy with other people when we observe them, without any experimentation needed. When a small child sees another child playing a game, that child feels as though actually playing even though only a spectator, and thus gets into the mindset of the playing child and empathises with that child's position.

However, autistic children tend to find difficulties in developing theory of mind: autism being a mental condition involving problems in communicating and relating to others.

RESEARCH STUDY

Baron-Cohen et al. (1985)

The work of **Baron-Cohen et al.** investigated the extent that autistic children have **theory of mind**. It had the strength of being a natural experiment in an environment strongly resembling reality involving 27 normally-developed child participants aged 4–5, 14 children with Down's syndrome (average age 11 years, average verbal mental age 3 years) and 20 autistic children (average age 12 years, average verbal mental age 5.5 years). Each viewed the Sally and Anne puppet show. They saw Sally put a marble in her basket and walk out. Then, Anne took the marble and put it in her box. Afterwards, Sally came back. The experimenters asked the children where the marble really was at that moment, where the marble was at the beginning of the study, and where Sally would look for the marble. The final question was the crucial false-belief question. The right answer, in the basket, would indicate a false belief to Sally.

Nearly all the normally-developed child participants and the older group with Down's syndrome answered the question correctly. Only four out of the 20 autistic children correctly attributed a false belief to Sally. The study indicated that autism could have developed out of difficulties in developing theory of mind, and that theory of mind and empathy are norms in human behaviour that develop at an early age, between 4 and 5.

This study had a high ecological validity, as the puppet show enacted scenarios that the children could easily identify with. It was well-controlled, using both autistic and non-autistic children. It was, however, relatively small scale, and it was based on the assumption that the errors that had taken place could be imputed to lack of empathy and theory of mind.

RESEARCH STUDY

Shahaeian et al. (2011) on theory of mind

This study researched influence of culture on developing theory of mind. There were 164 children aged from three to nine, from Iran and from Australia. Each child was individually tested with five different tasks designed to measure their capacities in theory of mind. The results showed similar results for both cultures. However, the Australian children scored significantly higher when the theory of mind involved different beliefs and viewpoints, whereas Iranian children scored significantly higher in tasks involving access to knowledge. The researchers concluded that theory of mind development may be culturally influenced: Iranians emphasising social conformity and Australia emphasising cultural diversity.

Its strengths include the distinct cultural diversity of the participating children, and the standardisation of tasks used for the investigation. Its limitations include its laboratory setting for testing which reduced ecological validity, and the generalisation of national stereotypes to explain the differences between the two sets of children.

5.3 Developing as a Learner

This section considers two aspects of developing as a learner: cognitive development and brain development.

5.3.1 Cognitive Development

'Cognition refers to all those processes by which sensory input is transformed, reduced, elaborated, stored, recovered, and used… cognition is involved in anything a human being might possibly do.' (Neisser, 1966).

Human beings are regarded as information processors, and cognitivists explain behaviour through these internal processes. This subsection looks at two widely-influential theories of brain development: Piaget's, and Vygotsky's.

Piaget's theory of cognitive development

Piaget's theory of cognitive development (1920s, and the decades until his death in 1980) predate modern brain-scanning methods.

Piaget's starting points in his theory of cognitive development are:

Intellectual development occurs through active interaction with the world: children do not passively receive their knowledge; they are curious and self-motivated. They are indeed experimenters.

Intellectual development occurs as a process: children think in qualitatively different ways from adults – intelligence, knowledge, and understanding develop in stages. They cannot be pushed to function at higher stages of cognitive development before they have passed through the lower stages of cognitive development. And these stages of cognitive development are age-bound (as described below).

The growing child builds increasingly complex schema: a unit of intelligent behaviour that enables the individual to interact with and understand the world. For example, the infant is born with certain reflex actions, such as sucking or gripping. These schemas continue to develop and increase in their complexity (e.g. that gripping a rattle and gripping a cup with a drink in it are two different forms of gripping) and adapt the individual to function in the environment. The child builds the schema by experimenting. The child is thus an active partner in the early process.

5. PAPER 2 OPTION – DEVELOPMENTAL PSYCHOLOGY

Piaget's stages in his theory of cognitive development

Sensory-motor stage (ages 0–2)	The baby goes from reflex, instinctive actions (e.g. sucking a bottle) to constructing knowledge by experience of what can be sucked and what cannot be sucked.
Pre-operational stage (ages 2–7)	Thinking is based on what the child sees, and from his/her point of view only. The child understands **object permanence** (will understand that, his or her favourite toy still exists even though it is out of sight), but shows **egocentrism** (will not succeed in task where someone else is placed in a different part of the room, and the child has to describe what that person sees from his/her viewpoint), and **lack of conservation** (for example, if an adult pours water from a short wide glass into a narrow tall glass, the child will say that there is more water in that second glass because it is taller).
Concrete operational (7–11 years)	Needs to witness things carried out; will not grasp concepts presented abstractly. In the example above, the child will understand that there is the same amount of water in the tall glass on seeing the water being poured and glasses being handled.
Formal operational (12 plus)	Can think abstractly, and work things out in the mind rather than have to reconstruct them physically. The older child can manipulate reasons, numbers, and ideas.

Strengths and limitations: Piaget's theories of child development

Strengths	Limitations
1. It has demonstrated that children of different age groups process information differently, and certainly different from adults. 2. It has placed emphasis on the teacher being a facilitator (to enable the child to learn through his or her own discoveries) rather than a disperser of knowledge.	1. Child development may be seen as a continuous process rather than a series of stages. 2. His research methods placed too much emphasis on deducing conclusions from the child's mistakes – to the degree that he may have overlooked abilities that children do possess, and may have wrongly deduced the reason for their failure. 3. Neglected other cognitive factors that could have accounted for the individual differences in development, such as memory span, motivation, impulsiveness, practice, and linguistic ability. 4. The child as an experimenter model seems to underestimate the importance of the involvement of adults and more knowledgeable peers. 5. Vygotsky (1896–1934, see below) argues that it is possible to speed up cognitive development provided that a suitable structure ('scaffolding') can be used to break down a complex topic and make it accessible to the child. This challenges the notion that teaching a child is only possible if he or she is within the appropriate stage of development. 6. Knowledge of the biological functioning on the brain through brain-scanning techniques has advanced since Piaget's day.

RESEARCH STUDY

McGarrigle and Donaldson (1975)

The study challenged one of the key principles of Piaget's stages of development: that children in the pre-operational stage (ages 2–7) have a lack of conservation as he demonstrated in the amount of water and shape of the glass test, above. Piaget had followed that with the counter test in 1960, where he laid out two rows of counters of equal number and length and asked the participating pre-operational age-group children how many were in each line, received the answer that they were the same, and then compressed one of the rows in full sight of the children, who said that the now shorter row had fewer counters. The researchers wanted to determine whether the reason that the children made that erroneous judgment was because they indeed had no sense of conservation, or because they did have a sense of conservation, but they believed that adults always changed things. Therefore, the researchers used a puppet named Naughty Teddy to compress the counters, and in contrast to when Piaget was carrying out the experiment, the children responded that both rows had the same number of counters. The researchers concluded that, in contrast to Piaget, children are very likely to have a sense of conservation even when in the pre-operational stage.

This study had the strength of removing the demand characteristics, namely what the children thought Piaget wanted them to say, which could have biased Piaget's results. They seemed to feel able to say what they thought to Naughty Teddy, but not to Piaget. In addition, this study's validity was supported as apart from Naughty Teddy it was an exact replica of one of Piaget's original tests. However, the nature of the test, like Piaget's, was of limited ecological validity due to the laboratory set up. In addition, the test as used by the researchers did not take into account other relevant motivational factors, such as motivation and impulsiveness.

RESEARCH STUDY

Vygotsky's Sociocultural Approach to Cognitive Development (developed in the early 1930s)

Whilst agreeing with Piaget that the child's mind differs from the adult's, Vygotsky views language and instruction as the key factors of cognitive development. This is not just through creating the environment to promote the child discovering for him/herself (as Piaget). It is chiefly through cooperative interaction with the child in the instruction process.

It is the quality of contacts with more skilled individuals that counts in child development. Vygotsky identifies the **zone of proximal development** which is the area beyond what the child can do unaided (within the child's zone of competence), but what the suitably-motivated child can achieve when 'stretched' by someone with more knowledge and skills. An experienced educator and/or the demands and resources of the environment can prompt that development-promoting stretching.

This area is made accessible and achievable to the child by **scaffolding** (term introduced by Wood et al. in 1986 as an extension of Vygotsky's zone of proximal development theory). That involves the instructor breaking down the new concept, skill, or task into suitably structured units through which the child can access the new areas, stage by stage.

Thus, even a very young learner can master complex material so long as the material is appropriately scaffolded.

5. PAPER 2 OPTION – DEVELOPMENTAL PSYCHOLOGY

Strengths and limitations: Vygotsky's theories on child development

Strengths	Limitations
1. It puts forward the notion that children can handle more complex material than Piaget-age-appropriate – so long as it is suitably presented and broken down (scaffolded).	1. Some lack of empirical support. His ideas are difficult to test as his emphasis is on the learning process rather than on the learning outcome.
2. It views child development from the continuous process of instruction and interaction, rather than from the outcomes expected at the end of each stage of cognitive development.	2. His heavy emphasis of the importance of pedagogic and social interaction in the child's development may be seen as underestimating fundamental biological issues.
3. It incorporates sociocultural issues into the learning process and learning outcome.	3. Knowledge of the biological functioning on the brain has advanced since Vygotsky's day, through brain-scanning techniques.
4. It also incorporates the linguistic ability and motivation of the child.	

However, Vygotzky died when his work was in its infancy. Had he lived longer, he might have incorporated the criticisms of his work following peer review.

RESEARCH STUDY

Wood et al. (1975)

This purpose of this study was to demonstrate the role of scaffolding in enabling the learner to optimise access to the zone of proximal development. The participants were four-year-old children, with access to support from their mothers. They were shown a picture with an object. Their task was to use the building blocks and pegs provided to produce a three-dimensional model of the object that they saw in that picture. The task was too difficult for the children to do by themselves, but it the children could carry it out if they were given the proximal support where needed by their mothers.

There were observers that were recording the individual children's progress with the task, and the nature of support from their mothers.

The researchers found that they succeeded as the mothers adjusted their support to the needs of their own children. This was done though their general words of encouragement, giving them specific advice on how many blocks to use when they were stuck, and helping them practise correctly laying one block on another. They did not intervene when the child was managing on his/her own.

The study had the strength of containing a task that was designed to be accomplished with varying degrees of scaffolding. It also made use of mothers for the scaffolding, who probably would be the most likely to know what their children could and could not realistically achieve. However, it is possible that the mothers might have offered more support than necessary: the study was not followed by a task of similar difficulty without the support of the mother that would indicate whether or not the mothers' support had indeed been part of the learning process. In addition, the mother influence might have been primarily reassuring in the particular situation rather than providing vital scaffolding.

5.3.2 Brain Development

Much current research in developing as a learner is linked with the biological perspective – especially the extremely complex brain function and neurological systems. This is the neurobiological approach to human development.

Brain Development and Cognitive Function

The work of Giedd (2004) involved an MRI-brain-scan-based longitudinal study of how the brain structure of healthy children develops with age. By the time the child reaches six, 95% of the brain structure is formed. However, the part of the brain that deals with the focus of attention, planning, and decision-making takes the longest to develop – typically becoming fully mature at around age 25.

The Effect of Deprivation on Neuroplasticity

Brain plasticity is the brain's capacity to adapt to the challenges placed on it by developing appropriate new neurons that adapt the brain to environments and situations faced. For example you might find maths very difficult, but with regular practice, the part of the brain that deals with maths on a challenging basis 'thickens', and is able to handle maths more effectively. Thus the more your brain is exercised, the more powerful it becomes. In fact, every time we learn something new, the neurons connect to form a new trace in the brain. This is called **dendritic branching** because the branches (dendrites) of the neurons grow in numbers and connect with other neurons. Thus there appear to be neurological correlates with the learning process.

Perry and Pollard (1997) looked at Romanian orphanages in the 1990s, concluded that as a child grows, the brain absorbs all kinds of experiences – so, if a child is not held, touched, talked to, and interacted-with, the neurons will cease to make enough connections to remain functional, and will simply die.

Indeed, the work of **Chugani et al. (2001)** on Romanian children who had spent time in orphanages before being adopted highlighted lack of development of the pre-frontal part of the brain, such as attention and social cognition. That is because there was a lack of socially-challenging stimulus to enable growth of that part of the brain through neuroplasticity.

Social and environmental factors

The biological approach to cognitive development takes into account the role of genes in brain development. However, it is not the only factor: stimulating social and environmental elements may strongly and positively influence the brain development process. And brain development may be undermined by a lack of stimulating social and environmental factors.

Strengths and Limitations: Neurobiological brain-development theories

Strengths of neurobiological brain-development theories

1. They show the connection between deprived social and environmental stimulation, and poorer brain development.
2. They provide evidence that suitable educational opportunities can biologically enhance brain development.

5. PAPER 2 OPTION – DEVELOPMENTAL PSYCHOLOGY

Limitations of neurobiological brain-development theories

1. Non-experimental nature of the studies including lack of a control population makes it difficult to establish a direct relationship between brain neurobiological development and cognitive growth.
2. Brain scanning methods have not been used for long enough for complete longitudinal studies to be carried out on the same participant from birth to age 25.

 RESEARCH STUDY

Brain Development and Risk-Taking Behaviour: Barkley-Levenson and Galván (2014)

The experimental work of Barkley-Levenson and Galván investigated the influence of different stages of brain development on risk-taking behaviour.

The hypothesis was that teenagers of both genders (aged 13–17) would be more inclined to take risks than adults of both genders (aged 25–30) for the following reason. The teenage brain biologically expects and experiences more pleasure, more 'reward', on winning than the adult brain in the same situation. The ventral striatum in the teenage brain responds more intensely than in the adult brain, releasing a more intense dopamine-influenced feeling in anticipating winning and on actually winning.

The experimenters briefed and placed each group in the same laboratory-structured series of gambling situations, with their brains connected to fMRI scanners that were focused on registering the degree of activity in the ventral striatum region. The greater the degree of pleasure experienced, the greater degree of activity was expected to register in that part of the brain.

For information on the location of the different regions of the brain, see section 1.2.

The results indicated that teenagers displayed significantly more risk-taking behaviours when the rewards on winning a gambling activity were raised. The scans indicated more activity in the ventral striatum as hypothesised, and also less activity and thus less fear in the amygdala section of the brain than with the adults who gambled at the same levels of risk.

The study concluded that these biological correlates help to explain the association of risk-taking at teenage rather than at adult stages of brain development.

Strengths and limitations: Barkley-Levenson and Galván (2014)

Strengths	Limitations
1. Supported by significant biological correlates in the ventral striatum and the amygdala. 2. The laboratory procedures were standardised and replicable. 3. The results contribute to explaining why the teenage years are associated with ill-advised activities including extreme sports and dangerous driving.	1. The sample was small, with a total of 20 teenage and 17 young adults whose data contributed to the study. The expensive and time-consuming nature of fMRI scanning meant that relatively few could take part. 2. The study was of independent measures design, meaning that it was not possible for the same person to be involved in both the test (teenagers) and control (adults) conditions.

5.4 Ethical Considerations

Ethical considerations in researching issues in development psychology are common to other areas of psychology, including:

- Informed consent: participants must know the object of the study, that their involvement is voluntary, what the data will be used for, and if necessary be debriefed at the end of the study. In extreme cases, the ethical requirement for informed consent may be waived, when the focus of the study is of public importance and there is no other way to obtain the sought-after information.
- Avoiding deception, except possibly where the research cannot be carried out in any other way.
- Protection from harm: particularly important when handling potentially sensitive material that may be found when studying the individual's childhood background.
- Making the participants anonymous to protect them, even at the risk of reducing the authenticity of the research and of preventing any follow-up study.
- The right for any participant to withdraw from the study at any point, and communicating that right before the commencement of the study.
- All participants are to be debriefed at the end of the study.
- Bearing in mind that research involving associated cultural issues is extremely sensitive with many ethnic groups. Typically, the elders of the society must be consulted for permission to work with members of their group.

5.5 Key Research

5.5.1 The roles of biological, cognitive, and sociocultural factors in influencing human development

For biological influences, look at the following:

- The neurobiological approach to human development.
- The Rutter et al. (2007) investigation of the long-term effects of severe deprivation in childhood on cognitive development and attachment disorder.
- Hormone-based psychosexual differentiation theory.
- The work of Barkley-Levenson and Galván (2014) on the influence of different stages of brain development on risk-taking behaviour.
- The work of Pollitt et al. (1995) on the relationship between children's diet in early life and their learning skills

For cognitive influences, look at the following:

- Piaget's theory of cognitive development.
- McGarrigle and Donaldson (1975) on pre-operational stage conservation
- Theory of mind development
- Bowlby's theory (1973) on the development of attachment.
- The study of Russ et al. (2010) on types of play and the degree of divergent thinking in children
- Gender-schema theory.

5. PAPER 2 OPTION – DEVELOPMENTAL PSYCHOLOGY

- Felitti et al. (1998): the ACE (adverse childhood experiences) study.
- Shahaeian et al. (2011) on cultural differences in theory of mind

For sociocultural influences, look at the following:

- The study of Ladd (1990) on the quality of children's peer relationships and their adjustment to school at kindergarten level.
- The work of Ainsworth on attachment patterns.
- The work of Fagot (1985) in investigating the role of adult feedback on children's behaviour in terms of gender-appropriateness.
- The study of Hazan and Shaver (1987) on adult styles of attachment relating to previous attachments made in infancy.
- The High/Scope Perry Preschool project, on measure the degree of early-age resilience training can prevent juvenile delinquency.
- Felitti et al. (1998): the ACE (adverse childhood experiences) study.
- Vygotsky's sociocultural approach to cognitive development.
- Wood et al. (1975) in the role of scaffolding in the learning process
- The work of Mead (1935) on different gender-roles in different tribes.

5.5.2 Evaluate psychological research relevant to developmental psychology

For influences on cognitive and social development, look at the following:

- Bowlby's theory (1973) on the development of attachment.
- The study of Russ et al. (2010) on types of play and the degree of divergent thinking in children.
- The study of Ladd (1990) on the quality of children's peer relationships and their adjustment to school at kindergarten level.
- The 'strange situation' study of Ainsworth et al. (1978), designed to investigate the presence and nature of infants' attachment.
- Felitti et al. (1998): the ACE (adverse childhood experiences) study.
- The study of Hazan and Shaver (1987) on adult styles of attachment relating to previous attachments made in infancy.
- The work of Fagot (1985) in investigating the role of adult feedback on children's behaviour in terms of gender-appropriateness.
- Baron-Cohen et al. (1985) on the lack of theory of mind in autistic children
- Shahaeian et al. (2011) on cultural differences in theory of mind
- The study of Barkley-Levenson and Galván (2014) on the influence of different stages of brain development on risk-taking behaviour.
- The Rutter et al. (2007) investigation of the long-term effects of severe deprivation in childhood on attachment disorder.
- The work of Pollitt et al. (1995) on the relationship between children's diet in early life and their learning skills.
- The High/Scope Perry Preschool project, on measure the degree of early-age resilience training can prevent juvenile delinquency.

PSYCHOLOGY SL & HL

For developing an identity, look at the following:

- The work of Ainsworth on attachment patterns
- The study of Hazan and Shaver (1987) on adult styles of attachment relating to previous attachments made in infancy.
- Hormone-based psychosexual differentiation theory, and the case study of David Reimer (Money, 1974).
- Gender-schema theory.
- The work of Fagot (1985) in investigating the role of adult feedback on children's behaviour in terms of gender-appropriateness.
- The effect of social learning theory on gender roles (Bandura, 1977).

For developing as a learner, look at the following:

- The effect of deprivation on neuroplasticity (1997).
- Piaget's theory of cognitive development
- McGarrigle and Donaldson (1975) on pre-operational stage conservation
- Vysgotky's sociocultural approach to cognitive development.
- Wood et al. (1975) in the role of scaffolding in the learning process
- Development of theory of mind
- The High/Scope Perry Preschool project, on measure the degree of early-age resilience training can prevent juvenile delinquency.
- The work of Bhoomika (2008) on the effects of malnourishment on the cognitive performance of elementary school children.
- The Rutter et al. (2007) investigation of the long-term effects of severe deprivation in childhood on cognitive development.
- Barkley-Levenson and Galván (2014) on the influence of different stages of brain development on risk-taking behaviour.

PRACTICE QUESTIONS

Essay-response Exam Questions: Developmental Psychology

1. Discuss strategies to build resilience.
2. Discuss possible effects of childhood deprivation and/or trauma on later development.
3. Contrast two theories of cognitive development.

Chapter 6: Paper 2 Option – Abnormal Psychology

Overview

Abnormal psychology looks at how abnormal behaviours may be defined and diagnosed, how abnormal behaviours might be caused, including the roles of culture and gender, and how they may be treated.

The IB specifies that *one or more* types of abnormal behaviour may be chosen from any of the following categories: eating disorders, depressive disorders, anxiety disorders, OCD (obsessive compulsive disorder), trauma and stress-related disorders. Our focus in this chapter will be on major depression (depressive disorders), though much of this chapter's overall approach applies to other disorders as well. The IB requires detailed knowledge of one disorder only.

Remember that you are applying the biological, cognitive, and sociocultural perspectives to specific issues within the field of abnormal psychology.

KEY CONCEPT

The goal of studying abnormal psychology is to identify the causes of abnormal behaviour and consider how to treat them most effectively: whether by clinical and/or therapeutic means.

Learning objectives of this unit include an understanding of:

- The criteria used in defining and diagnosing abnormality.
- The role of biological, cognitive, and sociocultural elements in causing psychological disorders.
- The use of medication and placebos in aiding recovery from abnormal conditions.
- The use of non-biologically-based methods for the treatment of abnormal conditions.

The work of this unit covers three main sections: **factors influencing diagnosis**, **etiologies of abnormal conditions**, and **treatment of the disorder**.

6.1 Factors influencing diagnosis

Influences on cognitive and social development are examined under four headings:

1. Normality versus abnormality
2. Classification systems used for the diagnosis of abnormalities
3. Validity and reliability of diagnosis
4. The role of clinical biases in diagnosis

6.1.1 Normality versus abnormality

Abnormally may be defined in terms of illness in the psyche. This is based on medical diagnosis: psychiatry is a branch of medicine. Thus a mental disorder may be classified as an illness, as would be a physical disorder.

In contrast, normality as defined by **Jahoda (1958)** in terms of the components of ideal mental health, includes:

- **Self-esteem**: a positive attitude to yourself. Even if you know you're far from perfect. You have a realistic and positive perception of who you are.

- **Personal growth**: you see yourself on the way to positive goals. You are becoming a greater person in your own way, not in somebody else's way. Your life is mainly growth, development, and self-actualisation.

- **Environmental mastery**: you feel that you can cope and positively interact with the situations and people around you. Your independence gives you both the choices and the resources to cope with routine situations and stressful situations.

- **Interaction with others**: you can form and develop deepening relationships, including romantic ones.

- **Integration**: you can fit into your surroundings without sacrificing your identity.

Substantial deviations from any these norms would suggest abnormality.

In fact, this list seems to describe the characteristics of particular well-adapted individuals who would be a minority in any society. These ideas may be challenged by:

- The list is a summary of the ideals, rather than the realities of Western society.
- The list is ethnocentric, as it is culturally Western. The norm of people in many societies is to turn to superiors and cultural tradition for advice, rather than to their own assessment of the situations and to their own coping strategies.
- Many people's perception of who they are is not positive and realistic, but over-positive and unrealistic. That would hardly be abnormal, even though it is a faulty self-perception.

Abnormality has been defined by **Rosenhan and Seligman (1989)** as including seven criteria to determine whether a person or a behaviour pattern is normal or not:

1. Is any suffering involved?
2. Is the person's behaviour the source of his or her own troubles?
3. Does the person manage to communicate his feelings in a rational and reasonable way?
4. Is an unpredictable pattern shown in dealing with situations?
5. Is a particular situation experienced quite differently from the ways others go through it?

6. Is the behaviour causing awkwardness and embarrassment to others?
7. Is the person's way of doing things in violation of his/her accepted cultural standards?

This list shows a careful balance between the mental well-being of the individual and the realities of society at large. However, it needs to take into account that social (and political) realities change:

- The work of Read et al (2004) exemplifies behaviour that would not be considered abnormal today, but was once. Examples include a sexual interest in a person of the same gender, and a woman deliberately choosing to be single rather than marry.
- The behaviour of the person may be categorised as abnormal when it is seen to threaten powerfully-backed regimes and interests. For example, the Soviets' categorising of dissidents as mentally abnormal and forcing them to undergo clinical treatment.
- Many behaviours that are different to the dominant culture are normal conduct for the minority-culture that the individual identifies with. This is exemplified in the manual of the American Psychiatric Association (DSM-5, see below), which classifies various disorders as culture-bound syndromes.

Most psychological abnormalities cannot be traced to physiological (biological) disorders, despite advances in brain-scanning technology. Indeed, the psychiatric diagnosis of mental illness relies on professionally-produced diagnostic manuals (for classification purposes), clinical interviews, and the patients' self-reporting. The difficulties in making a diagnosis include:

- The possibility of a diagnosis causing the patient to suffer the stigma of mental illness, which may a greater threat to the patient than the illness itself.
- The possibility of a patient diagnosed as mentally ill being no longer held fully responsible for often violent or anti-social behaviour.
- The lack of medical evidence in diagnosis of most conditions, due to the difficulties in understanding the workings of the brain.
- **Serious errors can occur in diagnosis:** see the study of **Rosenhan (1973)** Section 6.1.4: "On being sane in insane places". This possibility can be reduced by data triangulation, where more than one mental health professional independently diagnoses the patient with the findings subsequently compared.
- **Cultural issues**, such as those exemplified by the research of **Parker et al. (2001)**, Section 6.1.4.
- **Gender issues**, such as exemplified by **Swami (2012)**, Section 6.1.4.
- **Various types of bias, such as an anchoring bias** exemplified by the research of **Friedlander and Stockman (1983)**, see Section 6.1.4.

6.1.2 Classification systems used for the diagnosis of abnormalities

Diagnosis is the identification of disease on the basis of symptoms, clinical tests, observations, interviewing those connected with the patient, and information from the patient.

Classification systems involve a standardised set of criteria for each abnormal condition. These are tools designed to improve the reliability of diagnosis, so that the patient would be more likely to be diagnosed the same way by any competent professional using the criteria within the manual.

There are several systems of classification of identifiable mental disorder. Three of them are:

1. **DSM-5**: The American Psychiatric Association's *Diagnostic and Statistical Manual of Mental Disorders*, fifth edition 2013, with updates in succeeding years. Produced by the American Psychiatric Association, DSM-5 is based on the U.S. experience. This publication is constantly revised in order to make diagnosis more valid, by including the most recent developments in medical and psychological knowledge. Since 1987, this source has shown increasing awareness of viewing people's problems more holistically, within an integrated bio-psycho-medical framework.

   The manual presents abnormal conditions with their respective symptoms, rather that the elements that may have contributed to the condition. A positive diagnosis may be made where the prescribed types and number of symptoms are evident.

2. **ICD-11**: The International Classification of Diseases. Multilingual availability, and in the 11th Revision, released in 2019. It is produced by WHO (World Health Organization), and it is approved by the health ministers of all its 193 member countries. Though its sections on mental disease have differences from DSM-5, it is becoming increasingly similar to the DSM. It tends to place a stronger focus on causes as well as symptoms than the DSM-5. In contrast to DSM-5, ICD-11 is relatively inexpensive, with discounts for low-income countries and free availability on the Internet.

3. **CCMD-3**: The Chinese Classification of Mental Disorder. In both Chinese and English, it is devised for and often used in preference to the ICD-11 by Chinese practitioners for the following reasons:

   - Chinese culture traditionally tends to consider nervous disorders as physical disorders in general: as arising from lack of harmony between vital organs and *qi*: the life energy that flows through a person. Thus, a condition that in the West would be diagnosed as depression may be categorised as *shenjing shuairuo*, a form of neurasthenia that strongly emphasises the somatic symptoms of depression. Such a diagnosis is much less stigmatising in Chinese culture than depression.
   - There are abnormal conditions that are cultural-specific to China and Southeast Asia. One example is *koro*, meaning genital-retraction syndrome where the individual is fully-but-wrongly convinced and horrified that his or her own genitals are shrinking and will soon disappear. This abnormality has been suggested as being cultural-specific, arising from the Chinese emphasis on balance, as well as fertility.
   - The ICD-11 in Chinese has tended to cause serious problems for practitioners due to the complexities arising from cross-cultural translation issues.

The psychological profession uses the ABCS framework of describing the symptoms of a disorder, which forms the basis of a diagnosis within an interview or observation session:

(a) **Affective symptoms** – emotional elements such as euphoria, sadness, fear.

(b) **Behavioural symptoms** – observations such as excessive laughter, weeping, looking away in conversation.

(c) **Cognitive symptoms** – such as personalisation (attempting to give a false impression of who you really are).

(d) **Somatic** (physical rather than psychological) **symptoms** – such as "butterflies in the stomach", stomach cramps, sudden jerky movements.

Research studies have indicated that patients experiencing similar conditions tend report them differently according to culture (Parker et al., 2001, Section 6.1.4). And manuals also depend on the psychiatrist's level of accuracy in applying criteria to the patient's condition, including possibilities of bias (Friedlander and Stockman 1983, Section 6.1.4 below).

6.1.3 The validity and reliability of diagnosis

Validity relates to how accurately the diagnosis fits the patient's reality, according to professional criteria.

Reliability is about how likely different psychiatrists will give the same diagnosis if they use the same diagnostic procedures, without that diagnosis necessarily being valid.

It is much harder to make a valid diagnosis of a psychological condition than a physical condition, as its symptoms are less likely to be apparent, and rely on observation and self-reporting. Both validity and reliability of diagnosis may be affected by the degree of clinical bias in diagnosis, and the issues arising are examined in Section 6.1.4.

6.1.4 The role of clinical bias in diagnosis

Clinical bias may occur to varying degrees given the following realities:

1. **Bias in diagnosis arising from interpretation of classification systems.**

    Standardised manuals such as DSM-5 that define and specify symptoms of abnormalities are designed to promote both validity, as the diagnosis criteria are clearly defined, and reliability, as psychiatrists use the same standard manual.

    However, manuals still do place the responsibility on the individual psychiatrist to decide whether the degree of severity of the patient's symptoms actually meets the criteria for the diagnosis. The symptoms may be an individual's coping strategy with life's difficulties rather than evidence of a particular abnormality. As such, the diagnosis of abnormality could be invalid. Inaccurate diagnosis, even supported by the manual, could negatively label the patient, affect his/her job, require medical treatment and even hospitalisation. This argument might well be less important with the advance of brain scanning technology, especially in the diagnosis of conditions such as Alzheimer's disease.

2. **Bias in diagnosis arising from differences in the style, theoretical orientation, culture, and personality of the clinical interviewer.**

    The work of **Cooper et al. (1972)** investigated **professional reliability** in the diagnosis of depression and schizophrenia. The study involved New York and London psychiatrists observing a series of movies of the same clinical interviews of patients, whom they had to diagnose. Significantly, twice as many of those viewed were diagnosed as suffering from schizophrenia by the American psychiatrists as by the British psychiatrists, who significantly and more frequently diagnosed mania and depression. This indicated the importance of reliability becoming more robust by including professionals of different rather than similar backgrounds.

3. **Bias in diagnosis arising when a patient presents himself/herself as having an abnormal behaviour.**

    This is exemplified in Rosenhan, below.

RESEARCH STUDY

Rosenhan (1973)

The work of **Rosenhan (1973)** "On being sane in insane places" sought to test the validity of diagnosis of schizophrenia in an ecologically valid setting. Could psychiatrists demonstrate **validity** in diagnosis in distinguishing between normal and abnormal behaviour?

Each of the eight participants (including Rosenhan himself) was to attempt to gain admission to a specific psychiatric hospital (a total of 12, within the USA). This was done by claiming to have heard "voices", but otherwise giving a normal background. The ruse worked as an anchor. All instances were diagnosed as schizophrenia, except one which was classified as manic depression.

Once admitted, their aim was to be discharged as soon as possible – which was dependent on their convincing the staff that they were sufficiently mentally healthy. They thus acted perfectly normally when hospitalised, except for taking notes. That was vital, for all the participants were observing the hospital staff without their knowledge (covert observer participation).

In fact, the note taking was interpreted as evidence of insanity by the staff members, who did not seem to pay much attention to the content of the notes. On average, it took 19 days for them to be released, most commonly with a diagnosis of 'schizophrenia in remission'. (The findings caused considerable embarrassment to the psychiatric profession.)

The follow-up study took place when the staff at one psychiatric hospital was told that some fake patients would present themselves, and they should be on the lookout for them. Out of 193 patients, 43 were rejected by at least one member of staff. In fact, all the patients were genuine.

Strengths and limitations: Rosenhan (1973)

Strengths	Limitations
1. Ecologically valid, and no issues in determining cause (the faked hearing of 'voices') and the effect (the admission to the psychiatric ward as a patient). 2. Highlighted the need to improve existing diagnostic tools, including the manuals.	1. Needs to address the ethical issues of covert participant observation. May well be justifiable in this case as the findings were of paramount public importance and could not have been obtained in any other way. 2. Possibility of research bias as the note takers were psychiatrists, adversely affecting validity. 3. Possibility of bias from the psychiatrists at the hospitals, as the researchers were presenting themselves as being in an abnormal condition, adversely affecting reliability. 4. That imposters would be present in the follow-up study raises the ethical issue of genuine patients not receiving necessary treatment. 5. Only one abnormal condition was addressed: the hearing of voices. This creates problems in transferring the finding to the diagnosis of other abnormal conditions.

6. PAPER 2 OPTION – ABNORMAL PSYCHOLOGY

RESEARCH STUDY

Friedlander and Stockman (1983)

This experimental study is based on the practice of the psychiatrist interviewing the patient several times before making a diagnosis. It aimed to examine the possibility of an anchoring effect if information about the patient was given to the professional earlier rather than later in the series of clinical interviews. The hypothesis was that if the information about the patient is known to the professional earlier on, it might have a greater influence on the diagnosis than finding out later after getting to know the patient. Such bias could well adversely affect the **validity** of the diagnosis.

The study engaged 46 US mental health workers, including psychologists, psychiatrists, and social workers. Each was given two different cases: a more severe case of depression with an attempted suicide, and a less severe case of anorexic behaviours. Each case came with the transcripts of five clinical interviews. Each participant had to rate the level of functioning and prognosis after each interview. However, some of the professionals received the background information at the first interview stage, and other professionals received the background information at the fourth interview stage.

The results for the less-severe anorexia case showed that the early disclosure of the anorexic behaviour was significantly more likely to result in a severer diagnosis and prognosis than disclosure at the fourth interview. The early disclosure seems to have served as an anchoring bias. In contrast, the results for the more severe depression case did not seem to have been influenced by an anchoring bias, as suicide attempts seemed to have invited a more severe professional diagnosis at whatever stage that information was disclosed.

The strengths of the study were its experimental independent measures design, and its use of experienced health professionals. Its limitations include the relatively small number of participants in the study, and its focus on two abnormal conditions only.

4. **Bias in diagnosis arising from gender difference**

The rate of major depression diagnosis for women is about double that of men in most societies, raising the possibility of validity and even reliability issues because of possible gender bias within the profession. The research of Bertakis et al. (2001) indicates fundamentally similar prevalence of depressed feelings in both genders, raising the possibility of gender bias in professional diagnosis, which has been countered by the possibility of women more readily being prepared to seek help than men (e.g. Brommelhoff et al, 2004), which is also supported by Swami (2012).

RESEARCH STUDY

Swami (2012)

This study on gender bias focused on the fundamental question of whether seeking help for depression may be influenced by the attitude of the people the individual is in contact with. The participants were 1218 adults in the UK. Each participant was given a description of either a male or a female patient. The participants were not told that they satisfied the diagnostic conditions for depression as set in the DSM-4 manual. Each was asked whether the patient had a mental health disorder.

The study found that significantly more participants rated the description of the female as suffering from a mental disorder than those rating the description of the male. This suggests that there is a tendency in society for associating mental ill-health with females rather than with males, who might be described as being under stress and overworked.

The research indicated that gender stereotypes might well influence the tendency for individuals to seek help, and supports the possibility that more females are diagnosed with depression because society encourages them to seek help.

The research had the strength of a large sample of participants, and a standardised procedure as described above. It supports the argument that the correlation between gender and incidence of diagnosis depression could be illusory. However, the wholly UK-base of the study may limit the degree the findings can be generalised. It also does not address claims of gender bias in diagnosis at the professional level.

5. **Bias in diagnosis arising from socio-cultural issues**

The differences in cultures between the psychiatrist and the patient may create severe difficulties in the validity of effective psychiatric diagnosis.

There is the possibility of the psychiatrist not being able to identify signs of (for example) depression that are expressed in a non-recognisable way in a different ethnic group. Some cultures tend to play down emotionally-expressed disorders, and only address them when they are expressed somatically.

STUDIES

Zhang et al. (1998) carried out a research study that reported that only 16 out of over 19,000 people from twelve different regions in China reported suffering from a mood disorder at least once in their life. This might indicate that depression hardly exists amongst the Chinese. However, many did report **somatic** symptoms that indicated depression, such as 'a weakness of the nerves' 'fatigue' and often 'lower-back pains'. That fits in with the Chinese approach. The Chinese view holistically sees the body and its organs as integrated together, instead of each organ being an independent part. It thus views disease as arising out of disharmony in the body between the "energy flow" and the different organs in the body. Indeed, the work of Kleinman (1984) argued that the somatisation of symptoms makes it difficult to "join the dots" and identify a depressive situation even where one exists. There is also the consequent danger of too readily accepting physical pain by itself as a symptom of depression with Chinese patients.

This study can also be used for Etiologies of major depression (6.2), Prevalence of disorders (6.2.2), as well as Normality versus abnormality (6.1.1).

Parker et al. (2001) carried out a research study to investigate the ways in which patients of contrasting cultures (Australian of Western ancestry, and Chinese living in Malaysia) who had already been diagnosed for major depression emphasised somatic and psychological symptoms as reasons for seeking help. This study thus investigated the cultural validity of manual-based criteria, as their use depends on the self-reporting of the patient. They were first asked what their primary symptom was in seeking help. Then, using a 39-point questionnaire listing somatic and psychological symptoms, the Chinese participants tended to rank somatic elements, whereas the Australian tended to rank psychological elements as well as somatic elements in causing them distress.

This study had the strengths of having 100 participants, a relatively large number, incorporated psychiatrists that understood the Chinese community, and included somatic elements that were not included in the then DSM-4 manual. Its limitations include being based on self-reporting, and that it was etic: the Malaysian Chinese that participated had already been diagnosed with depression under the Western DSM-4 criteria. That may have excluded people from the sample whose depression may not have been recognised as such with Western diagnostic tools.

Other cultural issues involve a fear of giving a diagnosis of (for example) depression, as it can create disproportionate harm to the patient in his/her own society (stigmatisation, see below). It can make the patient especially wary of reporting affective, behavioural, and cognitive symptoms.

There is also the possibility that the distress that the person experiences is a product of the belief system. Mental suffering is the divine-imposed consequence of a past misdeed, rather than a fundamental underlying disorder. This may influence the patient to play down the symptoms and thus be at risk of not receiving an appropriate diagnosis and treatment.

The psychiatrist working together with a bilingual/bicultural person trained in mental health may help to address these cultural issues. He or she can relate and present the various symptoms reported by the patient to the framework of the psychiatrist's understanding.

6.1.5 Ethical considerations in diagnosis: the issue of stigmatisation

The reality of psychiatric diagnosis is that it gives the patient a new identity, which can be a label for life, such as schizophrenic or depressive, rather than a person with schizophrenia or a person with depression. This is a stigma that can continue after the symptoms are over: schizophrenia in remission and depression in remission. It is very likely to affect marriage prospects, job prospects, and indeed his or her sense of personal identity. The work of Doherty (1975) points out that those who reject their mental illness label tend to improve more quickly than those who accept it. Being diagnosed may become a crutch that patients lean on too much.

The ethical considerations are all the more serious where members of certain groups are at higher risk of receiving a stigmatising diagnosis than others, including:

- In the UK, a patient is nine times as likely to be diagnosed as suffering from schizophrenia if coming from an Afro-Caribbean background rather than from a white British one. Morgan et al. (2006) account for this with racially-biased diagnostic error rather than genetics.
- Women are more likely to be diagnosed with depression, as above. In addition, the work of Rosser (1992) argues that to be partially due to the large number of male psychiatrists in the profession who might 'over-diagnose' and stigmatise a woman as being depressed. In reality, she could be bored and frustrated with her role traditional home-based routines and misses her honoured role in the workplace.

Ethically, there remains the very grave issue of the risk of over-diagnosis and the unjust consequences flowing from stigmatisation (including 'in remission' conditions) needing to be balanced with the potential denial of treatment to those who need it, which can prevent suicide or grievous bodily harm to a third party. The consequences of stigmatisation are hard to identify as the findings of studies of stigmatisation are correlational in nature due to the problems in isolating the precise elements influencing it.

There is also the ethical problem of confidentiality: which may, and should, be waived when the condition is such that the condition endangers the patient or society. Such situations may override the usual ethical rights to consent, anonymity, right to withdraw, deception, and debriefing, although there is still the requirement of avoiding more than the minimum stress.

6.2 Etiology of abnormal conditions

Etiologies of abnormal conditions are examined under two headings:
1. Explanation for disorders: biological, cognitive, and socio-cultural
2. Prevalence rates and disorders.

You need to have studied only one disorder in detail. The material below is mainly on **major depression**.

Etiology involves the explaining of the cause of the abnormal behaviour. Etiology connects to psychiatry in that the treatment given should take into account the causes of the disorder. These may be biologically, cognitively, and/or socio-culturally rooted.

Depressive disorders are those that relate to mood, one example being **major depression** whereby the symptoms persist without a break at least two weeks

Major depression affects about 15% of the world's population (Charney and Weismann 1988). Major depression, which is the depression studied in this chapter, is more than simply feeling in a depressed mood. It is where symptoms have continued without interruption for at least two weeks. In the UK, some 25% of admissions to psychiatric hospitals are because of diagnosed depression. Its main symptoms are:

- Affective symptoms: distress, lack of signs of interest or pleasure.
- Behavioural symptoms: not wishing to be together with other people, difficulty in sleeping at night, difficulty in getting through a normal day's work, observable agitated or unusually slow movements, self-destructive and even suicidal behaviour.
- Cognitive symptoms: problems in staying focused on what is going on, inappropriate feelings of guilt, and negative attitudes to oneself and one's surroundings.
- Somatic symptoms: fatigue, loss of appetite, and significant weight loss or significant weight gain.

6.2.1 Etiologies for major depression: biological, cognitive, and socio-cultural

Though common, depression is typically a complex condition with one or more influencing factors that might be biological, cognitive, and/or socio-cultural.

Biological etiologies: the serotonin hypothesis

Serotonin is a neurotransmitter. When functioning normally in neurotransmission, serotonin is released in suitable quantities, and is not taken up too quickly to lose its pleasurable effect. Depression happens where these neurons do not function well, and can thus adversely influence brain development, emotional regulation, and sensitivity to stressors.

Evidence supporting the serotonin hypothesis
    (a) Positive response of patients to SSRI (serotonin re-uptake inhibitors) drugs designed to increase the level of serotonin activity in synapses.

(b) Research studies investigating genotypes, such as Caspi et al. (2003) in section 1.5.3, finding a correlation between a short allele variation of the 5HTT gene and the incidence of depression following stressful events and situations. This study involves accepting the serotonin hypothesis by its investigating the possibility that it is that gene's transporting role which is vital for serotonin to be effective.

Evidence questioning the serotonin hypothesis

(a) SSRI current success rate in effectively treating the depression is about 25%, relatively low.

(b) Cognitive symptoms of depression are not always supported by malfunctioning serotonin.

(c) It is not possible to determine the serotonin levels in the brain.

(d) It is unclear whether it is the depression that influences the lower serotonin levels or whether it is the lower serotonin levels that influence the depression.

(e) It does not consider the possibility that depression may be associated with lack of neural regeneration in the hippocampus. This is a focus of the cortisol hypothesis, below.

Biological etiologies: the cortisol hypothesis

The underlying focus of the cortisol hypothesis is the **neurogenesis theory of depression**, that not enough new neurons are being regenerated in the hippocampus and in the brain neural networks that are associated with serotonin, dopamine, and norepinephrine. According to this hypothesis, the under-generation of new neurons is due to over-secretion of cortisol that leads to reduced neurotransmitter activity in the brain.

Evidence supporting the cortisol hypothesis

(a) Depressed patients seem to have small hippocampal volumes, as concluded by the meta-analysis of Videbech and Ravnkilde (2004) using brain scans to compare the volume with individuals with depression and individuals without depression, indicating less growth of neural networks.

(b) The above meta-study was based on a total of 351 people diagnosed with depression and 279 that did not have depression.

Evidence questioning the cortisol hypothesis

(a) The above meta-study did not indicate whether depression might cause the lower-volume hippocampus or whether it was the pre-existing lower-volume hippocampus that might be more susceptible to depression.

(b) The researchers used cross sectional data rather than longitudinal data. Their findings were correlational: they were not able to determine the size of the hippocampi before the diagnosis of depression.

Biological etiologies: the influence of genes

This is considered in Chapter 1, Section 1.5.

Research studies for biological etiologies of depression

- **Caspi et al. (2003)** an experimentally-designed study on the possible influence of genetics in depression – Chapter 1, section 1.5.3. Using linkage analysis, its aim was to examine whether the degree of an individual's susceptibility to depression following stress is influenced by the person's genetic makeup.
- **Weissman et al. (2005)**, a prospective family study on the possible influence of genetics in depression over three generations – Chapter 1, section 1.5.

Cognitive etiologies: Aaron Beck's cognitive theory of depression (1976)

Beck's cognitive approach considers the **depressogenic schemas** that can develop out of negative experiences (such as excessive criticism, abuse, and bullying) especially in childhood and early adolescence, through parents, siblings, and other people of importance. Experiencing persistent rejection in childhood or later on can lead to feelings of hopelessness and worthlessness as an adult. Being rejected plays and replays the message of the soundtrack of:

(i) **the negative self**: "everyone hates me, I wish I was different",

(ii) **the negative interaction with the world**: "nobody takes any notice of me, I don't matter to anyone", and

(iii) **the negative future**: "there's no point in trying as things will only be worse".

These soundtracks interact to create an over-arching negative schema with the combined framework: "everyone will always hate me because I am worthless".

In other words, Beck observed that depressive patients show evidence of a distorted "cognitive triangle" set of schemas: about oneself "I'm useless"; about the future "Nothing will ever change"; and about what is going on all around "Nobody cares for me".

Figure 6.1: **The cognitive triangle**

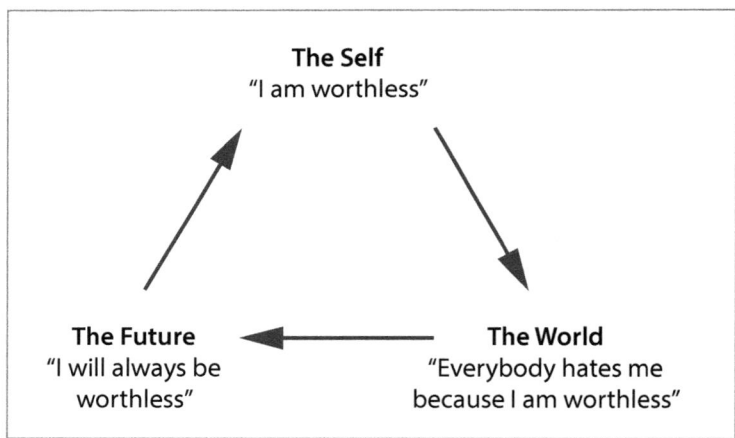

This negative set of schemas can be strengthened by **confirmation bias** as events take place, whereby the depressed person focuses on information and interpretations that confirm pre-existing negative schemas and expectations whilst disregarding those that contradict them. See Lord et al. (1979), in Chapter 2, Section 2.6.

Confirmation bias can lead to the support of negative schemas, for example:

- drawing negative conclusions about oneself from insufficient evidence.
- focusing on negative aspects of an interaction rather than the whole picture.
- thinking in "black and white" (dichotomous thinking): it's either perfect or a disaster.
- assuming self-blame for whatever goes wrong.

Evaluation: Beck (1976)

Beck's cognitive theory of depression creates a framework to show how those suffering depression think more negatively about themselves and the world even when they are not actually depressed. For the depressogenic schema remains. This would strengthen Beck's assertion that it is the negative schema that is a cause of depression, rather than a product of a depression with, for example, biological roots. On the other hand, it does not rule out **bidirectional ambiguity**: are the negative schemas a cause of depression or a symptom of depression?

Research studies for cognitive etiologies of depression

RESEARCH STUDY

Alloy et al. (1999)

The aim of this study was to determine whether negative thinking and **negative cognitive schemas increased vulnerability to depression**. 347 first-year university students took part. The research was prospective and longitudinal; the participants who did not suffer from depression at the outset were checked at intervals over a two-and-a-half year period for any developments of depression.

At the beginning of the study, the researchers gathered information on the thinking style of the individual participants through questionnaires and semi-structured interviews. They used it to identify whether the participant had a depression-susceptible thinking style or not, classifying as high-risk or low-risk for depression. The point of the investigation was to find out whether a negative thinking schema was likely to influence the future development of depression.

The study found 17% of the high-risk students developed depression over the period of study, in contrast to only 1% of the low risk students. The research concluded that negative cognitive styles contribute to the development of depression, and thus supports Beck.

The strengths of the study were that it was prospective (none of those who took part had depression at the start of the study), and it used a large sample. The tests used for depression were standardised for that condition and had shown a high level of reliability. Its limitations include being quasi-experimental in design, as the researchers had no control of the independent depression-causing factors that would have varied from participant to participant. Therefore they were unable to demonstrate cause and effect: that negative schemas caused depression rather than were affected by depression. In addition, there may well be biological and socio-cultural elements influencing the development of depressive symptoms.

RESEARCH STUDY

Nolen-Hoeksema (2000)

This study researched whether negative cognitive thinking influenced depression. This study focused on the rumination aspect of negative thinking: where the individual thinks constantly and deeply about the symptoms and causes of the distress, rather than the solutions. The researchers aimed to investigate whether high levels of rumination influence depression.

Participants were over 1,000 adults in San Francisco. At the beginning of the study, the researchers gathered information on the thinking style of the individual participants through standardised questionnaires and a clinical interviews. They then used the questionnaires to gather information on patterns of rumination and patterns of coping.

The study found that those whose questionnaire responses identified them with symptoms for major depression had significantly higher scores for rumination than those with responses that did not. The researchers concluded that negative cognition patterns put a person at higher risk for depression.

The strengths of the study were that it used a large sample and investigative tools that had been shown to be reliable in previous studies, such as the Hamilton rating scale for depression. However, its limitation was that it relied on symptoms of depression indicated by the questionnaire rather than professional diagnosis of depression. In addition, it did not take into account the degree of support received by the participants with depressive symptoms.

Socio-cultural etiologies: social vulnerability factors, and cultural explanatory factors

Social vulnerability factors: environment and circumstances, such as poverty, death of spouse or an unsatisfactory relationship with spouse, or lack of social support, have been associated with depression.

RESEARCH STUDY

This study can also be used for 6.2.2: in using differences in social vulnerability as an explanation for prevalence of depression.

Brown and Harris (1978) investigated the social causes of depression in South-East London. This semi-structured-interview-based study involved a sample of 458 women, between 18 and 65. Within that sample, 37 had been diagnosed for depression within the previous year.

Using evidence from this study, Brown and Harris developed the theory that severer levels of social vulnerability increase the likelihood of depressive symptoms. Social vulnerabilities that the study indicated as being significant were:

(a) Stressful events and environments: Over four-fifths of the first group had suffered a major life-cycle-event (such as a death of a close relative) or a prolonged severe difficulty (e.g. coping with the children at home), compared with only a third of those who were not in a depressed group.

(b) Poverty: there were poverty-linked tendencies to depression, with those in the poorer, working class having a significantly greater likelihood of depression than those in the more affluent middle class.

(c) Single living: substantially higher rates of depression were found in women who were separated, divorced, or widowed, than those who were married.

On those bases, the researchers proposed that socio-cultural factors that influence the development of depression include: **lack of protective elements** (such as family or community support), **presence of elements raising the risk of depression** (including loss of mother before age 11, not having anyone to confide in, having more than three children at home under age 14, and being unemployed), and **provoking elements** of ongoing stress.

This study has the strength of supporting the view that social factors seem to influence depression, irrespective of biologically-rooted and cognitively-rooted personality factors. It has been argued that this study supports the view that women are more susceptible to depression because they tend to be exposed to more risk factors. The semi-structured interview helped to identify the stressors most linked to the cause of depression. It also used a relatively large sample. However, this study was confined to women, creating problems in generalising it to men. The correlational design of the study created difficulties in establishing cause and effect; bidirectional ambiguity: for example, did poverty create the depression, or did the depression create the poverty?

Cultural explanatory factors: culturally-based models of depression may indicate that different cultures show different symptoms for the development of depression. A patient's expressed symptoms for depression can differ from culture to culture, which in turn can draw attention to different elements influencing the condition, as indicated by the study of Parker et al. (2001) above (Section 6.1.4, review this study): the Malaysian Chinese tending to emphasise somatic symptoms pointing to somatic factors influencing the depression, and the Australians tending to emphasise psychological symptoms as well as somatic symptoms, pointing additionally to psychological factors influencing the depression.

Becker et al (2002), a self-reporting-based prospective study of the influence on adolescent girls of globalisation-caused cultural variations in eating disorders, is described in section 6.2.2 as it can also be used to exemplify culturally explanatory factors as etiologies of abnormal behaviours.

6.2.2 Prevalence of Disorders

Prevalence means the proportion of people in a population with a particular disorder. Lifetime prevalence means the proportion of people in a population who have experienced that particular order at least once in their lives. Prevalence rates are not globally and culturally universal, and they tend to change over time.

The prevalence of major depression, the world's most prevalent psychiatric disorder (Marsella, 2002) is a subject of many studies and theories, including:

- Gender differences in prevalence: In the USA, a lifetime prevalence of 13% for men, and 20% for women (Kessler et al. 2005). The gender differences are almost completely the same cross-culturally, with one exception: depression has been found to be as prevalent with Jewish men as with Jewish women (Levav, 1997).

- Explanations for women being more susceptible to major depression include: different biological mechanisms in coping with stress, reflected in the way they think about themselves, and the styles they use to handle difficulties with tendency for rumination (Nolen-Hoeksema, 2001). Chronic stress can lead to being vulnerable to depression, expressed in Beck's schema of depression.

- Socioculturally: the higher women's prevalence rates in depression reflects their low social status in many societies, which comes with poorer access to resources, the brunt of the hard work of child-rearing, the chronic strains and frustrations of being a housewife and mother, sexual abuse, and poverty (Brown and Harris 1978, Nolen-Hoeksema 2001).

- Weisman (1996) conducted a cross-cultural study of the prevalence of depression in ten locations/cultures worldwide. Heading the list was recently war-torn Beirut, Lebanon (19%), with peaceful Paris, France not far behind at 16%. The Far Eastern island of Taiwan showed the lowest rate at 1.5% - just over half of that of neighbour South Korea at 2.9%.

- Very low prevalence rates for depression in the Middle East and China. However many patients that would be likely to be diagnosed with depression tend to be given a diagnosis of a condition that is less culturally stigmatised, e.g. neurasthenia.

- In the city of Chennai, Southern India, the overall rate was 16%. It was more than three times as high with those having lower incomes than with those having high incomes. Over a quarter of those divorced had suffered or were suffering from major depression, higher than those widowed (one fifth), and those currently married (just over one seventh). (Poongothai et al., 2009, using a sample of 25,000 people and using a self-reporting questionnaire.)

- The increased in the incidence of depression in young people today has been argued to be that more people seek treatment. There is less of a stigma today in seeking help that in the previous generation (Twenge, 2015).

It should also be borne in mind that the ***statistical variations in depression may well be under-reporting the real situation***, as:

(a) The stigma of reporting and diagnosis varies worldwide. Where it is high in e.g. China, people tend to report depression symptoms somatically, emphasising physical pain (Sartorius et al., 1983, Parker et al., 2011).

(b) The geographical process of urbanisation (rural-urban migration) means that a greater percentage of the world's population lives in cities and with it, the unfamiliar strains of city life. These include living in overcrowded accommodation, underemployment (earning insufficient for basic living standards), and insufficient adaptation skills to cope with the rapid change of modern living. Access to psychiatric systems could be beyond the reach of those lacking urban navigation skills and basic literacy (Marsella, 1995).

(c) Despite the wider recognition of depression as a disorder, individuals may not recognise the symptoms that they do experience as indications of depression. The condition is thus left untreated, with possibilities of becoming more severe.

Research studies on prevalence of disorders

Brown and Harris (1978), a largely self-reporting-based study of the influence of social vulnerability on the prevalence of depression in women – Section 6.2.1, above.

Becker et al (2002), a self-reporting-based prospective study of the influence of globalisation-caused cultural variations in the prevalence of eating disorders with adolescent girls.

Explanations for the prevalence of bulimia include the globalisation of culture. This involves imposing western ideals on the ideal body shape, being socially reinforced worldwide through slim female figures on globalised television, movies, and women's magazines. That puts social pressure on women worldwide to conform to the model of the "affluent and successful Western society".

RESEARCH STUDY

Becker et al (2002) researched the prevalence of eating disorders in adolescent girls in a remote area of the Fiji Islands before the then introduction of TV (1995), and three years after the introduction of TV (1998). The study used a questionnaire and follow-up semi-structured interviews on girls' eating patterns from two secondary schools. The 30 girls taking part in the 1995 study were from the same years in school as the 30 girls

6. PAPER 2 OPTION – ABNORMAL PSYCHOLOGY

taking part in the 1998 study, and were thus different groups of participants. The results indicated that there had been a change in the ideal body profile from fairly round and robust before television introduction, to the slim Western model afterwards. There was no dieting before the introduction of TV. Three years later, more than 10% of the girls reported dieting and self-induced vomiting as a means of working towards the western-idealised body shape. The study indicated that cultural change may help to explain eating disorders, and changes in prevalence of eating disorders.

The study had the strengths of being prospective in design and ecologically valid. It used students from the same schools and age group in the 1995 and 1998 studies. However, the results were correlational: the possibility of eating disorders in the 1998 group may have explanations other than exposure to the newly-available media, such as peer pressure. Also, the behaviours were self-reported: none of them had been diagnosed for eating disorders.

6.3 Treatment of disorders

You need to have studied the treatment of only one disorder in detail. The material below is on **major depression**.

Depressive disorders are those that relate to mood, one example being major depression whereby the symptoms persist without a break at least two weeks.

Make sure that you are familiar with the main symptoms of depression as stated under 6.2.

This section considers:

1. Biological treatments of disorders, and their effectiveness
2. Psychological (including cognitive and socio-cultural) treatments of disorders, and their effectiveness
3. The role of culture in treatment

6.3.1 Biological treatments of depression and their effectiveness

Biological treatment can include drug therapy and electro-convulsive therapy (ECT), as well as psychosurgery and brain stimulation.

Drug therapy involves the use of appropriate drugs to restore the body to health where the etiology of the depression indicates biological roots. For example, **imipramine**, a **tricyclic antidepressant**, that appears to work by increasing levels of serotonin and norepinephrine.

Low levels of the neurotransmitter serotonin (see earlier in this chapter) are characteristic of depression and, following the serotonin hypothesis (Section 6.2.1), a major cause. Therefore biomedical treatment should aim to restore serotonin activity to normal levels.

Commonly used to restore serotonin levels are **serotonin re-uptake inhibitors (SSRIs)**. These make each unit of neurotransmitter serotonin more effective. Instead of the serotonin being immediately reabsorbed, it stays longer in the synaptic gaps, operates at an increased level, and is therefore more effective as a unit of pleasure. The aim is to improve serotonin-based energy, lifting the depression.

Bear in mind, however, that SSRIs are devised on the basis of the influence of serotonin and thus a reductionist approach to the causes of depression, whereas there may well be other elements influencing depression such as neurogenesis (section 6.2.1) whereby insufficient new neurons are being regenerated in the hippocampus and in the brain neural networks that are associated with serotonin, dopamine, and norepinephrine. One possible explanation of neurogenesis is the cortisol hypothesis (section 6.2.1).

In addition, SSRIs directly address low serotonin levels rather than the causes of major depression. A study by **Hollon et al. (2005)** indicated that more than three quarters of those who withdrew from Prozac, an SSRI, relapsed after withdrawal. Serotonin levels cannot be directly measured: assessing the effects of SSRIs depends on professionally standardised rating scales for depression that rely on self-reporting and professional observation.

SSRI users also face the risk of the side-effects of nausea, headaches, insomnia, and sexual problems. As they affect the workings of the brain, there is also the possibility of side-effects from withdrawal adversely affecting the brain's natural self-regulation which may aggravate the depressive symptoms.

Overall, drug treatments are generally quicker to take effect than psychological treatments, but they tend to address the symptoms rather than address the cause of the depression as exemplified by Hollon et al. (2005), above.

Ethically, drugs may only be used if the patient gives informed consent unless unable to do so or in a threatening condition such as suicidal.

RESEARCH STUDY

Elkin et al. (1989)

This study can also be used for 6.3.2: Psychological treatments, as it includes treatments and the effectiveness of the outcomes of biological treatments and psychological treatments.

This was an outcome-focused study on the success of different means of treating major depression. 250 patients participated, and were allocated randomly into four groups for the following treatments:

- biomedical treatment – real: anti-depressants (imipramine, a tricyclic antidepressant) plus normal clinical management
- biomedical treatment – supposed: placebo plus normal clinical management
- psychological treatment – CBT (Section 2.2.1)
- psychological treatment - IPT (interpersonal psychotherapy; unlike CBT, it is designed for clients to identify their problems in relating to others as these are felt to be a root cause of depression).

The treatment lasted for four months. Patients were assessed three times: before treatment, after six weeks of treatment, and after a year-and-a-half. The results were that medication plus clinical management performed the best at over 50%, CBT and IPT both almost as well (catching up with medication in the final weeks of the 4-month period of the treatment), with significant improvements to only 29% of the placebo plus clinical management group. This suggests that both medication and psychotherapy work to some degree, but neither by themselves are even nearly successful for all those being treated for major depression.

More generally, this study indicates that causes of major depressive disorder are complex and may well have different causes in individuals. A consequence is that some respond to biological treatments and others to psychological treatments.

Strengths and limitations: Elkin et al. (1989)

Strengths	Limitations
1. The divisions into four groups ensured that the study was well-controlled. 2. The findings were quantitatively supported by the sample size.	1. As an outcome-based study, it addressed the outcome of treatment for major depression, rather than the cause of major depression. 2. A total of one third of the medication plus clinical management participants dropped out of the study: significantly more than from the other treatment groups. The higher success rate for medication plus clinical management may have been reduced by the possible reasons for dropout, including adverse side-effects of the drugs.

RESEARCH STUDY

Riggs et al. (2007)

This study aimed to determine whether biologically-based SSRIs were able to increase the improvement rates of those already in CBT psychological therapy.

There were 126 participants aged 13–19. All had diagnosis of depression and substance use disorder and conduct disorder.

The participants were put into two groups: one receiving CBT and SSRIs and the other receiving CBT and placebos. It was a double blind: neither the researchers nor the participants knew what particular treatment was being given.

The results showed that 76% of those given SSRIs were rated as much improved or very much improved. Those given placebos showed 67% in the much improved and very much improved categories.

The research team concluded that though CBT therapy with SSRI drugs was effective, CBT without SSRIs, but using placebos was almost as effective. The study also showed that medications could enhance the more holistic psychological approach of CBT

> This study can also be used for 6.3.2: Psychological treatments, as it includes treatments and the effectiveness of the outcomes of psychological treatments when augmented by biological treatments, implying the comparative limitations of psychological treatments.

Strengths and limitations: Riggs et al. (2007)

Strengths	Limitations
1. The study was experimental in design, enabling the effects of the SSRI and placebo to be compared. 2. The findings were quantitatively supported by the sample size. 3. It is supported by findings from studies such as Kirsch et al. (2008), which found similar progress from both SSRIs and placebos, except in the most severely depressed participants.	1. As an outcome-based study, it addressed the outcome of treatment for major depression, rather than the cause of major depression. 2. Despite the effectiveness of SSRIs in assisting recovery from depression, the link between low serotonin levels in the brain and depression (the serotonin hypothesis) is not yet proven. The success rate of anti-depressants (e.g. Prozac) is based on its use by many patients, rather than clear demonstration that blocking the serotonin reuptake capacity does actually address the depression.

6.3.2 Psychological Treatments

These treatments are non-invasive. They typically involve psychotherapy, whereby the professional and the client directly interact. They aim to address and treat the causes rather than just the symptoms of the depression.

Cognitive behavioural therapy (CBT)

Individual (cognitive) treatment can involve **cognitive behavioural therapy (CBT)**. CBT is a form of psychotherapy, whereby the professional and the client directly interact. CBT is based on the idea that depressed thinking patterns are a cause rather than just a symptom of depression. CBT works on the basis that suffering persistent rejection in childhood or later on can lead to feelings of worthlessness as an adult. However, its focus is on current symptoms and issues. Being rejected plays the soundtrack of "everyone hates me, I'll never be accepted". It will cause negative feelings about oneself, which in turn will play the soundtrack of: "I am useless. I am worthless. I am good-for-nothing". Both soundtracks interact to build a negative schema in processing one's environment, creating the combined message: "everyone hates me because I am worthless". As previously explained Beck (1976) observed that depressive patients show evidence of a distorted cognitive set of schemas about the self, about the future, and about what is going on all around.

CBT therapy typically operates on a one-to-one basis, though it can also be used at a group basis. It seeks to enable the depressed person to:

1. Identify what the negative beliefs and thinking patterns are.
2. Test out whether these beliefs are actually true – reality testing, whereby the therapist asks the client to defend a negative belief, which the client typically fails to do flawlessly, and the therapist then challenges.
3. Move on to accept that parts of the thinking patterns are flawed. Then proceed to activities that produce positive feelings and seek more positive problem-solving capacities and skills.
4. Cognitively restructure: replace the previous thought patterns with ones that are more accurate and positive.
5. Test the new thought patterns by modifying behaviour, especially when interacting with others.
6. Ultimately develop new skills to cope with their life's challenges.
7. Support the improvements by becoming involved in activities that they find enjoyable and fulfilling.

In addition, CBT has more recently incorporated **mindfulness-based cognitive therapy (MBCT)**, a form of therapy using exercises in meditation. These are designed to help the patient let go of possible stresses that are fuelling the depression, as well as negative and harmful thinking patterns that include rumination over negative thoughts and behaviours at past events. This process in turn enables the therapist to help the client to build more positive schemas, including about the self, the future, and the world. This will be examined in the study of Kuyken et al. (2008), below.

Overall, psychological treatments have the advantages being personally supportive, involving personal interaction of the therapist with the client, and little risk of biochemically-based side effects. They also aim to address the root causes of depressed condition rather than just the symptoms, and thus have lower relapse rates than biological treatments following completion of treatment. However, their limitations include time involved in therapy, cost of therapy, time for treatment to take effect, and being unsuitable for depression that has stemmed from neurological or hormonal imbalances. In addition, there are possible communication issues when the treatment is cross-gender or cross-culture (Section 6.3.3). Moreover, CBT has been criticised for not sufficiently focusing on past events, which may be crucial for having generated the depressive condition. Indeed studies such as Riggs et al. (2007) indicate that combining both biological and psychological treatments seems to produce the best improvement rates.

RESEARCH STUDY

Kuyken et al. (2008)

This was a 15-month experimental study investigating the effectiveness of MBCT in a study of 123 depression-suffering participants with at least three episodes of depression. All participants were initially on anti-depressants, but instead of continuing on those drugs, the test group reduced medication and substituted MBCT. After the 15-month period, the medication stopped. The control group showed a relapse rate of 60%. The test group showed the substantially lower relapse rate of 47%. And those in the test group that received MCBT reported a much higher quality of life and feelings of physical well-being.

Strengths and limitations: Kuyken et al. (2008)

Strengths	Limitations
1. The experimental nature of the study made it possible to show cause and effect. 2. The findings were quantitatively supported by the sample size.	1. The study did not categorise the patients according to the severity of their major depression. Anyone suffering from three or more episodes of depression could have qualified. 2. It addressed the outcome of treatment for major depression, rather than the cause of major depression.

In addition, see Elkin et al. (1989, Section 6.3.1), which can also be used psychological treatments, as it focuses on the effectiveness of the outcomes of psychological treatments as well as biological treatments. Also see Riggs et al. (2007, Section 6.3.1), which includes the effectiveness of the outcomes of psychological treatments when and when not augmented by biological treatments, implying the comparative limitations of psychological treatments.

6.3.3 The role of culture in treatment

The role of culture in treatment is a vital element in the effective reaching of those with abnormal conditions worldwide.

Professional methods of treatment have tended towards the culture of Western-type industrial nations

The treatment of mental health by conventional means exemplified in this chapter is (like psychology in general) largely a product of Western experience, with its tendency to focus on abnormal conditions being caused by the biological functioning of the nervous system. WHO (2005) estimated that more than 90% of mental health resources are in high-income countries. More than 10% of the national health budget in the USA is spent on mental health, in contrast to typically less than 1% in the countries of Latin America, Africa, and S.E. Asia. The work of Mathers and Loncar (2006) forecasts that depression will take the greatest segment of the world disease burden by 2030 after HIV/AIDS. The lack of academic focus on non-Western perspectives and mental-health conditions indicates the likelihood that the Western economically-supported understanding of mental health is likely to be superimposed over time-honoured local tradition and understanding (Timini, 2010).

Against this, Kleinman (1977) proposed a new cross-cultural psychiatry that would avoid exporting Western-culture-bound psychiatric theories and treatments. It would accept that trans-cultural psychiatry should work in harmony with local social, cultural and moral concerns to be effective and beneficial. This may be supported by the claim that despite the high investment in treatment for abnormalities in mental health, there is no conclusive evidence that Western treatments have more successful outcomes than the traditional treatments available in non-Western societies (Alem et al., 2009; White, 2013).

Culture-bound barriers to diagnosis

Social norms and expectations can obscure considerable psychological distress. In the example of Japan, Hubert Tellenbach's proposal in the 1960s that depression was not an abnormal condition, but part of a serious-outlook, hard-working, and thoughtful personality type became highly influential in that society. As late as 2000, there was little market demand for anti-depressant drugs in Japan. Since then, there has been a change in national perception of this condition, and has been brought in line with Western-based psychiatry. That has been claimed to have been fuelled by anti-depressant drug companies seeking to create a market in Japan who at the same time have been sponsoring international consensus groups on cultural society (Ballenger et al., 2001). Such bodies claimed that the prevalence of depression was vastly under-estimated in Japan.

Psychological effects of globalisation on non-Western countries

Journalist Ethan Watters in *Crazy like us: The globalization of the American psyche* (2010) argues that abnormal conditions that include Western-generated concepts of depression, eating disorders, and other conditions like PTSD (post-traumatic stress disorders) have been exported around the globe, like other Western products ranging from movies to junk food. Based on his experiences in Sri Lanka, Japan, Tanzania, Peru, and other countries, he puts the case that West has, possibly inadvertently and with the aid of often well-intentioned, but culturally-Western health professionals actually caused specifically Western cultural abnormalities to spread to non-Western countries. Among his examples are the well-intentioned efforts of Western trauma-counsellors helping survivors of Sri Lanka's 2004 tsunami that actually adversely interfered with the local family and friends culture-grounded phases of grief, suffering, and healing. Those affected tended to express themselves in terms of somatic symptoms and family relationships. This led to the erroneous reporting of post-tsunami PTSD being much lower than expected. Another example (see above) is the marketing of anti-depressant drugs in Japan, whose culture-based concept of depression was very different from the West. In the process, he accuses the companies of marketing the condition with the highly profitable drugs.

RESERACH STUDY

Marian and Neisser (2000)

The basis of this study is that it is the client's recollection of past events that often reveals vital information for use at both treatment and diagnosis level. This study hypothesised that the language that the therapist uses can affect the level of detail in the client's memory recollection.

The study used a **purposive sample**, meaning that eligibility for participation is determined by possessing the characteristics of what is being researched. In this case, the participants – university students - were fluent in both English and Russian, all having migrated to the US in their teens.

6. PAPER 2 OPTION – ABNORMAL PSYCHOLOGY

The researchers read two lists of words to the participants (e.g. neighbours, getting lost, cat) which were used as prompts for telling stories about what happened in their childhood. One list was in English and the other was in Russian. After each list, they then told the first story that came to mind, and could respond in English or Russian.

The researchers found that incidents that had taken place in Russia were better recalled in Russian than in English, and those that had taken place in the US were better recalled in English than Russian. This indicated that the depth and range of information yielded by the client will be influenced by the language, and by extension, the culture in which the experience recalled took place.

Strengths and limitations: Marian and Neisser (2001)

Strengths	Limitations
1. Used a rigorously-determined purposive sample: bilingual, experience of two contrasting cultures, and change of culture at the beginning of teens. 2. Used controls to cover for recency effect: some of the participants were interviewed in Russian first, and then in English; others, in English first, then Russian.	1. Sample size: 20 only. 2. All were students. Both these factors create problems in generalising the findings to other populations.

RESEARCH STUDY

Dein and Sembhi (2001)

This study aimed to determine the degree that minority populations are likely to make use of culturally traditional methods for treating psychological abnormalities where Western facilities are available. They addressed the issues of the extent that those receiving Western psychiatric treatment are also likely to be treated by healers of their culture, and why they make that choice. They sought to elicit the patients' experience of healing.

The participants were 25 psychiatric patients (mean age 42, 9 male, 16 female) from the Indian subcontinent living in the London Borough of Waltham Forest. That district has a large population from that part of Asia. All were receiving psychiatric healthcare at local healthcare facilities. A practicing psychiatrist interviewed each participant, with an interpreter present.

The study found that 28% of the patients supplemented their Western psychiatric care with the treatment of a traditional healer, with a significantly greater tendency for older patients. Among the trends that the researchers found was the belief that religious practices were at least as important as psychiatric procedures in treating the condition. Traditional healing was considered as effective, but its practitioners were expensive and not always trustworthy. Not all patients claimed to understand how healing was intended to work.

Strengths and limitations: Dein and Sembhi (2001)

Strengths	Limitations
1. Use in depth interviews, making it possible to recapture the two types of treatment from the patient's standpoint. 2. Interpreters familiar with the patients' language were involved in the interviewing process.	1. The size of the sample and the population was of mixed origins (India, Pakistan, Bangladesh), religions (Hindu, Muslim), and levels of religious affiliation and practice. 2. All were currently in Western treatment for their conditions, limiting the transferability of the findings to those receiving culturally traditional treatment only without Western treatment.

6.4 Ethical Considerations

Ethical considerations in researching abnormal behaviours (see also in section 6.1.4 on ethics in diagnosis) are common to other areas of psychology, including:

- Informed consent: participants must know the object of the study, that their involvement is voluntary, what the data will be used for, and if necessary be debriefed at the end of the study. In extreme cases, the ethical requirement for informed consent may be waived, when the focus of the study is of public importance and there is no other way to obtain the sought-after information.
- Avoiding deception, except possibly where the research cannot be carried out in any other way).
- Protection from harm: particularly important when handling potentially sensitive material such as genetic information (e.g. Caspi et al.).
- Making the participants anonymous to protect them, even at the risk of reducing the authenticity of the research and of preventing any follow-up study.
- The right for any participant to withdraw from the study at any point, and communicating that right before the commencement of the study.
- All participants are to be debriefed at the end of the study.
- Bearing in mind that research involving associated cultural issues is extremely sensitive with many ethnic groups. Typically, the elders of the society must be consulted for permission to work with members of their group.

6.5 Key research studies

6.5.1 Research relevant to abnormal behaviour

For diagnosis of psychological disorders
- The work of Cooper et al. (1972) in investigating reliability in the diagnosis
- The ease of error in diagnosis: the research of Rosenhan (1973)
- Anchoring bias in diagnosis: Friedlander and Stockman (1983)
- Gender bias in diagnosis: Swami (1972)
- The work of Zhang et al. (1988) and Parker et al. (2001) on how cultural considerations may affect the diagnosis of abnormality.

For etiologies of psychological disorders:
- Biological etiologies: the role of genetics in causing psychological disorders: the work of Caspi et al. (2003) on depression based on linkage studies, and Weissman et al. (2005) on depression based on family studies.
- Beck's cognitive theory of depression (1976).
- Psychological: the influence of negative schemas on depression: Alloy et al. (1999), and Nolen-Hoeksema (2000).
- The work of Brown and Harris (1978) in investigating social causes of depression, and of Becker et al. (2002) on the social causes of bulimia nervosa
- The work of Becker et al. (1994) in investigating the role of social pressure creating at risk conditions for bulimia nervosa.

For implementing treatment:
- The study of Elkin et al. (1989) and Riggs et al. (2007) on the relative success of both biological and psychological means of treating major depression.
- The work of Kuyken et al. (2008) investigating the effectiveness of MBCT as an alternative to medication.
- Culture and treatment: the work of Dein and Sembhi (2001) on the use of culturally-based traditional treatments, and Marin and Neisser (2000) on the cultural significance of use of language in treatment.

6.5.2 The roles of biological, cognitive and sociocultural elements involved in field of abnormal behaviour

For biological influences, look at the following:
- The role of genetics in causing psychological disorders: the work of Caspi et al. (2003) on depression based on linkage studies, and Weissman et al. (2005) on depression based on family studies.
- The study of Elkin et al. (1989) and Riggs et al. (2007) on the relative success of both biological and psychological means of treating major depression.

For cognitive influences, look at the following:

- The ease of error in diagnosis: the research of Rosenhan (1973).
- Anchoring bias in diagnosis: Friedlander and Stockman (1983).
- Gender bias in diagnosis: Swami (1972).
- Beck's cognitive theory of depression (1976).
- Psychological: the influence of negative schemas on depression: Alloy et al. (1999), and Nolen-Hoeksema (2000).
- The study of Elkin et al. (1989) and Riggs et al. (2007) on the relative success of both biological and psychological means of treating major depression.
- The work of Kuyken et al. (2008) investigating the effectiveness of MBCT as an alternative to medication.

For sociocultural influences, look at the following:

- Sociocultural criteria used in defining and diagnosing abnormality: the example of CCMD-3.
- The issue of cultural variation in the diagnostic process: Parker et al. (2001).
- The work of Brown and Harris (1978) in investigating social causes of depression, and of Becker et al. (2002) on the social causes of bulimia nervosa.
- The work of Becker et al. (1994) in investigating the role of social pressure creating at risk conditions for bulimia nervosa.
- Culture and treatment: the work of Dein and Sembhi (2001) on the use of culturally-based traditional treatments, and Marin and Neisser (2000) on the cultural significance of use of language in treatment.

PRACTICE QUESTIONS

Essay Response Practice Questions: Abnormal Psychology

1. Discuss the role of one or more clinical biases in diagnosis.
2. Discuss a cognitive approach to explaining the etiology of one disorder.
3. Discuss the effectiveness of one treatment of one disorder.

Chapter 7: Paper 2 Option – Human Relationships

Overview

The psychology of human relationships in this program looks at three areas: formation of human relationships, group dynamics, and social responsibility.

The biological perspective emphasises the work of evolution, genes, neurotransmitters, and hormones. Cognitive theorists apply schema theory, focusing on how we 'read' and interpret the behaviour of others. Sociocultural psychologists concentrate on social cognitive theory, attribution theory, social identity theory, and the influence of culture on the individual and the group. These perspectives, which do not necessarily exclude one another, may be directed at the issues discussed in the main body of this chapter.

KEY CONCEPT

The goal of studying the psychology of human relationships is to understand and enhance the ways in which individuals interact with one another in various contexts and levels of intensity that may or not be mutual.

Remember that you are applying the biological, cognitive, and sociocultural perspectives to specific issues within topics under the heading of human relationships. Pay special attention to the methodologies and ethical issues in each research study.

Learning objectives of this unit include:

- The formation and ending of personal relationships.
- The role of communication in personal relationships
- The dynamics of group behaviour: cooperation, competition, conflict, and conflict resolution
- The nature and the promotion of pro-social behaviour.
- Approaches to research and ethical considerations in understanding human relationships.

7.1 Personal Relationships

Relationships are a major source of fulfilment and happiness, and lack of relationships can be a major source of feelings of emptiness and discontent. Relationships exist in many forms: family, work, friends, shared interests, and romantic relationships. The lack of social relationships has been associated with ill-health; among the elderly at a similar level to smoking, obesity, and lack of physical activity (Lou et al, 2012), and more generally with poorer antibody production and antiviral responses (Cole, 2007). The focus of this chapter is on the formation of one type of relationship only: romantic, and between the opposite sex.

7.1.1 Formation of Personal Relationships

Biological origins of attraction and love have been explained by a variety of theories. Among them are the workings of the neurobiologically-based motivation system on selecting a partner, and the influence of genes on selecting a partner.

1. **The neurologically-based motivation system on selecting a partner**

Fisher et al. (2005) in Chapter 1 (Section 1.2) is recommended as a research study on the neurologically-based motivation system on selecting a partner.

These create a deep craving to cause lovers to mate and reproduce, as an evolutionary force to promote long-term survival. Romantic love has the biological correlates of higher levels of adrenaline, adjustment of serotonin levels (which speeds up the nervous system), secretions of oxytocin (a powerful hormone released by both men and women during touching and in sex, which deepens and intensifies feelings of attachment), and vasopressin (released during sex, which promotes long-term commitment). The palms tend to sweat and the mouth tends to feel dry in the presence of that special someone.

2. **The influence of genes on selecting a partner**

Natural selection tends to favour those with the greatest capacity to adapt to adverse conditions, which would enhance any offspring's likelihood of survival in adverse conditions. Capacities to overcome adversities may include positive physical, social, and financial characteristics. Underlying our mate selection is evolutionary pressure: the fundamental desire to produce the healthiest and most-likely-to-survive-and-flourish offspring as possible, and give the best long-term scope and highest chances of survival for our genetic input.

RESEARCH STUDY

Wedekind (1995)

This study can also be used to explore the possible influence of pheromones on behaviour, linking with Chapter 1, section 1.4.

This research study aimed to investigate the role of **genetic compatibility** in **major histocompatibility complex** (**MHC**) in guiding individuals in partner preferences. MHC, a group of genes related to one's immune system, involves cell-surface proteins enabling it to recognise and protect the body from invading viruses, bacteria, and cancerous cells. MHC genes are co-dominant, meaning that both sets of inherited genes have an effect on the child's immune system. That means that the more diverse the MHC genes of the parents, the stronger the immune systems of the children. Both sexes have evolved to ensure their own survival by applying their genes to the creation of the healthiest possible children.

The hypothesis was that females would identify and choose males whose immune system was most likely, in combination with their own, to complement and boost the immune systems and chances of survival of potential offspring.

7. PAPER 2 OPTION – HUMAN RELATIONSHIPS

The study has become known as the "dirty shirt experiment". The participants were 49 women and 44 men with a wide range of MHC genes. The men had to avoid aftershave with odor and eat non-spicy food for two days, and wear the new t-shirt supplied for two nights in row, keeping it in a plastic bag when not in use. The women had to smell the t-shirts after they were returned, used, but unwashed. Three of the boxes of t-shirts were from MHC-dissimilar, three were from MHC-similar t-shirts, and one contained an unworn t-shirt as a control. The women were asked to rate the odors of each of the t-shirts as pleasant or unpleasant. Overall, the results showed that women preferred the scent of men with dissimilar genes, though those on oral contraceptives preferred those with similar genes.

The study concluded that attraction was influenced by the presence or absence of genetic factors that would maximise the resistance to disease in possible offspring.

With the 'dirty shirt' experiment, Wedekind demonstrated that women preferred the scent of men with dissimilar genes, though those on oral contraceptives preferred those with similar genes. It might be argued that those shirts released pheromones that influence sexual attraction.

However, no specific substances functioning as human pheromones were found in this study.

Strengths and limitations: Wedekind (1995)

Strengths	Limitations
1. It was experimental and repeated measures in design, in that the same participants evaluated their reactions to the test (worn) condition in the control (unworn) condition.	1. The relatively small size of the sample, with reporting from 49 female participants only
2. It was controlled for odors from other, non-MHC sources.	2. No specific substances functioning as human pheromones were indicated in this study.

Cognitive origins of attraction and love have been explained by a variety of theories. Among them are the similarity-attraction model, and self-esteem in relationship-forming.

A. **The similarity-attraction model puts forward the view that individuals are attracted to those they perceive that they have things in common: personality, culture, religious beliefs, intelligence, and outlook.**

 RESEARCH STUDY

Markey and Markey (2007)

The study assessed the extent that similarity was a factor as a basis of choosing partners. The participants were self-selected university students. The research team used questionnaires where the participants reported on:

1. The characteristics and attitudes of their ideal romantic partner without thinking of anyone in particular
2. Their own characteristics and attitudes: they were asked to describe themselves

In a follow-up, similar questions were asked to 106 couples who had been together for more than a year. They were recruited through the local press and university campus.

Both studies confirmed that people want partners similar to themselves. The study is supported for the relatively large sample (including 106 couples), and the detailed information yielded by each questionnaire. It may, however, be criticised because in reality it may not be just that *similarity promotes attraction*, but that *attraction promotes similarity*. The study of **Davis and Rusbult (2001)** demonstrated that attraction can also foster similarity: as one idealises the partner's behaviour, he/she adjusts to its flow. Indeed, the above research of Markey and Markey (2007) raised the issue of **reciprocity**: people often view their own partners more positively than they view themselves. And in idealising their behaviour, they tend to find themselves influenced by them. In addition as the study was based on self-reporting, it may have been influenced by demand characteristics.

B. **The presence of self-esteem in relationship forming puts forward the view that people's capacity to attract a quality partner is a function of their level of self-confidence, high self-esteem powering higher quality choices of partner.**

RESEARCH STUDY

Kieser and Baral (1970)

Kieser and Baral evaluated the importance of self-esteem in relationship formation and aimed to test the hypothesis that high self-esteem results in proactivity and success in making the moves to attract a quality partner. They investigated their hypothesis by giving a fake IQ test to a group of heterosexual men. The scores they gave them were entirely untrue. One group (individual by individual, in privacy) was told that they scored "off the charts", the highest scores ever seen on the IQ test. The second group was told (individual by individual, in privacy) that there must have been something wrong, because their scores were so low, and that they should arrange to redo the test in the near future. After the scores were given, the individual men sat in the waiting room to be paid for taking part in the study. During that time, a classically-attractive female walked into the room. The experimenters found that the men who had received the self-esteem boost of high scores readily engaged in conversation with her, in contrast with the low scorers who tended not to.

This study had the strength of having a relatively high ecological validity: each participant believed that he had gone through a real-life situation and had been given a real-life judgment about his intelligence. The study was also used a confidence-demanding situation, approaching an attractive woman who ostensibly was not connected with the program. Its limitations include that the simulated feelings of achievement or failure were temporary moods rather than fundamental personality changes: the capacity to open a conversation is only the first step towards the possibility of it going much further. In addition, individual men may have approached the woman for reasons other than high self-confidence after hearing the results of the test.

Socio-cultural origins of attraction and love have been explained by a variety of theories. Among them are physical proximity and cultural factors

7. PAPER 2 OPTION – HUMAN RELATIONSHIPS

C. **Physical proximity:** the theory holds that the more often you see someone, the greater the probability of becoming attracted: becoming friends and more.

RESEARCH STUDY

Festinger et al. (1950)

The aim of this study was to investigate friendship patterns in a housing development for students. The researchers observed the friendship patterns that were developing among the students, and interviewed them regularly.

The results showed that students were more than ten times as likely to form friendships with a given person in the same building (whom they saw on a daily basis) that in other buildings, and even more likely with students in rooms next door.

The researchers concluded that proximity increases familiarity, and thus the chance for relationship-forming.

Strengths and limitations: Festinger et al. (1950)

Strengths	Limitations
1. It supports the view that more exposure to the other can the feeling of trust that facilitates relationship-forming. 2. It is supported by later research, such as Jorgensen and Cervone (1978), whose work indicated that people rated the photographs of strangers more highly the more often they saw them.	1. It may have overemphasised the social, rather than underlying biological and cognitive elements (above) in choice of a friend/partner. 2. It was dependent on the validity of the reports given by the observers, and the replies in the interviews which could have been influenced by demand characteristics.

D. **Cultural factors:** even though evolutionary theory indicates the importance of biological factors, research indicates that they are moderated by cultural factors in some instances, for example chastity.

RESEARCH STUDY

Buss et al. (1989)

The aim of this study was to investigate how far evolutionary explanations in human mate preferences are based on cultural factors: different cultures, locations and religions.

The research team obtained data from some 10,000 participants from 33 countries using a multi-lingual comprehensive questionnaire designed to identify the characteristics most desired for an exclusive relationship with the person of the opposite sex.

Both genders in nearly all cultures (not just Western) rated mutual attraction and love as the most important in forming a relationship. The male respondents reported factors that were biologically determined and would tend to optimise reproduction, with culture placing limits on availability. Irrespective of upbringing and way of life, men prized youth and physical attraction, virginity tending to be a limiting factor in the more traditional societies only, such as Iran, India, and China. Associating pleasing appearance with health, the findings supported the theory that cross-culturally men compete for the women that will most enhance their genetic material, and that are physically in the best position to bring up children. Characteristics reported as being most valued by females were also biological: they wanted the male partner that was physically and by extension economically able, supporting the theory that females desire the opposite-gender partner that can provide the desired optimum levels of security and support.

Overall, the study showed far more similarities than differences in the conception of the ideal partner between different cultures. It indicated that with the exception of virginity of females, differences in culture, religion, and locations were of limited importance compared to biological factors in selecting a mate.

Strengths and limitations: Buss et al. (1989)

Strengths	Limitations
1. It was cross-cultural, sought to be linguistically sensitive, and it used a large sample. 2. It emphasises the important of economic success as a human evolutionary strategy, particularly in males.	1. Relied on self-reporting, with possibilities of translation inaccuracies 2. Possibility of respondents finding themselves influenced by perceived demand characteristics of the researchers. 3. The mean age in the study was mid-20s: it is possible that different results might have been obtained a similar group of old participants.

7.1.2 The Role of Communication

Communication involves how information is sent and how information is received. They are not always identical. Sometimes that can strengthen the relationship, and sometimes it can threaten it.

Strategies

The work of **Canary and Stafford (1994)** identified five communicative strategies that keep a relationship alive:

1. Spontaneity: doing things to make your partner feel good (unpredictability keeps a fun edge to the relationship).
2. Self-disclosure: sharing intimate things about oneself.
3. Assurance and empathy: make the partner feel that his/her feelings are respected.
4. Social networking together: doing things together with friends and family.
5. Sharing tasks together (the dishes: he washes, she dries).

Collins and Miller (1994) found that people who share personal information are more liked than those who are more secretive. They also found that people disclose more intimate information to those they like. And giving one's partner the feeling of being liked is in itself a positive force in maintaining a relationship.

Two additional vital elements in communication are **attributional styles** and **elements that can harm communication.**

7. PAPER 2 OPTION – HUMAN RELATIONSHIPS

A. Attributional styles

Interpretation of one's partner's communication is a window to the current character of the relationship.

Where the relationship is positive, partners tend to attribute the other's role with a positive bias. When something went well, it was thanks to the partner: prompting a positive **dispositional** style in communication. Where something went badly, it was because of the realities of the situation and not because of the partner: indicating a **situational** interpretation of the situation. The bias in communication is in favour of the partner: a **relationship-enhancing pattern**.

Where the relationship is negative, partners tend to attribute the other's role with a negative bias. When something went well, it was despite the partner: prompting a **situational** interpretation of the situation. Where something went badly, it was because of the partner and not the realities of the situation: indicating a negative **dispositional** style of communication. The bias in communication is against the partner: a **distress-maintaining pattern**.

Bradbury and Fincham (1992) found that where wives communicated blame to the husband (made dispositional judgments) in negative situations within a distress maintaining pattern, they were also more likely to behave negatively towards the husband in general as in the research below.

RESEARCH STUDY

Bradbury and Fincham (1992)

This observational study aimed to examine whether spouses' attributions for events in their marriage are related to their patterns of communications. The participants formed a volunteer sample, recruited by the local media. 47 married couples took part. The sample was both a volunteer sample and a purposive sample, as couples had to be married and never been to marriage counselling in order to be eligible to participate.

Each participant completed a questionnaire design to determine the level of marital satisfaction. They also completed a questionnaire to determine the greatest problem in the marriage. The researchers then picked a common problem from the questionnaires for each couple.

At the individual interview stage, they were separately about what caused the problem and who was responsible. They were also asked about problems that that appeared in their response but not in that of spouse.

At the couple interview stage, they were asked to discuss a possible solution to the problem they had both identified.

All interviews were videotaped and then coded by two independent researchers for identifying relationship-enhancing and distress-maintaining patterns of communication and attribution styles.

The study indicated that wives who made distress-maintaining attributions were more likely than those who made relationship-enhancing attributions to behave negatively in response to negative behaviour from their husbands. This held irrespective of whether marital satisfaction was low or high.

> Bradbury and Fincham (1992) may be used for theory and for research study in both the role of communication and explanations of why relationships change or end.

Strengths and limitations: Bradbury and Fincham (1992)

Strengths	Limitations
1. The researchers used a detailed questionnaire to obtain an accurate picture of the level of marital satisfaction with each couple, so that it would not interfere with the analysis of communication patterns 2. The study video-recorded the interviews that enabled the coding of the data by two independent researchers who did not conduct the interview, reducing the possibility of researcher bias, and increasing the reliability of the data.	1. The study did not take into account the possibilities of metal health issues such as depression that may have been more significant to marital satisfaction than the role of communication. 2. The sample relied on observers whose interpretations could have been subjective. 3. The participants were all from a Western cultural background, raising issues of generalising the findings to other cultures.

B. Elements that can harm communication: The Four Horsemen of the Apocalypse

John Gottman's *Why Marriages Succeed or Fail* on marital stability is based on his working with some 2,000 couples over the previous decades, a series of peer-reviewed published papers based on his scientific direct observation in his practice, and the patterns that he has observed in that clinical experience.

RESEARCH STUDY

> Gottman (1994) may be used for theory and as research study in both the role of communication and explanations of why relationships change or end.

On the basis of his research, Gottman identified four destructive patterns that would sink a relationship in his 1994 book *Why Marriages Succeed or Fail*. Whilst anger and conflict can by themselves sometimes actually open communication, they can both block communication and cause the relationship to change or end if they are accompanied by the following: criticism, contempt, defensiveness, and stonewalling.

- **Criticism**: where the partner's complaint is overgeneralised and attacks the other's character. For example, a true complaint "You forgot to take out the garbage" is replaced with criticism and character assassination: "You are always lazy! Why do you always give me the work to do? You're dishonest! You don't care about me at all! You're worthless!" This can lead to:

- **Contempt**: where the partner's words and body language are highly destructive, consistently and persistently directed at causing unhappiness to the partner. It typically includes behaviours that as a matter of course include deliberately looking away, insults, sneering, unpleasant nicknaming, and teasing designed to hurt the other. This in turn can lead to:

- **Defensiveness**: where the other perceives him/herself as the victim, and shields themself in anticipation of the next attack. The flood of emotions released by defensiveness makes it difficult for the other to tune in to what is being said, frequently causing the conflict to escalate rapidly and get out of control. For example "You spill things and never clean up" is met with: "So what? At least I'm nice to your parents when they come to visit." Defensiveness can give way to:

- **Stonewalling**: remaining silent, not responding, deliberately changing the subject, or leaving the room in order to avoid suffering yet more conflict. It is a shut-down type of response to relentless criticism, contempt, and the defensive nature of previous responses.

Strength and Limitations: Gottman (1994)

Strengths	Limitations
1. His model of the four elements that cause communication to deteriorate and ultimately destroy relationships are based on his experience of working with some 2,000 relationships in a career spanning several decades, as well his peer-reviewed papers showing patterns highlighting those four elements. 2. Recognises that suitable therapy can address the "Four Horsemen" with the potential of improving communication and preventing the change for the worse and breakup of a relationship. These include telling your partner how you feel rather than firing insults, drawing attention to the annoying action rather than using it for a character assassination, being open to apologising, and validating the partner's feelings "I know how you feel..." even if you do not agree. Strive for an ideal of five positive interactions for every negative one. 3. Gottman has continued in practice counselling couples and has claimed a 90% accuracy rate for predicting divorces to a great extent based on the model above.	1. Reductionist approach: using the four elements as explanations and foundations of improving communication and stability marriage may overlook fundamental and irreconcilable cultural and mental stability issues that can undermine communication and stability within a relationship. 2. Gottman's research is largely based on the Western experience, raising the question of to what extent its claims can be generalised.

7.1.3 Explanations for why relationships change or end

The work of **Levinger (1980)** indicates that relationships tend to go through five stages, ABCDE:

- Attraction
- Building (dating, making the relationship steady)
- Continuation (with the possibility of things being left to become routine)
- Deterioration (couple tend to drift apart finding interests outside their relationship)
- Ending (breakup of relationship or divorce), likely to take place where:
    - Problems seem insoluble, with a divorce/break-up as the only means of escape to a new life. This could include situational issues such as completely different working hours, and prolonged pressure of work.
    - Little faith that the marriage will endure, and lack of commitment to make it succeed.
    - Other more 'desirable' partners are readily available.

The work of **Canary and Dainton (2003)** goes even further when suggesting that relationships by nature have a natural tendency to end. Problems tend to accelerate the process of leaving a relationship and changing partners.

In addition, studies show that the breakdown of relationships will occur where there are:

Negative patterns of accommodation	The process of responding to a partner's negative behaviour can cause the nature of the relationship to be changed (Rusbult et al. 1991). Positive accommodation includes discussing problems openly, waiting for the situation to improve naturally, and forgiving each other. Negative accommodation includes physical avoidance, silent treatment, and recounting previous failures.
Relationship without equity	The equity theory of love predicts that people are happiest where benefits and costs are balanced, so that both partners contribute and receive more or less the same. In a study of 2,000 couples, Hatfield (1979) found that those who felt they were not getting a fair, equitable deal in the relationship were the most likely to cheat on the relationship.
Fatal attraction (Felmlee, 1995)	Where the same trait that attracted leads to the breakup of the relationship – e.g. the 'good-girl / bad-boy' – the excitement of being with a 'bad-boy' with motor-biking adventures gives way to the unpleasantness of dealing with his irresponsibility and abuse. Also, a partner who travels a lot may bring the initial attraction of fascinating conversation, but the relationship may dissolve when facing the reality of the other never being at home.

Other factors highlighted by **Duck (1982, 1998)** include pre-existing compatibilities not apparent or ignored in the early building stage, a sudden trauma such as discovering previously unknown negative information about one's partner, and subsequent maturing in different directions creating harder-to-bridge differences.

In spite of best intentions, relationships do not always survive the many changes they experience over time, as explored in **Duck's relationship dissolution model (1982).** This was based on his research: a meta study of previous research on breakdown in relationships, including longitudinal studies. On the basis of its findings, Duck proposed that a relationship goes through the following four stages between failure and final termination:

1. **Inter-psychic stage:** sense of disappointment and unhappiness in the relationship, possibly with seemingly better prospects outside it.
2. **Dyadic stage:** confronts partner with view to break up (which could alternatively lead to reconciliation), communicating the wish to bring relationship to a close as being the best thing to do.
3. **Social phase:** presenting a socially-acceptable version of the forthcoming break-up to family and friends.
4. **Grave-dressing phase:** each person presenting their own version of the story of the breakdown, typically blaming the other, and aiming to move further on in life.

7. PAPER 2 OPTION – HUMAN RELATIONSHIPS

Strengths and limitations: Duck's relationship dissolution model (1982)

Strengths	Limitations
1. It is based on the consensus of previously-conducted research studies on why relationships change or end. 2. The model provides a workable framework for understanding the breakup of relationships with widely differing histories and circumstances. 3. It accommodates repair and reconciliation.	1. It is limited by giving insufficient attention to gender differences, such as men becoming dissatisfied when the relationship yields less fun, and women when it bears less support (Argyle, 1988). 2. It does not extend to cultures where social stigmas form a significant barrier to breakup. 3. It does not allow for a sudden traumatic event (such as infidelity) that results in the estranged partner to instantly and permanently exit.

In addition, *relationships can change or end when there are serious communication issues*.

The following studies earlier in this chapter may be used for theory and for research study in both the role of communication and explanations of why relationships change or end:

- Bradbury and Fincham (1992);
- Gottman (1994).

7.2 Group Dynamics

Chapter 3 looks at thinking and behaviours towards people outside one's group. A group is where two or more, maybe many more people, interact with each other and see themselves as a distinct social unit. Groups form in settings such as schools, workplaces, sports, and religious affiliations.

Groups tend to establish norms that influence which behaviours are approved and encouraged within the group, and which behaviours are disapproved, ridiculed, and result in exclusion from the group. Psychology also recognises that group norms often contribute to their members' individual thought processes, value systems, and behaviours.

This area of study takes things further and looks at thinking and behaviours towards people both within one's group (intragroup dynamics) and outside one's group (intergroup dynamics). Its purpose is to understand the positive and negative outcomes that happen as people interact, and to enable those contacts to be as pro-active as possible.

This topic considers group dynamics in terms of cooperation, competition, prejudice, discrimination, and conflict with the psychological factors that have bearing on them, whose origins may be biological, cognitive, or socio-cultural. It then applies psychological theory and research towards considering means of resolving conflicts.

7.2.1 Co-operation and Competition

Among the factors that influence whether behaviours within groups and between groups are likely to be co-operative or competitive are:

(a) The degree that members of each group see their **goals as being shared**: the greater this is the case, the more the potential for co-operation. This is likely, for example, in a team with a strong sense of team cohesion.

(b) The **behaviours of other people in the group: informational social influence**. When members see others co-operating and that co-operation is the norm, they are likely to behave in the same way. The reverse is likely to promote competition.

(c) Whether or not **super-ordinate goals** are present: people and nations coming together to best respond to a common challenge, such as with the Covid-19 virus of 2020.

RESEARCH STUDY

Deutsch (1949)

Deutsch (1949) described attitudes and behaviours within groups (for example, in the workplace) as being on the spectrum between **co-operative** and **competitive**, as below.

Co-operative approach	Competitive approach
Characterised by effective listening throughout the group, focusing on what each member can bring to the issues being handled.	Characterised by inflexible thinking and management, lack of trust, mutual suspicions, and a feeling that the success of one member is at the expense of another.
Maximised where group goals are clearly communicated, common objectives are shared, roles within the group are clearly defined, and members of the group support one another in their roles.	Maximised where there is poor communication, suspicion of the motives of others, and seeing an increase in the other's success as a threat.

Deutsch argues that both cooperation and competition are self-perpetuating: more cooperation promoting more trust between individual members of a team, and more competition promoting poorer communication and increased mutual suspicion.

Team cohesion encourages the necessary cooperation to achieve the team goal, for example in sports when the team's overall objective is to win. It involves cohesion in both working as a team and also socially. Problems with team cohesion are evident, for example in soccer, Player A will avoid taking the easy move of passing the ball to B, and opt for the much riskier option of passing it to C. His hostility towards B (either sportingly or personally) could mean that through him, the team lowers its chance of scoring that winning goal. Or perhaps A takes a long shot for goal, instead of passing to B or C. His ego wants the goal to be in his name. To serve the team, he is much better off simply kicking the ball to one of the other players positioned closer to the goalmouth. Following Deutsch, the degree of team cohesion is likely to depend on whether the athletes have developed a history of working well together in previous team events, the degree that the team members' interaction with the coach is mutually beneficial, and the degree of sensitivity of both the coach and team members to the internal dynamics of the team.

Though Deutsch's early research was laboratory based, it is supported by studies such as Aaronson et al. (1978) that indicated that promoting competition within the school classroom produces poorer results than promoting interpersonal working together. Deutsch's framework also has wide applications where people combine: in the workplace, in schools, and in sporting and cultural organisations.

7. PAPER 2 OPTION – HUMAN RELATIONSHIPS

RESEARCH STUDY

Kerr (1983)

This is an experimental study, which aimed to investigate the possible role of **informational social influence** on the degree of willingness to co-operate. Informational social influence is taking cues for behaviour by observing others in the group.

The participants were 75 university undergraduates, who were given the same task: pumping air using a rubber bulb for set period of time. The amount of air pumped was measured by a spirometer.

Each participant was assigned to one of four conditions, this research being independent measures in design. They were, doing the task: without anyone else (the control condition); with a capable partner who was working hard; with a capable partner who was not working hard; and alone but with a person who was doing the same activity without much effort. The dependent variable was the amount of air pumped.

The results showed that those who worked the hardest in pumping air were those who worked alone. Those who worked with a capable hard-working partner pumped less (thus co-operated less) as they tended to rely on the partner to do the work (the free-riding effect). Those who worked with the capable lazier partner also pumped less. Their behaviour indicated a lower-producing norm, and a feeling that it was not necessary to work hard if the other was not working hard (the sucker effect). Those working individually, but with someone working individually at the same task at the same time produced similar results to the control individuals that worked alone.

The findings of this study thus indicate that deciding on how far to co-operate within a group situation depends on the behaviours of other group members that are in close proximity.

Strength and Limitations: Kerr (1983)

Strengths	Limitations
1. True experimental design, testing for a series of different informational social influences in deciding how far to co-operate.	1. Laboratory setting: low ecological validity, as the task of pumping air from a rubber bulb with or without a partner was highly artificial.
2. Supports the view that people's decisions on how far to cooperate are influenced by proximate informational social influences.	2. Participants were all university undergraduates, raising the question of how far the study's findings may be generalised to other populations.

RESEARCH STUDY

Sherif et al. (1956)

The purpose of this study was to assess whether co-operation is likely to be promoted where previously conflicting groups find themselves facing super-ordinate goals.

Active dislike of "the other group" has been shown to thrive where there is competition for scarce resources – demonstrated by the 'Robber's Cave' experiment conducted by Sherif et al. He wanted to understand the dynamics of social identity, group conflict, prejudice, and discrimination. He selected a group of 22 white 11 year-old boys who were unknown to each other. They were taken to a remote summer camp in Robber's Cave State Park

This study may also be used for origins of conflict and conflict resolution. It may also be used for prejudice and discrimination.

161

in Oklahoma, USA, randomly put in to two groups, neither knowing of the existence of the other. The first week was dedicated to team-building activities, hiking and swimming together. Each group chose a name for itself: Eagles and Rattlers, with those names on their shirts and flags.

Then they were introduced to each other through a series of competitions, with prizes for the winners and nothing for the losers. Tensions rose between them, demonstrating their prejudices and showing discriminatory behaviour: derogatory songs on the other, burning each other's flag, and refusing to eat together with the other group.

Following was the integration phase. The two groups watched movies together. The hope was that these face-to-face encounters would reduce tensions. But meetings broke up with the two groups throwing food at each other.

Finally, the researchers arranged situations in which a problem arose which threatened both groups at the same time. It included a blockage of the supply of drinking water to the camp. The two groups managed to work together to remove it, and celebrated when they succeeded. By the time these trials were over, they stopped having negative images of the other side. On the final bus-ride home, the members of one team used their prize money to buy drinks for everyone.

The conclusions of Sherif et al. were: (a) that competition over scarce resources is a vital element in the active dislike of another group, and (b) super-ordinate goals promote cooperation between formerly conflicting groups. Combining together to defeat the common threat creates a bond between two different competing groups and, in turn, wipes out the negative stereotypes one group has of the other.

Sherif et al. had the strength of taking place in a natural environment, with real-life situations exemplified by the cooperation-requiring water supply and bus scenarios. It showed how competition may give way to cooperation when both groups together face super-ordinate goals: such goals may be set to encourage prosocial behaviour as exemplified in this study. It may be criticised as the researchers may have subtly communicated their behaviour expectations to the young participants, and the ethical issues of possible inducement of hostile thinking and behaviour and lack of chance to withdraw once the program was in progress.

7.2.2 Prejudice and Discrimination

Prejudice is an unjustifiably negative attitude towards members of an out-group. **Discrimination** is an unjustifiably negative behaviour towards members of an out-group, such as refusing the other person a job or a service on the grounds of group membership (e.g. age, gender, religion, or political group), rather than on the grounds of individual merit. **Stereotyping** occurs where an individual belonging to a group is thought to have the characteristics commonly attributed to members of that group.

Among explanations for prejudice and discrimination are:

▶ **Availability heuristic (Section 2.6)**: the research of Tversky and Kahneman indicates that thinking and decision-making (which can be behind prejudice and discrimination) is often based on the information that is most easily accessible.

▶ **Confirmation bias (Section 2.6)**: research such as Lord et al. indicates that we tend to focus more on information that confirms and less on information that rejects our currently held opinion. Thus confirmation bias is used to explain a tendency to filter information that confirms stereotypes, which can in turn influence prejudicial attitudes and discriminatory behaviour.

- **Social identity theory (Section 3.2):** where the research of Tajfel indicates that discriminatory behaviour is likely to take place where the other is a member of the out-group.

- **Competition with out-groups for scarce resources:** as observed, for example, the discriminatory behaviour shown by the 11-year-old participants in Sherif et al. (Section 7.2.1).

- **The theory of threatened egotism:** the research of Fein and Spencer (1997) indicates that those with lower self-esteem are more likely to stereotype and have prejudicial attitudes towards members of out-groups than those with a higher self-esteem. This could also explain findings in studies such as Rogers and Frantz (1962, below), where longer-established immigrants may support discriminatory practices against the out-group, as they come to increasingly identify with the in-group community.

- **The integrated threat theory:** (**Stephan et al. 1998**) holds that prejudice occurs due to the perception of three types of threats:

    (i) **negative stereotyping** which in turn creates negative expectations for people belonging to that group,

    (ii) **realistic threats**, such as competition for jobs

    (iii) **symbolic threats**, such as having to face culturally-based behaviours that do not fit in with the values of the host society.

    The research of Novotny and Polansky (below) indicates that an in-group can show prejudice and discrimination towards an out-group that it perceives as a possible threat.

- **Evolutionary based theory (Sections 1.2, and 1.6):** negative reactions to out-groups could have evolved in order to protect the gene pool of the community.

> Harris and Fiske (1992) (Section 1.2) may be used as biological evidence of evolved mechanisms in brain that support prejudice and discrimination against an out-group.

RESEARCH STUDY

Novotny and Polansky (2011)

This was a self-reporting, questionnaire-based study designed to investigate the degree that the level of fear of out-group Moslem immigration into the Czech Republic and Slovakia might result in in-group prejudice towards them: the integrated threat theory. Both countries had relatively little experience of Moslems compared to other countries in Europe.

The participants were 716 undergraduates at Czech and Slovak universities. All responded to a questionnaire designed to measure the participant's (i) personal characteristics (ii) knowledge about Islam (iii) personal views of Islam and those who practiced it, and (iv) geographic knowledge of the Islamic world.

The findings indicated that less than a quarter of the participants had ever met a Moslem, and only one in ten had a Moslem friend. Overall, those who had more experience of Islam and Moslem communities though contact and travel felt less threatened by Moslems in their own country.

Strength and Limitations: Novotny and Polansky (2011)

Strengths	Limitations
1. Large sample size drawn from students of different departments in universities of the Czech Republic and Slovakia.	1. The findings were based on participant self-reporting, with the possibility of bias through demand characteristics.
2. Considered a wide range of indices that would measure levels of prejudice towards an out-group population, such as levels of impulsiveness, fanaticism, and respect to women.	2. The attitudes and behaviour that the participants claimed that they might show were based on the respondents' thoughts at the time rather than real-life encounter with members of Moslem communities.
3. It supports intergroup contact theory, and contact hypothesis (Section 7.2.3) whereby conflicts may be reduced, resolved, and avoided, where groups encounter and work together in a co-operative framework.	3. Participants were all university undergraduates, who were more likely to have travelled widely, raising the question of how far the study's findings may be generalised to other populations.

The theory of threatened egotism takes the view that people are more likely to show intergroup prejudice and discrimination when they feel that their own self-perception is being threatened.

RESEARCH STUDY

Rogers and Frantz (1962)

The aim of this cognitive-type research study was to investigate the prevalence of discriminatory attitudes of Europeans in Rhodesia (today, Zimbabwe) towards the country's African population, which was then under laws promoting racial segregation.

500 adult Europeans participated by responding to a questionnaire on their opinion of the many aspects of the racial segregation currently in practice, including separated public spaces and forbidden cross-racial sexual relations. They responded to each question on a semantic scale, whose spectrum ranged from strong support to keep the system to strong support to change the system.

The results indicated that the Europeans in Rhodesia who were most disposed to change were those living there for less than five years, with those there for more than five years significantly preferring the segregation and discrimination then in force. This could be because those there for longer felt threatened egotism, preferring to identify with their own group than the African population.

The study had the strengths of using a large sample, and a design that distinguished relatively new arrivals from the longer-established European population. Its limitations include demand characteristics in responding to the questionnaire, at a time when views today regarded as racist were more fashionable. Furthermore, the claimed relationship between number of years of residence and support of discriminatory practices was correlational: it might have been a product of series of events that the newcomers had not experienced.

7. PAPER 2 OPTION – HUMAN RELATIONSHIPS

 RESEARCH STUDY

Croucher et al. 2013

This **cognitive-based** research applied **Stephan's integrated threat theory** to examining the degree of prejudice towards the growing Moslem populations in the UK, France, and Germany. There were 432 non-Moslem participants from the three countries, who responded to a questionnaire designed to measure the respondent's degree of contact with the Moslem population, and the perception of realistic threats, symbolic threats, and stereotyped understanding towards the Moslem population.

The results indicated the following statistically significant trends. Firstly, the greater perception of realistic and symbolic threats, the more they expressed the stereotype that the Moslem population did not wish to integrate. Secondly, the higher level of nationalism in the host countries, the greater the perceived level of threat from the Moslem population. Thus Moslem immigrants were considered to be a greater threat in the UK and France, countries suffering relatively high unemployment and anti-Moslem rhetoric at the time, than Germany which was experiencing much less of both.

The research thus supports Stephan's cognitively-based integrated threat theory, whereby negative stereotyping is fuelled by realistic threats and symbolic threats.

Strengths and limitations of Croucher

Strengths	Limitations
1. Large sample from across the social spectrum in two countries then experiencing social and economic tension, and one that was experiencing considerably less of both. 2. The questions were controlled for the potential confounding variable of degree of contact with the Moslem population.	1. The results were correlational: findings on realistic and symbolic threats could have been rooted in pre-existing stereotyping that had developed for different reasons. 2. The study was based on self-reporting, with possible demand characteristics.

7.2.3 Origins of Conflict and Conflict Resolution

Conflicts are disputes behind which are incompatible viewpoints, such as mutually opposed goals, or scarce resources, which can be at the interpersonal, intergroup, and international levels.

Among the *reasons conflicts occur* are:

(a) Where **groups have opposing goals** and/or are **competing for scarce resources**, known as **realistic conflict theory**. This can lead to each group developing intra-group norms, with in-group bias in favour of members, and negative stereotyping, prejudice, and discrimination towards out-group members. This is exemplified in the research of Sherif et al. (Section 7.2.2). It also forms part the research of Novotny and Polansky (Section 7.2.2), whose findings could imply that socio-economically vulnerable people are more likely to oppose immigration due to fear of competition for scarce resources.

(b) **Perceiving the out-group as a possible threat**, known as the **integrated threat theory**. The research of Novotny and Polansky) implies that an in-group can

165

show prejudice and discrimination towards an out-group that it perceives as a possible threat, as explained in that section.

(c) **Evolutionary based theory** (Sections 1.2, 1.6, and 7.2.2): negative reactions to out-groups could escalate to conflict could have biologically evolved in order to protect the gene pool of the community.

Amongst *approaches to conflict resolution* are:

(a) **Intergroup contact theory**, where conflicting groups are enabled to meet in a non-threatening situation. The key is non-threatening and also on an equal basis. If the groups are still in a conflict situation, intergroup contact is likely to exacerbate the conflict, as demonstrated in the integrative stage of Sherif et al.

(b) The **creation of superordinate goals**, whereby the formerly conflicting groups find themselves putting their previous hostilities to the side in working together to face common threats or challenges, as demonstrated in the final phase of Sherif et al. with the failed water supply and with having to get the bus back on to the road.

Studies linked to conflict and conflict resolution include:

- **Sherif et al. (1956)** may be used for both the origins of conflict and conflict resolution.
- **Novotny and Polansky (2001)** may be used to examine the origin of conflict, and support suitable inter-group contact as a means of conflict resolution.
- **Harris and Fiske (2006)** (Section 1.2) may be used as biological evidence of evolved mechanisms in brain that support conflict (as well as prejudice and discrimination) against an out-group.

7.3 Social Responsibility

Social responsibility in psychology focuses on **prosocial** thinking and **behaviour** that is intended to benefit others. It considers the phenomenon of able people assisting and not assisting strangers when in need. Such behaviour is **altruistic** when the person assists without any expectation of recognition or reward. **Bystanderism**, on the reverse side of prosocial behaviour, is where individuals do not step forward to help a victim when others are present.

This area of inquiry is explored under three headings:
1. Bystanderism
2. Prosocial behaviour
3. Promoting prosocial behaviour

7.3.1 Bystanderism

In 1964, Kitty Genovese was stabbed to death by a serial murderer and rapist, over a half-hour period. Though witnessed by 38 of her neighbors, not one of them even telephoned for help; an example of bystanderism. Research by Latané and Darley suggests that bystanderism occurs for two reasons: diffusion of responsibility and pluralistic ignorance.

Explanations for bystanderism include **diffusion of responsibility, arousal-cost-reward of helping**, and **pluralistic ignorance**.

▶ **Diffusion of Responsibility**: this explanation holds that individuals are less likely to step forward when others are present, as the psychological costs of not helping are fewer. The more people around, the less the individual is likely to come forward, relying on other people to come forward.

7. PAPER 2 OPTION – HUMAN RELATIONSHIPS

RESEARCH STUDY

Latané and Darley (1968)

This was a laboratory experiment. Student participants (13 male, 59 female) were interviewed individually in separate rooms over a microphone connected to an intercom system, on the subject of living in a university environment under stress. They were told that this procedure was to ensure that their responses would be anonymous, but it was designed for the necessary deception to take place. This was that, at a specified point in the discussion, a confederate claiming to be a participant would produce some loud choking noises over the microphone, indicating an immediate emergency. The independent variable was the number of people that the experimenters led the participant to believe were taking part in the discussion. The dependent variable was how long it took for the participant to step forward, in this case by contacting the experimenter.

The results were that those who were told that they were the only participants attempted to help 85% of the time. When they were led to believe there were a few others there, 65%, but when it went up to four others, the number went down to 31%. This supported the researchers' theory of diffusion of responsibility: the more people present, the less the individual is likely to come forward, relying on other people to volunteer.

Strengths and limitations: Latané and Darley (1968)

Strengths	Limitations
1. The experimental design of the study made it possible to show cause and effect. 2. The findings were quantitatively supported by the sample size.	1. Ecological validity issues: laboratory setting where the participants could only hear rather than see the "victim". 2. Ethical issues: participants were deceived and were placed in an anxiety-creating situation.

▶ **The arousal-cost-reward model of helping**: this explanation holds that individuals make a cost-of-not-helping versus benefit-of-helping analysis of the situation in deciding whether or not to step forward and assist. Costs of not helping include feeling bad, and what other people present would think of them for not helping. Benefits of helping would include the anticipated feel of satisfaction, achievement, and social approval for having successfully intervened. This theory was put forward following Piliavin et al. (1969).

RESEARCH STUDY

Piliavin et al. (1969)

This was a field experiment on factors involving helping behaviour. Piliavin et al.'s experimental research involved set-up "crises" at various locations on the New York subway, between 11am and 3pm. The "victims" who in reality were confederates were young men aged 25–35. One acted as a drunken man, smelling of alcohol, with a bottle of drink in his bag. The other acted as a sober victim with his cane. A confederate "model helper" was instructed to come forward if no help was offered within 70 seconds. There were covert observers recording the findings.

The observers noted both qualitative and quantitative data: speed of help, gender of helper, frequency of help, verbal comments, and degree of tendency to move away from the victim. Thus non-participant covert observation was the means of obtaining data for this experimental research.

Results: in the 103 trials, 93% of the time someone helped spontaneously, and 60% of the time, more than one helper was involved. The cane victim received help all the time, but the drunk just over 80% of the time. There was no diffusion of responsibility (see above) observed, even with increase in-group size.

Conclusions: Piliavin argues that the theory emerging from the responses to the crises may be based on a very quick cost-reward analysis, involving weighing up the cost of helping (e.g. chance of physical harm) against cost of not helping (e.g. feelings of guilt). Also taken into account are the rewards of helping (e.g. approval of those watching) against the rewards of not helping (e.g. time saved). Thus the findings on the New York subway experiment may be explained by the arousal-cost-reward model, such as someone stepping out to help in each scenario with the cane-carrying person (cost of help is low and cost of not helping is high), and the fewer people stepping forward to help the drunk based on the commonly-perceived revulsion towards drunken behaviour, and in the notion that he should never have been drunk in the first place.

Strengths and limitations: Piliavin et al. (1969)

Strengths	Limitations
1. The research was designed a highly-ecologically-valid field experiment, which could demonstrate cause and effect. 2. The procedures in the field were standardised.	1. Assumes that the decision of whether or not to help depends on a rational cost-benefit analysis rather than on impulse. 2. The arousal-cost-reward model of helping associated with this study assumes that the decision to help is based on egoistical rather than altruistic motives. 3. Relying on observers raises the possibility of inaccuracies in their recording of the information. 4. Ethically: would have to account for deception, lack of consent, and lack of debriefing.

▶ **Pluralistic Ignorance**: people look around at others to see their reactions as cues in how to act in an emergency situation. If people are not sure what to do, they look round to other people present for cues on whether to act or not to act. Tested by **Latané and Darley (1969)**, a set of emergency screams associated with a call and a female cry were set up next door to a waiting room. When a single individual was alone in that waiting room, he or she would be more likely to help. However, there was less altruistic behaviour when there were many in the waiting room. Thus the presence of others in the room tended to reinforce the inherent ambiguity in the situation.

7. PAPER 2 OPTION – HUMAN RELATIONSHIPS

7.3.2 Prosocial Behaviour

Prosocial behaviour is when one's conduct is intended to benefit others. It involves the phenomenon of able people assisting and not assisting strangers when in need. Such behaviour is **altruistic** when the person helps without any expectation of recognition or reward, as opposed to the norm of **reciprocity**, whereby the helper expects to experience a reward of some kind. For example, when someone anonymously donates a sum of money to a worthy cause. An example of prosocial, but non-altruistic behaviour was investigated in Piliavin et al's research (see Section 7.3.1), which illustrates coming forward to help possibly to avoid unpleasant feelings and possibly to get the benefits of recognition. That would be prosocial, but not altruistic.

As well as the psychologically-based arousal-cost-reward model (Section 7.3.1), the theories that may be used to explain pro-social behaviour include:

- the biologically-based kin selection theory,
- the psychologically-based empathy-altruism model.

A.   Biological explanation of pro-social behaviour, and altruism: kin-selection theory

Kin-selection theory (as exemplified in Dawkins 1989: 'The Selfish Gene') theorises that we have an innate drive for the preservation of our species as a whole, and this drive becomes more acute as those suffering are closer to ourselves. "Closer" means immediate relatives and friends, the closer you are related to the person, the more you feel their pain. Kin-selection theory suggests that we should favour close family members when times are hard. It applies to humans and animals alike, since those many groups share many genes, prosocial (and altruistic) behaviour promotes the preservation of the many genes very similar to our own, and ensures that they are passed to the next generation. In evaluation: this is supported by the tendency to go to extreme lengths to protect those biologically closest to us. The individual strives to maximise the passing on of the genes of those biologically closest even if that individual personally does not survive. Though this may appear to be highly altruistic, this theory claims that such extreme behaviours are biologically driven in order to protect the gene pool.

 RESEARCH STUDY

Madsen et al. (2007)

This study was designed to investigate the hypothesis that humans are more likely to help relatives (kin selection) in emergency situations than complete strangers. This study used male and female students in two locations: the UK and South Africa.

All participants supplied the researchers with a list of blood relatives of various degrees of closeness. One relative (close or distant) was selected randomly by the researchers. Then each participant had to sit in an uncomfortable position: thighs parallel to the ground, back to the wall. They were paid for every 20 seconds that they sat in that painful way. The money would not be given to them, but to the selected relative. Results: the closer the relative, the longer the endurance of the painful position, and this was even more distinct in male participants than in female participants. The degree of closeness was slightly less marked amongst the Zulus of South Africa, who tended to equate siblings and cousins in their desire to support them. The study concluded that its findings supported that hypothesis that the people are prepared to go to more extreme lengths to show prosocial and indeed altruistic behaviour to those with whom they share more genetic material.

Evaluation: Madsen et al. (2007)

It does appear that kin-selection is a strong motivator for altruistic behaviour. In addition, two cultures were selected on the grounds of their having different social concepts of the meaning of 'kin' and 'family'. Therefore the biological evolutionary argument is strengthened as the biological degree of closeness appears to determine readiness to help, as evidenced in two very difficult cultures. In addition, studies with animals also suggest the biological base for kin-selection. For example, squirrels are more likely to warn relatives than non-relatives for predators (Sherman, 1980).

This study can be criticised on the grounds that the gifts to family members were relatively trivial in terms of the needs of the family-member recipients (though in the UK, the initial financial reward was raised during the course of the study), and that some participants might have had sufficiently high pain thresholds to take the sitting position in their stride. In addition, neither this study nor its underlying kin-selection explain why people have been observed to show highly altruistic behaviour towards people unrelated to them, and towards complete strangers. It also does not explain why frequently people feel much closer ties with individuals outside their families than with individuals within their families.

You may also use the arousal-cost-reward model (Section 7.3.1) as psychological explanation of pro-social behaviour, and use the research of Piliavin et al. (1969).

B. Psychological explanation of pro-social behaviour, and altruism: the empathy-altruism model

The empathy-altruism model (Batson et al.,1981) suggests that the decision to help is influenced by the person's:

- **Empathic concerns**: feelings of sympathy to another person's situation, positive emotions.
- **Personal distress** (fear, anxiety) towards the situation of the other, negative emotions.

Batson argues that those who most likely feel high levels of empathic concerns and/or personal distress are individuals who have been in similar situations themselves, or are close to the person to person in need of help. In the absence of either feelings of empathy or personal distress, help is likely to be given on the basis of the cost: whether the cost of assisting is likely to be less painful than the cost of knowing and being known to have not assisted. This is supported by the study of Toi and Batson, (1982).

RESEARCH STUDY

Toi and Batson (1982)

Toi and Batson (1982) experimentally tested the validity of empathy-altruistic theory. The researchers investigated the participants' motives to choose to help when they had a chance of not helping without any consequences.

The participants were a sample of female psychology students listening to audio tapes about a student named Carol. She talked about having been in an accident, the injuries she sustained, and her anxiety on not being able to complete the program. They were then confronted with the question: would they help Carol by writing to her, or meet up with her and sharing their lecture notes?

This was an independent measures-designed experiment. One group of students had the tapes presented with a high level of empathy, where the experimenter described the experiences in terms of getting the students to focus on how Carol was feeling. The second group was told not to be concerned with her feelings: a low level of empathy. The researchers also divided the participants into two groups: high cost for not helping, and low cost for not helping. The high-cost group was told that Carol would see them again in class: "difficult escape", and the low cost group were informed that she would complete her studies out of class: "easy escape".

The results were that those in the high empathy group were as likely as not to help Carol whether they believed they would see Carol again in class, whereas those in the low-empathy group were more prepared to help where they were informed that Carol would return to class. Thus participants with high levels of empathy helped whether escape was difficult or easy, but those with low levels of empathy were far less inclined to help unless escape was difficult, that they would be seeing Carol again.

Evaluation: Toi and Batson (1982)

The results appear to support the empathy-altruism model: that people offer help when they feel empathy for the individual in need irrespective of whether they will see that person again or not. However, in the absence of empathy and personal distress, people are likely to make the decision whether or not to help on the basis of the ease of escape: would they be likely to see Carol again. In effect, they would consciously weigh the costs and benefits in deciding whether or not to help. Also, the study was rigorously controlled for levels of empathy and ease of escape.

However, this experiment did not take into account the personalities and backgrounds of the participants. Indeed, it is not clear whether empathy is something learnt (sociocultural) or something biologically based. In addition, the participants were psychology students, and also female, limiting the scope to generalise the findings to other populations. Moreover, as the participants were studying psychology, it is possible that some of them guessed the purpose of the experiment, which might have influenced their responses. Finally, some of the students may have had personality traits that were altruistic or non-altruistic.

7.3.3 Promoting Prosocial Behaviour

Psychology's aims in promoting pro-social behaviour include encouraging individuals to respond to situations that support others in need, including overcoming bystanderism. Methods of promoting pro-social behaviour include empathy training, peer counselling, and also parental and teaching styles. Some countries have penalties for people who are able to give aid in a life threatening situation and do not respond: in Australia the law makes the person liable to imprisonment for up to seven years.

RESEARCH STUDY

Flook et al. (2015)

This study aimed to investigate the effect of a mindfulness-based kindness program with pre-school children. This program was designed to develop pro-social awareness of situations needing help, empathy, compassion, and a promote culture of caring. 68 pre-schoolers took part. 30 formed the test group, which received two weekly sessions is the program for up to half-an-hour, over a 12-week period. 38 formed the control group, who were put on the waiting list for the program.

The findings indicated that the children who received the training showed significantly more social skills and more generosity towards the situations of others than those in the control group who did not receive the training, as reported by their teachers. In addition, children who had shown the lowest pro-social scores before the program had benefitted most from the program.

The study had the strengths of being experimental and independent measures in design, with high ecological validity as the children's behaviour that was being observed and reported was within their real-life pre-school environment. In addition, ethically the children in the control group were not to miss out on the prosocial training, as they were assigned to a waiting list for the same treatment after the duration of the study. Its limitations include judging the extent its findings on promoting pro-social behaviour can be generalised to other age groups, and to other societies. There is also the issue of assessing the validity of the teachers' reports as evidence of child behaviours, and the capacity for such programs to promote pro-social behaviours over the long as well as the short term.

RESEARCH STUDY

Carlo et al. (2007)

This study aimed at investigating the influence of parental style of upbringing, and the degree of prosocial behaviour shown by American high school students. 223 took part, their average age just under 17. Each participant completed a questionnaire that reported on their experience of parenting styles and their own pro-social behaviours.

The study found a significant positive relationship between children brought up on a basis of empathy with others (as well as mutual respect and valuing self-control), and relatively high incidences of pro-social behaviour. The researchers used their findings to support the view that the home plays a vital role in influencing the level of the individual's pro-social behaviour.

The study had the strengths of a large sample base. In addition, the questionnaire covered a wide range of parental styles. Its limitations include its reliance on adolescents' self-reporting, and associated demand characteristics. Furthermore, its applications are limited when considering the value of pro-socially-orientated programs in workplaces and universities, as these influences are likely to have been part of the participants' home socialisation from birth.

7.4 Ethical Considerations

Ethical considerations in researching human relationships are common to other areas of psychology, including:

- Informed consent: participants must know the object of the study, that their involvement is voluntary, what the data will be used for, and if necessary be debriefed at the end of the study. In extreme cases, the ethical requirement for informed

consent may be waived, when the focus of the study is of public importance and there is no other way to obtain the sought-after information.
- Avoiding deception, except possibly where the research cannot be carried out in any other way).
- Protection from harm
- Making the participants anonymous to protect them, even at the risk of reducing the authenticity of the research and of preventing any follow-up study.
- The right for any participant to withdraw from the study at any point, and communicating that right before the commencement of the study.
- All participants are to be debriefed at the end of the study.
- Bearing in mind that research involving associated cultural issues is extremely sensitive with many ethnic groups. Typically, the elders of the society must be consulted for permission to work with members of their group.

7.5 Key research studies

Research relevant to human relationships

For biological influences, look at the following below:

- Wedekind (1995): evolutionary theory focusing on the characteristics of the other's immune systems in the choice of partner.
- Fisher et al. (2005) on elements that might stimulate the nervous and endocrine systems into falling in love.
- Harris and Fiske (2006) on an evolutionary-based explanation of prejudice, discrimination, and conflict
- Madsen et al (2007), on degree of closeness of kin in deciding whether to step forward in helping a person in need.

For cognitive influences, look at the following below:

- Markey and Markey (2007) on the recognising of loveable similarities in one another as cue for forming an exclusive relationship.
- Piliavin et al. (1969) on the degree of perceptions that in turn arouse unpleasant feelings, in deciding whether to step forward in helping a person in need.
- Rogers and Frantz (1962) on discriminatory behaviour and the theory of threatened egotism.
- Novotny and Polansky (2011), and Croucher (2013) on integrated threat theory.
- Kieser and Baral (1970) on the importance of self-esteem in forming relationships.
- Toi and Batson (1982) on the effect of empathy arousal in deciding whether to help.

For sociocultural influences, look at the following below:

- Collins and Miller (1994) on the degree of openness and acceptance in communication as a factor in choice of partner.
- Festinger et al. (1950) on the degree of familiarity with the person present prior to choosing him/her as a partner.
- Bradbury and Fincham (1992) on communication strategies in relationships, and why relationships change and end.
- Gottman's "Four horses of the Apocalypse" in explaining communication strategies in relationships, and why relationships change and end.
- Kerr et al. (2003) on the effect of informational social influence on willingness to co-operate.
- Sherif et al. (1956) on competition, co-operation, prejudice, discrimination, origins of conflict, and conflict resolution.
- Latané and Darley (1969) in diffusion of responsibility as an explanation of bystanderism
- Carlos et al (2007), and Flook et al (2015) on the respective roles of the home and of pre-school specialised programs in promoting pro-social behaviour.

Some studies (e.g. Buss et al. 1989 on choice of partner) are based on empirically-collected data, and can have elements of all three approaches to behaviour.

Evaluate psychological research relevant to the psychology of human relationships

For personal relationships, look at the following:

- Wedekind (1995): evolutionary theory focusing on the characteristics of the other's immune systems in the choice of partner.
- Fisher et al. (2005) on elements that might stimulate the nervous and endocrine systems into falling in love.
- Buss et al. (1989) on elements influencing choice of partner.
- Kieser and Baral (1970) on the importance of self-esteem in forming relationships.
- Markey and Markey (2007) on the recognising of loveable similarities in one another as cue for forming an exclusive relationship.
- Collins and Miller (1994) on the degree of openness and acceptance in communication as a factor in choice of partner.
- Festinger et al. (1950) on the degree of familiarity with the person present prior to choosing him/her as a partner.
- Bradbury and Fincham (1992) on communication strategies in relationships, and why relationships change and end.
- Gottman's "Four horses of the Apocalypse" in explaining communication strategies in relationships, and why relationships change and end.

7. PAPER 2 OPTION – HUMAN RELATIONSHIPS

For group dynamics, look at the following

- Harris and Fiske (2006) on an evolutionary-based explanation of prejudice, discrimination, and conflict
- Rogers and Frantz (1962) on discriminatory behaviour and the theory of threatened egotism.
- Novotny and Polansky (2011), and Croucher (2013) on integrated threat theory.
- Kerr et al. (2003) on the effect of informational social influence on willingness to co-operate.
- Sherif et al. (1956) on competition, co-operation, prejudice, discrimination, origins of conflict, and conflict resolution.

For social responsibility, look at the following:

- Madsen et al. (2007) on degree of closeness of kin in deciding whether to step forward in helping a person in need.
- Piliavin et al. (1969) on the degree of perceptions that in turn arouse unpleasant feelings, in deciding whether to step forward in helping a person in need.
- Toi and Batson (1982) on the effect of empathy arousal in deciding whether to help.
- Latané and Darley (1969) on diffusion of responsibility as an explanation of bystanderism
- Carlos et al (2007), and Flook et al (2015) on the respective roles of the home and of pre-school specialised programs in promoting pro-social behaviour.

PRACTICE QUESTIONS

Essay Response Practice Questions: Psychology of human relationships

1. Discuss explanations for why relationships change or end.
2. Discuss the origins of conflict and/or conflict resolution.
3. Discuss a socio-cultural approach to social responsibility.

Chapter 8: Paper 2 Option – Health Psychology

Overview

Health psychology in this program looks at three areas: determinants of health, health problems, and promoting health.

> Remember that you are applying the biological, cognitive, and sociocultural perspectives to specific issues within the field of health psychology.

KEY CONCEPT

The goal of studying health psychology is to recognise and understand the issues in people's lifestyles that are often risky and detrimental to the maximum enjoyment of health. Health psychology is important in the development of prevention strategies, and enabling the individual and community to implement health-promoting decisions. Our foci in health psychology includes research from stress, addiction, and obesity, but chronic pain and sexual health are also acceptable alternatives.

Learning objectives of this unit include an understanding of:

- The long-term relationship between poverty and ill-health.
- The relationship between higher stress levels and less-effective resistance to disease.
- The role of social support as a means of coping with ill-health.
- Addiction to an unhealthy lifestyle forming a barrier to quitting.
- The role of genetics in obesity caused by overeating.
- Models and programs of health promotion.

8. PAPER 2 OPTION – HEALTH PSYCHOLOGY

8.1 Determinants of Health

Health behaviours divide up into habits that promote health, such as a healthy diet, regular exercise, and responsible sexual activity, and behaviours that can threaten health, such as an unhealthy diet, lack of exercise, smoking, drinking, high stress levels, and irresponsible sexual activity. This section considers the following subtopics:

1. The biopsychosocial model of health and well-being
2. Dispositional factors, and health beliefs
3. Risk and protective factors

8.1.1 The Biopsychosocial Model of Health and Well-Being

Proposed by Engel (1977), this integrative model proposes that the level of health that the individual enjoys is influenced by three sets of factors:

Biological factors	Physical health, level of physical fitness, genetic vulnerabilities and absence/presence of disease.
Psychological factors	Thoughts, feelings, and behaviours. These include social skills, coping skills, and self-esteem. Professional practice can include, for example, counselling in facing stressors or tackling addictive behaviours.
Social factors	Social class, ethnic background, wealth and poverty, peers, family situation, and school / employment.

As with other options, be aware of the ethical issues and the different research methods in the research studies in health psychology. Some examination questions allow a trade-off for more depth and narrower scope with less depth and wider scope. Either are acceptable.

The strengths of the biopsychosocial model include its incorporation of three distinct sets of elements involved in health and well-being. The model is support by research studies, such as **Reed et al. (1999)**, and **Wayment et al. (2006)** that both indicate that despairing, pessimistic attitudes weaken the immune system though the stresses they create. The model also includes and emphasises the potential and importance of developing counseling skills within the medical profession, and the range of available options to assist coping. However, the model's validity is limited by its simplicity: there is a huge range of possible biopsychosocial factors that can influence levels of health that are not always immediately apparent in the individual. In addition, the model is limited by its emphasis on individuals taking responsibility for their own health, which may not be possible for those finding themselves confined to inescapable high-stress environments, compounded with lack of social support. The model's limitations also include the practical difficulties in quantifying the psychological situation and progress of the individual, and also differing ease of access to the range of treatments under the biological and psychological/cognitive headings.

Applied to stress, the model focuses on *biologically* the sympathetic nervous system and endocrine system working together with *cognitively* the perception of threat: preparing the individual to either confront (fright, fight) or run away (fright, flight) from the source of stress, and *socially*: for example access to resources that assist coping, moving toward improving well-being. These systems combine, for example, in energising and supporting the body to confront, or quickly get away from the threat.

RESEARCH STUDY

Kiecolt-Glaser et al. (1984)

This study is a natural experiment that considers the effects of stress in lowering resistance to disease. The researchers looked at the T-cell (immune system, fight disease) count in a group of medical students for one month (control) and then the day before their final examinations (test). The study therefore had a repeated measures design. Each participating student also completed a questionnaire with scales of bodily symptoms (biological), life events, and levels of satisfactions with interpersonal contacts (cognitive and social). The researchers found that the second blood sample taken on the day before revealed a lower T-cell count. So did the counts from students with a higher level of stressful events and loneliness. That indicates that cognitive and social stress may well influence the immune system, which in turn is likely to have a negative effect on well-being.

Since then, psychologists have become aware that long-term stress arising from conditions involving biological, psychological, and/or social stressors causes an increase in **cortisol**, whose hormonal influence not only leads to depression and memory problems, but also a decrease in the number of T-cells that cause the immune system to weaken.

Strengths and limitations: Kiecolt-Glaser et al. (1984)

Strengths	Limitations
1. The experiment used repeated measures. The same people were the source of data for the control and test situation. 2. The experiment was part of the medical students' real-life situation, and therefore ecologically valid. 3. More generally, the study suggests a link between one's psychological state (e.g. optimism or pessimism), one's social interpersonal contacts, and the efficacy of the immune system via the nervous system: thus supporting the biopsychosocial model.	1. As it was a natural experiment and not in laboratory conditions, it was difficult to establish cause and effect. The researchers did not have the power to adjust the independent variable. 2. The lower T-cell count could have been a result of something else that all the students had gone through that was not connected with the questionnaire (above). It might not have been directly connected with those stressors.

RESEARCH STUDY

Habtewold et al. (2016)

This study applied the biopsychosocial model to type-2 diabetes outpatients who were comorbid (an additional condition apart from the primary condition) with depression. It was based in Ethiopia. Its purpose was to determine the importance of social support in treating such patients.

Participants were a random sample of 276 type-2 diabetic outpatients. Using a patient health questionnaire, they were evaluated for the possible presence of depression, and also for elements in their personal situations that might be significant risk factors for depression.

The results indicated that just under half the patients had identifiable depression symptoms, indicating a high rate of comorbidity with type-2 diabetes. It identified the following factors increasing the risk factor for depression when already having

8. PAPER 2 OPTION – HEALTH PSYCHOLOGY

type-2 diabetes: low income, unpleasant life events, and poor social support as well as complications with the diabetes itself. It supported the biopsychosocial model in that cognitive and social as well as biological factors need to be considered in diagnosing and treating mental health issues.

Strengths of the biopsychosocial model

1. It does view health issues holistically, recognising that they have biological, cognitive, and sociocultural dimensions which need to be taken into account in treatment.
2. It identifies and accommodates the barriers that individuals face in both living healthily and in undergoing effective treatment, including health-promoting behaviours in diet and exercise, poverty-related issues, and stress management.

These may also be applied to Habtewold et al. In addition, Habtewold et al's study used a large sample.

Limitations of the biopsychosocial model

1. It opens complications when attempting to assess the relative importance of the varieties of different factors that might be influence a particular health challenge.
2. In practice practitioners tend view what they are best able to treat: medical doctors would be more likely to consider biological factors, and psychotherapists would consider sociocultural ones.

These may also be applied to Habtewold et al. In addition, the responses in Habtewold et al's study could have been influenced by the respondents' perceived demand characteristics.

8.1.2 Dispositional Factors as determinants of health

Dispositional factors are internal factors that are part of the individual's reality, and which can affect health. These include gender, genetic predispositions, and personality type. Not all of them are under the control of the individual. The following two research studies consider genetic predispositions and personality type.

Genetic predispositions: influence of specific genes on resisting weight loss following weight-losing activities

 RESEARCH STUDY

Claussnitzer et al. (2015)

An individual may find losing weight particularly difficult because of the influence of genes in resisting weight-losing activities. Claussnitzer et al. (2015) identified the FTO chromosome 16 as a controller of two other genes, IRX3 and IRX5. These determine rate of thermogenesis whereby the body burns energy as opposed to storing energy. Switched on, they accumulate and store fat and make it harder for the body to lose weight. Switched off, they let the body burn fat and make weight loss much easier.

This relationship was determined after experimental work with mice that were fed a high-fat diet. The researchers had blocked the fat-storing genes in the test sample and left them as they were in the control sample. Those in the test samples were 50% thinner than those in the control, continuing to burn energy even when asleep. Subsequently, the research focused on human fat whose test samples were genetically modified to block those genes' effects, which then appeared to show an increase in the rate of energy burning in the fat cells rather than storing.

This study advances research in obesity to a new level: from conclusions drawn from empirical data, to identifying the genetic material that seems to have a role in obesity. It could lead to the development of effective medication to switch off the fat-storing genes, combating obesity. Its limitations include the above genotype having been found in nearly half the white European fat samples, but in only 5% of the fat samples from black people. That indicates that other, currently unidentified genes may be involved. Also, the ethical issues common to genetic modification are likely to be present in developing such an obesity-treating drug on those lines.

However, research in being able to isolate the range of genes influencing obesity is still in its infancy. In addition, the presence of genes does not necessarily mean that they express themselves. Research in the field also needs to include studying the psychological conditions that can switch on and switch off those genes.

Personality type: ability to form friendships as a strategy for reducing stress and promoting health and well-being

RESEARCH STUDY

Graber et al. (2015)

This study embraces the personality disposition of the person's capacity to attract and keep a best friend. It researched the role of social support as a stress-coping and thus health-promoting strategy, framed within the following question: Does having a best friend during health-stressful times help the individual to become more resilient to health challenges? The researchers used a sample of 409 students aged 11–19 who reported through questionnaires designed to elicit information on the detailed nature of their closest friendships, their levels of resilience in coping with a series of stressful situations, and their means of coping with their problems. The results indicated a positive correlation between the reported quality of best-friend relationships and the degree of reported resilience to health challenges. Those with quality friendships were more likely to talk their issues over rather than blame their troubles on others and attribute their misfortunes to inescapable causes, reflecting a more positive set of dispositional factors. The study also found gender differences: boys in established mutual-trust male-male friendships could discuss their concerns with one another, whilst girls were more likely to try out risky behaviour such as alcohol and drugs.

The study concluded that having a best friend greatly supports resilience, including coping strategies with health issues. It had the strengths of being a large sample, and was also conducted in a relatively limited-resourced, high-stressed region in the north of Britain. However, the findings were correlational: it was not clear whether it was best friends who promoted resilience or people of a resilient nature tending to be good at attracting best friends. In addition, it was based on self-reporting (possibilities of demand characteristics) and on the 11–19 age group in a particular location, raising issues of applying the study to other cultures, locations, and age-groups.

8. PAPER 2 OPTION – HEALTH PSYCHOLOGY

8.1.3 Health Beliefs as determinants of health

Health beliefs refer to the degree that a person believes that he or she can make the necessary behavioural changes to improve health. This can include tackling habits that threated health such as over-eating and smoking, and habits that protect and promote health, such as regular exercise and regular check-ups. Among the determinants for health belief are awareness of **risk perception** and the danger of optimism bias, and **self-efficacy**.

Risk perception is our estimation of the effect of our behaviours on our health. A person with an **optimism bias** will believe that his or her habits are less health-threatening than they are, with the sense of "even if it happens to others, it won't happen to me." Such a cognitive bias can threaten health, as the individual that underestimates the risk is less likely to quit health-threatening behaviours.

Self-efficacy theory holds that "people who believe they have the power to exercise some measure of control over their lives are healthier, more effective, and more successful than those who lack faith in their ability to effect changes in their lives" (Bandura, 1997). Bandura identifies four factors in promoting an individual's self-efficacy, which applied to health belief would be: success in a previous behaviour change, seeing others successfully make the behaviour change, support from other people in making the behaviour change, and the cognitively being able to interpret the behaviour as being in one's power to change.

RESEARCH STUDY

Weinstein (1983)

This experimental study aimed to investigate the degree that people brought an optimum bias to elements that could threaten their personal health and safety. 88 undergraduate psychology students took part.

The participants were divided into three groups. All were given the same questionnaire on health and safety risks, including being injured in a car accident, and suffering diabetes, heart attack, and cancer. For each condition, they were asked the same question: "Compared to other people of your age and sex, what are your chances of getting [that condition]: greater/the same/less? They were also required to rate how far they worried about developing each of the above conditions.

Each group answered the question under different conditions. The control group responded without any guidance at all. The second group was primed with a list of better-established and poorer-established factors that put individuals at greater health risk. They responded on questions designed to make them assess how risky their own behaviours were before proceeding with the main questionnaire that was given to all groups. The third group was primed with list of risk factors and given information on how other similar students had already responded earlier that semester, and then proceeded with the main questionnaire.

The results showed that the greatest levels of optimism occurred in the second group, which could be interpreted as being presented with the risks might have stimulated an "it won't happen to me" optimism bias. The optimism bias was at a higher level than the control group. However the optimism level of the third group, which saw data about the optimism levels of their peers, was significantly lower than both groups.

The study indicated that people tend to overrate their optimism in health and safety, and do so even more when presented with information about health risks, possibly with an "it won't happen to me" attitude. On the other hand, knowledge of the risk status of their peers can reduce levels of optimism bias.

Strengths and limitations of Weinstein

Strengths	Limitations
1. It was a controlled experiment with high internal validity. 2. It is easily replicable and can be repeated with different populations.	1. It depended on self-reporting, which may have influenced demand characteristics. 2. Only a minority of the participants were smokers or solo drinkers, raising the possibility that the participants were in reality a low-risk group, whose findings could not readily be generalised to other populations.

RESEARCH STUDY

Brown et al. (2014) may be used as a research study to address the risk and protection factors (Section 8.1.4) that encourage smokers to try to quit.

Brown et al. (2014)

Brown et al. investigated the efficacy of the first **'Stoptober' campaign of 2012**: a UK national campaign aimed at the country's smokers, with the objective of persuading as many as possible to quit smoking in the month of October. This nation-wide campaign had the clear behaviour target of getting as many smokers as possible to abstain throughout that 31-day period, with the hope that many would quit and not resume smoking after that. It was theorised that the smoker would be encouraged to stop the habit when perceiving that many others were doing the same thing, all sharing the support and encouragement of the nation. October was chosen as it was the ideal month for promoting and evaluating the effectiveness of a mass campaign. It was not the time for New Year resolutions; indeed statistics from previous years showed fewer-than-average attempts to quit during that month. The idea presented to the smoker was: Quit for a month as part of a group and, with the hardest part of giving up being over in the first month, it should be easier to totally withdraw from smoking after that.

The nation-wide campaign was designed to foster self-efficacy in potential quitters by offering support to make the behavioural change, and by helping people cognitively to believe such a behavioural change was within their reach.

The results indicated that 'Stoptober' generated some 350,000 attempts to quit, with nearly 9,000 giving up permanently as a result of the campaign: a 50% increase in October compared with other months of the year. In cost-benefit terms, 10,400 estimated years of life were saved. That worked out at £415 (US$530) per year from the campaign's budget, considered a good investment in public health. In contrast with previous years, there were more attempts to quit in October 2012 than average.

The campaign had the strengths of successfully reaching the entire age-range spectrum of smokers, indicating that it is possible to promote a universal rather than age/gender-specific health campaign. It was presented in positive terms, avoiding fear-inducing negative consequences of smoking. It also indicated significantly higher attempts to stop smoking than in previous years during the same month.

Its limitations are that both the 2012 and subsequent campaigns did not elicit a mass movement to quit smoking, appearing to have been ignored by most of the nation's smokers. It is also possible that factors other than the campaign elicited the larger numbers of attempts to quit during that month.

8.1.4 Risk and Protective Factors

Risk factors are elements that promote undesirable health outcomes. **Protective factors** are elements that promote desirable health outcomes and/or reduces the risk of undesirable health outcomes.

Examples of risk factors are unhealthy eating, smoking, and drug abuse. Protective factors may include refusal to partake, avoiding events where such substances circulate, and living in a culture that does not tolerate those risky activities.

Risk and protective factors in smoking cigarettes

Risk factors in smoking cigarettes	Include the reality that nicotine is a significant ingredient. Nicotine is a stimulating substance that attaches itself to the neurotransmitter acetylcholine receptors, promoting the development of many more receptor sites that stimulate a craving for yet more nicotine. The work of **Weiss et al. (2008)** singled out six genes that appear to affect the likelihood of the brain becoming addicted to nicotine. Other possible factors appear to include the childhood experience of high levels of stress (Pampel et al., 2015), interaction with peers that smoke (O'Loughlin et al., 2009), and ethnicity: and the apparent trend for white teenagers being more likely to smoke cigarettes that black teenagers (Singh et al., 2016).
Protective factors in smoking cigarettes	Can include developing the capacity to mentally step back from stressors and addiction-based cravings (as exemplified by the practice of MSBR, above), and having the social support of quality friendships (Graber et al., 2015, details above) and quality family members (Akers and Lee 1996, focused on smoking behaviours of the 12–17 age group).

Inducing **competitive social pressure** on children at the age considered to be most vulnerable has shown significant results as a protective element. The "Be Smart. Don't Start" school-based program for over 2,000 12–13-year old children (age with a comparatively high vulnerability to start smoking) in Germany featured competitions with prizes and special benefits for the test-group (but not control group) classes that collectively decided be non-smoking for six months. The results indicated a third of the control smoked, in comparison with barely a quarter in the test group (Hanewinkel and Wiborg, 2002).

Workplace-based financial incentive programs to help adult smokers to quit have also shown significant results. The work of **Halpern et al. (2015)** was a large study involving over 2,500 participants, all of whom were CVS Caremark company employees or individuals connected with them. This was an independent measures study, with each participant (in addition to receiving basic smoking-cessation therapies) being randomly assigned to one of four incentive programs, two of which were individual based and two of them were group-of-six-participants based. Two programs – one individual and one group-based - required each participant to buy into the treatment, by making a $150 deposit that would be not refunded if resuming smoking during the 12 month period. If they did not resume, they would receive a $650 reward plus return of deposit, making $800. The other two groups were told that success in quitting would earn an $800 bonus without their having to buy into the scheme. The study showed that those who bought into the scheme were more than three times as successful in quitting (52%) during the

12-month period than those who had not personally invested in the scheme (17%). There were no significant differences whether the participants attended individual programs or group programs.

This research indeed indicated a way that a company might help their employees to live more healthily, and it also how it could reduce the overall cost of employee health benefits.

The strengths of Halpern included it being experimental in design and that it had a large number of participants in the sample. Its limitations include the possibilities that some participants might well have been less addicted than others, and that factors other than the campaign might have contributed to their success in quitting.

Brown et al. (2014) may be used as a research study to evaluate the role of programs that promote self-efficacy in smokers to help them quit.

8.2 Health Problems

The previous section introduced the biopyschosocial model as a general framework for understanding and explaining health problems. However, health issues take many forms, including stress, addictions (e.g. smoking, drugs), obesity, chronic pain, and sexual health. Each of them is complex, with biological, cognitive, and sociocultural origins and influencing factors. Understanding them is vital for the health psychologist in assisting both the prevention and the treatment of the particular problem. The IB requires in-depth focus on **one health problem only**: the material below considers **obesity**.

8.2.1 Explanations of health problems

Explanations of health problems, including obesity, are contributed-to from biological, cognitive, and sociocultural approaches to behaviour. According to many health scientists, the ideal weight is below a **BMI** (body-mass index) of 25. This is calculated by taking the person's weight (in kg) and dividing it by the square of the height (in meters). A BMI of 25 plus is overweight, and over 30 is obese.

Biological factors relating to overeating and development of obesity: two of which are genetic influences and hormonal influences

▶   **Genetic influences**: suggesting that natural selection has favoured those who, in millennia gone by, could adapt to store food as part of one's body when it was not available for long periods in the hunting-gathering way of life.

Stunkard et al. (1990) researched 93 pairs of twins who were reared apart, and compared their BMIs. They found that genetic predisposition accounted for about two-thirds of the variance in their body weight. The conclusion was that there were strong genetic factors in the development of obesity, and that genetics played an even greater role in those twins that were slim. That genetic factors may be more influential that environmental factors may be supported by the 23-year longitudinal study on adopted Danish children (**Sorensen et al.,1998**), which found that weight of the adoptees during the period of study was closer to the genetic parents than to the adoptive parents.

The genetic factor in obesity is hard to determine for the following reasons. It is not clear to what degree the main factor is the role of genes in metabolism, or the role of genes in determining the number of fat cells. In addition, critics of the role of genes in obesity argue that the phenomenon of widespread obesity has occurred over too short a period for the genetic makeup of the population to have changed substantially. Moreover in the adoptive study, the mother's eating habits and the child's nutrition before adoption may also play crucial roles in determining obesity earlier in life.

It has been hypothesised, but not proven, that humans are genetically programmed to overeat when food is available in order to store for times of shortage. This worked well during evolutionary (i.e. natural) selection, where Mankind was a species of hunter-gatherers, but is now biologically unsuitable, as food is abundant.

More recent studies have utilised the knowledge base from genome research (as considered in Chapter 1), for example of the influence of specific genes on resisting weight loss after weight losing activities. For example, **Claussnitzer et al.** (2015, see above in Section 8.1.2) identified the FTO chromosome 16 as a controller of two other genes, IRX3 and IRX5. These determine rate of thermogenesis whereby the body burns energy as opposed to storing energy. Switched on, they accumulate and store fat and make it harder for the body to lose weight. Switched off, they let the body burn fat and make weight loss much easier. This relationship was determined after experimental work with mice that were fed a high-fat diet. The researchers had blocked the fat-storing genes in the test sample and left them as they were in the control sample. Those in the test samples were 50% thinner than those in the control, continuing to burn energy even when asleep. Subsequently, the research focused on human fat whose test samples were genetically modified to block those genes' effects, which then appeared to show an increase in the rate of energy burning in the fat cells rather than storing. This study advances research in obesity to a new level: from conclusions drawn from empirical data to the identification of the genetic material that seems to have a role in obesity. Such knowledge might lead to development of effective medication to switch off the fat-storing genes, combating obesity. Its limitations include the above genotype having been found in nearly half the white European fat samples, but in only 5% of the fat samples from black people. That indicates that other, currently unidentified genes may be involved. Also, the ethical issues common to genetic modification are likely to be present in developing such an obesity-treating drug on those lines.

However, research in being able to isolate the range of genes influencing obesity is still in its infancy. In addition, the presence of genes does not necessarily mean that they express themselves. Research in the field also needs to include studying the psychological conditions that can switch on and switch off those genes.

▶ **Hormonal influences:** Strong desires to eat, as well as slow rates of fat burning at rest with no wish to exercise correlate with low levels of the hormone **leptin**. Normal levels of leptin are associated with feeling satisfied and more energetic. Low levels of leptin are also associated with losing fat: the body in its reluctance to lose fat reduces the level of leptin which in turn gives way to **ghrelin** (the hunger hormone) which indicates to the brain that the body urgently needs food. Both hormones act on receptors in the arcuate nucleus of the hypothalamus. Together, they are associated with the craving for food which dieters experience after initial weight loss: the hormone system induces a craving for food in order to save and increase the fat that the brain believes that the body needs. Thus the first few kilos are relatively easy to lose, but the next ones are very much harder, suggesting a possible explanation of why so many dieters do not succeed long-term.

Among the approaches to dealing with leptin regulation are changes in lifestyle: regular optimum hours of quality sleep, regular physical exercise, and a diet that is high in protein, low in carbohydrates, and avoids artificially-processed foods.

RESEARCH STUDY

Goldstone (2010)

Goldstone used a repeated measures experiment to determine the effect of ghrelin on hunger.

There were 18 healthy participants, 13 male and 5 female. In each of three conditions taking place on different days, the individual participants viewed a series of pictures illustrating low-calorie food (fish, vegetables, salad) and high-calorie food (pizza, chocolate), and were required to rate the level of appeal of the food in each picture.

In the first condition, the participants missed breakfast, and were shown the pictures in mid-morning. That was the control. In the second, test, condition, the same participants ate breakfast, but received injections of ghrelin 40 minutes before the task. In the third, also control condition, they received injections of salt water 40 minutes before the test, as a placebo, controlled condition. It was double-blind with neither those giving the injection nor the participants knowing whether the substance was the hormone or the placebo.

The results showed no significant difference in the appeal of low-calorie food in any of the three conditions. In contrast, high-calorie foods were of significantly greater appeal in the conditions of arriving hungry without breakfast, and after having eaten breakfast, but being injected with ghrelin. Those who had eaten and had been injected with a placebo showed significantly less interest in the high-calorie foods illustrated.

The research concluded that the increased level of ghrelin in the first and second condition has a significant influence in heightening desire for the high-calorie foods associated with obesity. The findings suggest that developing a drug that can effectively prevent the ghrelin reaching the brain may help to combat obesity.

Strengths and limitations of Goldstone

Strengths	Limitations
1. It was a controlled, easily replicable, experiment that be repeated with different populations. 2. It was experimentally designed to show cause and effect of a single hormone: ghrelin.	1. It depended on self-reporting, which may have influenced demand characteristics. 2. Small sample with only 18 participants. 3. Laboratory conditions, with lower ecological validity. It is possible that the participants may have reacted differently to real food in contrast to photographs of food.

Cognitive factors relating to overeating and obesity

There are a number of cognitive factors relating to overeating and obesity, two of which are what people think they have eaten, and the influence of branding.

▶ **What people think they have been eating**: people's level of hunger could be influenced by the number of calories they think they have eaten. If, for example, they believe they have been eating high-calorie items, their ghrelin-stimulated (see Biological factors above) hunger levels are likely to be lower and they are likely to feel more satisfied, than if they believe they have been eating low-calorie items. They might then be less likely to overeat as a result.

8. PAPER 2 OPTION – HEALTH PSYCHOLOGY

 RESEARCH STUDY

Crum et al. (2011)

Crum et al. tested this hypothesis experimentally, using a repeated measures design. There were 46 healthy participants, recruited by flyer from the local community. They were instructed that they would need to attend two milkshake tasting sessions, one week between them.

At the first session, they drank a shake labelled "Indulgence. Decadence you Deserve. 620 calories". At the second session a week later, they drank a shake labelled "Sensishake. Fat free. Guilt free. 104 calories". Nurses measured the ghrelin levels for each participant at each session at the beginning of the experiment to establish the baseline, when they were in anticipation of the milkshake just before drinking it, and finally an hour later after drinking it. In fact, the participants had drunk the same 380-calorie milkshake at both sessions.

The results indicated that ghrelin levels were significantly lower after consuming the Indulgence-labelled shake than after the fat-free, guilt-free shake. The researchers concluded that the level of feeling satisfied seemed to resemble what people believed they were consuming rather than what they actually consumed. This would suggest that the ghrelin hormonal activity of promoting hunger is influenced by the person's state of mind.

Strengths and limitations of Crum et al.

Strengths	Limitations
1. It was a controlled, easily replicable, experiment that could be repeated with different populations. 2. It was experimentally designed to show cause and effect of changes in cognition on the activity of ghrelin. 3. Ghrelin levels were monitored by medical professionals.	1. Small sample size of 46 people all of whom were under-36 raises the question of how far this study may be generalised. 2. Ethically, there was a deception issue, addressed by debriefing.

▶ **The influence of branding**: presenting healthy nutrition with fun characters may influence healthy choices.

 RESEARCH STUDY

Wansink et al. (2012)

Wansink et al. investigated the extent that branding healthy food might induce healthy eating habits and choices.

The researchers offered a choice of an apple or a cookie to each of the 208 participants aged 8–11 in seven socio-economically and ethnically-diverse schools during a consecutive series of lunchtimes. The first time, both products were unbranded: only 20% of the students chose the apple. That established the baseline for the study. The next three times involved branding, but the branding of the products was changed each time: a cookie with a known, popular character (Elmo of Sesame Street) and an apple;

an unbranded cookie and an Elmo sticker-branded apple, and an unbranded cookie and sticker-branded apple with a non-familiar character. Finally, on the fifth day they were offered the same choice of unbranded items as on the first day.

The results indicated a significant rise in the choices for apples – from 21% to 34% - only when branded with the familiar Elmo character. There was no difference when the cookie, the unhealthy choice, was branded with the same character. This indicates that branding healthy food with familiar, loved characters could well induce children to choose healthy rather than unhealthy items.

The study had the benefits of a large sample, which was also socio-economically and culturally heterogeneous. Its limitations include its having been conducted over one week only: it did not extend to considering whether the children would continue to eat Elmo-branded apples once the novelty had worn off.

Sociocultural factors relating to overeating and obesity

There are a number of cognitive factors relating to overeating and obesity, two of which are **sedentary lifestyle** and **stressful living environments**.

▶ **Sedentary lifestyles**: modern living in much of the world involves far less physical effort than in the past. Even where people eat the same amount as in previous generations, their lifestyle often sitting in the same place for hours facing a computer screen tends to burn less energy with the excess being stored into fat. In approaching obese clients, psychologists seek to increase the use of physical energy as well as means of changing nutrition habits.

RESEARCH STUDY

She, King and Jacobson (2017)

She, King, and Jacobson (2017) may also be used as a research study that investigates the role of public transport use in reducing the prevalence of obesity, in Section 8.2.2.

She, King and Jacobson investigated the effect of encouraging people to use public transport, instead of door-to-door travel by means of the private car. The research used data from U.S. national survey sources (CDC: National Center for Disease Control and Prevention) on behavioural risk factors of the population in over 300 counties (districts) in 45 states, and data from the 2009 National Household Travel survey on journeying by public transport. The hypothesis was that there would be a lower incidence of obesity among those using public transport due to the regular effort of walking to and from the access points, than among those using the private car.

The results indicated a significantly lower prevalence of obesity among those using public transport than the more sedentary private car. Specifically, a one-percentage point increase of frequent public transit riders in a county population was estimated to decrease the county population obesity rate by 0.473% points.

The researchers concluded that their findings support the view that the physical activity involved in using public transport can significantly reduce the prevalence of obesity. The study also recognised the importance of providing and encouraging public transport on that health-promotion basis.

8. PAPER 2 OPTION – HEALTH PSYCHOLOGY

Strengths and limitations of She, King and Jacobson (2017)

Strengths	Limitations
1. Used a very large database covering the overwhelming majority of the states in the US. 2. The national database contained detailed information from each respondent to control for potentially confounding variables including amount of leisure time physical activity, health care coverage, and distribution of income.	1. The research was correlational. The results did indicate a lower prevalence of obesity among public transport users, but it may not necessarily follow that using public transport decreases obesity. 2. Limited application: the research was conducted in the US where for most part the rate of use of public transport is lower than in Western Europe.

▶ **Stressful living environments**: stress can increase the release of cortisol, a hormone. This promotes obesity in two different ways: moves triglycerides from the liver to the abdomen where they are stored as fat, and also increases the appetite with consequent overeating.

RESEARCH STUDY

Koch et al. (2008)

Koch et al. investigated the possibility of high stress levels in the household increasing the prevalence of obesity in 5-year-old children.

Over 7,000 families in Sweden participated by responding to a questionnaire designed to elicit information on serious life events, parenting stress, parental anxiety levels, and the extent of lack of social support. They already had data on obesity, as those families had all been taking part in prospective study of childhood diabetes.

The data indicated that 4.2% of the children were obese. In correlating data on child stress with data on child obesity, two stress elements were found to be statistically significant: parental anxiety levels and serious life events. The other stress elements, parenting stress and lack of social support, did not show any statistical significance with the prevalence rate of obesity.

In conclusion, reducing prevalence of obesity in children at the household level is not just an issue of diet, but of seeking to reduce parental anxiety levels, and approaching stressful serious life events as calmly as possible.

> Koch et al. (2008) may also be used as a research study that investigates the role of family stress in increasing the prevalence of childhood obesity, in Section 8.2.2.

Strengths and limitations of Koch et al. (2008)

Strengths	Limitations
1. Large number of families in the sample. 2. The study broke parental stressors down into different types.	1. The data was based on self-reporting, with possible demand characteristics. The study was not designed to include the measurement of cortisol levels. 2. The research was correlational. The results did indicate a higher prevalence of child obesity in families experiencing certain types of parental stressors, but it may not necessarily follow that promoting lifestyles specifically to avoid those stressors will lead to reduced prevalence of child obesity.

8.2.2 Prevalence of health problems

Prevalence in this context means how common particular health problems are. For example, according to the American National Center for Health Statistics, prevalence of obesity in the US has risen from 30.5% in 1998 to 42.4% in 2018. Among the influencing factors with youth obesity are rises in the rates of fast-food consumption, reducing the numbers of those serving in the military, and reducing physical education in the school timetable. Elements from the biological, cognitive, and sociocultural approaches to understanding behaviour have been considered in the previous section.

Prevalence statistics are important for the following reasons. They raise public and individual awareness of health problems. They also inform local and national priorities when allocating resources to health improvements.

However, prevalence claims should be treated with caution for the following reasons:

- Diagnosis criteria for obesity, and rigor in applying the diagnosis criteria vary from country to country.
- Sources of statistics on obesity also vary: not all are based on comprehensive national medical records. Some countries rely on patient lists. These would exclude those with the condition who did not seek professional help.
- Those based on samples need to consider the degree that the participants represent the general population. If based on a self-reporting survey, people with language problems or busy lifestyles are likely to be underrepresented.
- Certain groups within the population are particularly hard to reach: recent immigrants with language difficulties, members of particular social and religious groups, and those with no fixed address.
- Studies of prevalence based on questionnaire surveys could be biased towards individuals with the characteristics of a willing respondent, and also on the accuracy of the reporting of information that could be personally sensitive.

Koch et al. (2008) may be used as a research study that investigates the role of family stress in increasing the prevalence of childhood obesity.

She, King, and Jacobson (2017) may be used as a research study that investigates the role of public transport use in reducing the prevalence of obesity.

8.3 Promoting Health

Health promotion may be defined as the encouragement of people to avoid health-threatening habits in the first place, and for those already indulging, to change their lifestyle to reach their optimum level of health.

Psychology has a distinct role in health promotion. It is accepted that healthy living is in the interests of the public. It also accepts that people in general will follow a suitably healthy lifestyle if they perceive that they will physically suffer by not doing so. For examples, avoiding smoking, excessive alcohol intake, not regularly exercising, or having too many sugary soft drinks.

Among psychology's contributions are models and research studies that promote health improvements and healthy habits and lifestyles. Psychology accepts that the models do not work for everyone, tending to regard significant falls in prevalence rates for unhealthy habits as a success. Psychology also recognises that the relationship between health beliefs and health behaviours is not fully understood. Thus, researchers tend to assess the outcome of health promotions empirically, on the basis of the success rates that indicate what works and what does not work.

8.3.1 Health promotion

Psychology attempts to understand the cognitive barriers to living healthily, and ways to motivate the person to identify the barriers, deal with them, and attempt to overcome them. Some or all of these may be framed in the following models: the **health-belief model**, and the **stages of change model**.

The health-belief model: Rosenstock et al. (1988)

This cognitive health-belief model focuses on two simultaneous sets of forces that motivate the individual to address behaviour adverse to health, such as smoking. In considering the example of a person's readiness to change smoking habits towards quitting:

The first set of forces comes from the person:

- How far do you believe your life is in danger by smoking? (perceived susceptibility, and perceived seriousness)
- Do you see benefits by not smoking? (perceived benefits)
- What problems do you see yourself facing in quitting smoking? (perceived barriers-to-change)
- Do you believe that you can give up smoking, given the benefits? (perceived self-efficacy)

The second set of forces comes from the environment: such as a persuasive anti-smoking media campaign, including the government health warning on the cigarette packet.

These forces combine. The more powerful they are, the more likely they are to promote a positive health change, such as serious determination to quit smoking.

RESEARCH STUDY

Quist-Paulsen et al. (2003)

This field experimental study focused on a total of 240 patients that were smokers and had received heart treatment. The baseline was the knowledge that, following heart treatment, between 30% and 45% of patients that smoke will quit on their own accord. They were divided into two groups. The control group was given supportive group counseling. The members of the test group were given additional individualised phone support from trained nursing staff, which sought to arouse fear by warning about the serious heart-disease-related dangers of relapsing into smoking. That group also had two consultations during the year after leaving the hospital.

Thus the elements of the health-belief model were applied to the test group: promoting the health dangers of increased susceptibility and seriousness of the condition, promoting the cognitive change of self-efficacy believing that one had the ability to overcome the barriers to change and quit, and promoting the environment that supports quitting the habit.

The researchers found that a significantly higher 57% of the test group, but only 37% of the control group managed to quit. The rest relapsed into smoking. That supported the model's emphasis of health campaigns needing to be designed to support the elements required to promote health changes with positive benefits.

Strengths and limitations of Quist-Paulsen et al. (2003)

Strengths	Limitations
1. Large number of participants in the sample. 2. Experimental structure of the research designed to show the effect of additional treatments for the test group.	1. It is not clear how many of those in the experimental group might have quitted on their own accord, without the additional treatment. 2. The research was conducted in Norway. There may be problems of generalising the findings to societies where healthy living does not form part of the culture to the same degree.

The **ethical issues** of fear arousal in the test group were justified by the substantially higher rate of successful quitting at the end of the program, and the support offered by the nurses such as advising medication to stop the craving. And ethically, in addition, the control group did not receive any treatment that was not at least up to the norm for patients in such a condition.

Strengths and limitations of the health belief model (1988)

Strengths	Limitations
1. Identifies the issues and paradigm shifts faced in seeking a healthier lifestyle. 2. Enables perceived barriers to be identified and addressed by psychologists. 3. Identifies the powerful environmental cues that are crucial in supporting lifestyle changes.	1. Does not sufficiently factor-in the difficulties of applying the consistent will-power and persistence required to follow effectively a healthier lifestyle. 2. Those on lower incomes may not be able to afford the supportive environment of a fitness centre or even the more expensive healthier food required.

8. PAPER 2 OPTION – HEALTH PSYCHOLOGY

The stages of change model

The stages of change model focuses on five stages of change that a person must go through to break a habit, e.g. smoking, excessive eating:

1. **Pre-contemplation**: "I know I shouldn't smoke, but that's me."
2. **Contemplation**: "I do need to quit, but I am not up to quitting."
3. **Preparation**: "I'm taking the first steps to quit by not smoking until midday."
4. **Action**: "I've stopped smoking."
5. **Maintenance**: "I've stopped smoking over a long period and will never go back." This comes from consistent will-power and persistence.

A serious quitter will try to *progress from stages 1 to 5*. However, his will-power and persistence might keep him on track during the busy week at school/work, only to *relapse* into smoking during a lonely weekend. He might go back to stage 2 or even stage 1.

This model has been criticised by **West and Sohal (2006)**. This study involving a cross-sectional survey of 918 smokers who seriously attempted to quit but relapsed at least once, and 996 smokers who had succeeded in quitting. They found little evidence to support the spectrum of change from stages 1 to 5 above. Indeed, they found that it was the unplanned efforts to quit smoking (like the cue from the environment that it's "stop now or die soon", or the influence and support of friend who successfully quit) that were more effective than those attempts that followed the spectrum.

Strengths and limitations: the stages of change model

Strengths	Limitations
1. Adaptable to wide variety of health-adverse behaviours including smoking, excessive alcohol intake, and overeating.	1. Does not sufficiently accommodate the social and cultural factors that might be involved in habit-changing decisions.
2. Enables the stages of progress and associated barriers to be identified and addressed by psychologists.	2. Does not place sufficient weight on the powerful environmental cues, such as those in West and Sohal (above).
3. Does factor-in the difficulties of applying the consistent will-power and persistence required to follow a healthier lifestyle effectively.	

Brown et al. (2014) (Section 8.1.3) may be used to examine the nature of the UK nationally-sponsored Stoptober health promotion program.

Halpern et al. (2014) (Section 8.3.2) may be used to examine the nature of a workplace health promotion program.

The two studies referenced above tend to focus on impact of the health campaigns from the environment on the individual. However, they do not address the particular barriers that the individual might be facing in making the necessary changes. These could include individually-perceived susceptibility, individually-perceived barriers to change, and individually perceived lack of self-efficacy in the health belief model, and the maintenance of continuing to quit smoking and/or eat healthily of the stages of change model.

8.3.2 Effectiveness of health promotion programs

Reminder: health promotion may be defined as the encouragement of people to change their lifestyle to reach their optimum level of health.

> Brown et al. (2014) (Section 8.1.3), may be used to examine the effectiveness of the UK nationally-sponsored 'Stoptober' program to promote quitting smoking.

Health promotion can be conducted through the national campaigns with the mass media, through the community at 'grass-roots' level, and through the workplace.

Health promotion through the community: 'grass-roots' level

The Florida-based **TRUTH anti-tobacco campaign (1998–9)** was aimed at changing teens' attitudes towards smoking, and encouraging them to form groups to influence yet more teens to do so. Central to this youth movement against smoking was its well-publicised confrontation with representatives of the tobacco industry, accusing them of manipulating the public to smoke. Its campaign to prevent and stop teenage smoking was wide ranging, including TV advertisements, billboards, the Internet, and local youth advocacy groups.

The communication efficacy of the campaign was measured after its first six months by a telephone survey. It showed that 92% of teens had heard of the campaign. And a survey of youth in the state conducted in 1999 showed that the number of smokers had gone down: by some 20% at middle schools, and 8% at high schools.

Schum and Gold (2007) studied the TRUTH campaign. Aware of the above statistics (making it one of the most successful anti-smoking campaigns in the United States), it cited the following reasons for the campaign's success – which are vital points to note when planning future health-promotion initiatives and strategies:

1. It was conducted at grass roots level. Being planned by teens for teens, it spoke to teens in ways that they could readily respond. Their passion for the campaign caught others, quickly.
2. It did much towards establishing a youth social norm: "It's not cool to smoke".
3. It made use of teens' own social networks, which were out of reach of more conventional approaches. It was indeed the teens who delivered the message. This highlights the potential of Facebook health-promotion programs at grass-roots level.

However, its limitations include its being based on self-reporting and possible demand characteristics. In addition, the study was correlational in design, not being set up to identify those who might have quit irrespective of the campaign.

Health promotion through the workplace

Many companies worldwide run such programs as the connection between health promotion and the workplace benefits both the company and the employees in terms of reducing the number of sick-leave absences, employee-borne health-insurance costs, and workers' compensation costs.

These programs tend to include health-promotion material on eating habits, smoking, and alcohol intakes, as well as on exercise and stress management. Typically, people from many different cultures meet at the workplace. Thus the workplace can reach many people from different cultural backgrounds. Through them, the health promotion messages spread through many cultures.

RESEARCH STUDY

Chapman (2005)

Chapman combined studies of a large number of very different workplaces conducted in the previous 23 years. He found that health promotion campaigns produced a drop of more than a quarter in worker absenteeism, health costs, and workers' compensation costs. Thus, the workplace seems to be an effective area for health promotion, with very likely non-factored-in spreading the message to friends and families of those who benefited from the campaign.

Workplace-based financial incentive programs to help adult smokers to quit have also shown significant success in health promotion.

 RESEARCH STUDY

Halpern et al. (2015)

Halpern et al. (2015) was a large study involving over 2,500 participants, all of whom were CVS Caremark company employees or individuals connected with them. This was an independent measures study, with each participant (in addition to receiving basic smoking-cessation therapies) being randomly assigned to one of four incentive programs, two of which were individual based and two of them were group-of-six-participants based. Two programs, one individual and one group-based required each participant to buy into the treatment, by making a $150 deposit that would be not refunded if resuming smoking during the 12-month period. If they did not resume, they would receive a $650 reward plus return of deposit, making $800. The other two groups were told that success in quitting would earn an $800 bonus without their having to buy into the scheme. The study showed that those who bought into the scheme were more than three times as successful in quitting (52%) during the 12-month period than those who had not personally invested in the scheme (17%). There were no significant differences whether the participants attended individual programs or group programs.

Strengths and limitations of Halpern et al. (2015)

Strengths	Limitations
1. It used a large sample. 2. It supported the view that a company might help their employees to live more healthily, and it also how it could reduce the overall cost of employee health benefits. 3. It draws attention to an element not explicitly inside the two health models considered in the previous section: the importance of individuals personally investing themselves in health improvements.	1. Its focus on personal investment may overlook other factors included in the health models considered in the previous section that may be of equal or even greater importance. These could include individually-perceived susceptibility, individually-perceived barriers to change, and individually-perceived lack of self-efficacy in the health belief model, and the maintenance of continuing to quit smoking of the stages of change model. 2. Similar work-based, or school-based campaigns carry the possible ethical issue of social stigmatisation for those who do not achieve what they may feel to be society-imposed goals. A smoker may personally be quite happy to smoke, and an obese person may be quite happy to continue overeating or the obese condition may be related to genetic and other psychological factors other than the socially-assumed character weakness and lack of will-power. Such health campaigns can also lead to instances of denigrating the person in need of help rather than offering suitable support.

8.4 Ethical Considerations

Ethical considerations in researching health psychology are common to other areas of psychology, including:

- Informed consent: participants must know the object of the study, that their involvement is voluntary, what the data will be used for, and if necessary be debriefed at the end of the study. In extreme cases, the ethical requirement for informed consent may be waived, when the focus of the study is of public importance and there is no other way to obtain the sought-after information.
- Avoiding deception, except possibly where the research cannot be carried out in any other way).
- Protection from harm. This includes stigmatisation in health campaigns (Section 8.3.2.) and also exemplified in humiliations such as "fat shaming", which can also compromise the requirements that those participating remain anonymous (below).
- Making the participants anonymous to protect them, even at the risk of reducing the authenticity of the research and of preventing any follow-up study.
- The right for any participant to withdraw from the study at any point, and communicating that right before the commencement of the study.
- All participants are to be debriefed at the end of the study.
- Bearing in mind that research involving associated cultural issues is extremely sensitive with many ethnic groups. Typically, the elders of the society must be consulted for permission to work with members of their group.

8.5 Key research studies

For biological influences, look at the following:

- The biopsychosocial model of health and well-being
- Kiecolt-Glaser et al. (1984) on the effects of stress in lowering resistance to disease.
- Stunkard et al. (1990) on genetic factors in the development of obesity.
- Claussnitzer et al. (2015) on how genetic factors might influence obesity.
- Goldstone (2010) on the importance of targeting the hunger-creating hormone ghrelin.
- Crum et al. (2011) on how the individual's state of mind affects ghrelin activity.

For cognitive influences, look at the following below:

- Weinstein (1983) on how optimum bias may threaten personal health.
- Goldstone (2010) on the importance of targeting the hunger-creating hormone ghrelin, which can be cognitively stimulated.
- Crum et al. (2011) on how the individual's state of mind affects ghrelin activity.
- Wansink et al. (2012) on the influence of branding products as a means of promoting healthy nutrition:
- The health-belief model for health promotion.
- The stages of change model for health promotion, and West and Sohal (2006) in challenging that model.

8. PAPER 2 OPTION – HEALTH PSYCHOLOGY

For sociocultural influences, look at the following below:

- Graber et al. (2015) on the role of friendships in a protective, stress-coping role, and as a health-promoting strategy.
- Koch et al. (2008) on the influence of household stress in promoting child obesity.
- She, King, and Jacobson (2017) on the use of public transport in preventing obesity.
- Halpern et al. (2015) on workplace-based financial incentive programs to help adult smokers to quit as a protective actor and as a health promoter.
- The use of mass media in health promotion: the Florida-based TRUTH campaign, and the UK 'Stoptober' campaign.

As you progress with this topic, you should be evaluating the theories and studies relevant to the study of health psychology. You should be aware of the strengths and limitations of various health and health-promotion models, the reality of research), and the especial importance of following ethical practices given the personal and sensitive nature of the findings. You, the student, should be considering the question: 'To what extent do biological, cognitive and sociocultural factors influence personal health and well-being?' in view of the theories and studies including those above.

Evaluate psychological research relevant to health psychology

For determinants of health, look at the following:

- The biopsychosocial model of health and well-being
- Kiecolt-Glaser et al. (1984) on the effects of stress in lowering resistance to disease.
- Stunkard et al. (1990) on genetic factors in the development of obesity.
- Claussnitzer et al. (2015) on how genetic factors might influence obesity.
- Habtewold et al. (2016) on the importance of social support in assisting Type-2 diabetes patients.
- Graber et al. (2015) on the role of friendships in a protective, stress-coping role, and as a health-promoting strategy.

For health problems, look at the following:

- Weinstein (1983) on how optimum bias may threaten personal health.
- Goldstone (2010) on the importance of targeting the hunger-creating hormone ghrelin.
- Crum et al. (2011) on how the individual's state of mind affects ghrelin activity.
- She, King, and Jacobson (2017) on the use of public transport in preventing obesity.
- Koch et al. (2008) on the influence of household stress in promoting child obesity.
- Wansink et al. (2012) on the influence of branding products as a means of promoting healthy nutrition.

For promoting health, look at the following:

- The health-belief model for health promotion.
- The stages of change model for health promotion, and West and Sohal (2006) in challenging that model.
- Halpern et al. (2015) on workplace-based financial incentive programs to help adult smokers to quit as a protective actor and as a health promoter.
- The use of mass media in health promotion: the Florida-based TRUTH campaign, and the UK 'Stoptober' campaign.

PRACTICE QUESTIONS

Essay Response Practice Questions: Health Psychology

1. Discuss health beliefs as determinants of health.
2. Discuss the prevalence rates of one health problem.
3. Evaluate research on health promotion.

8. PAPER 2 OPTION – HEALTH PSYCHOLOGY